PlayStation® 2 For Dummies®

Cheat Sheet

DVD/CD Controller Commands

Press	To
Directional pad buttons	Navigate menus and move the cursor
✖	Enter a command or select a menu item
●	Stop a disc from playing
▲	Access the DVD menu
■	Access the Title menu
L1	Go to previous chapter or track
R1	Go to next chapter or track
L2	Search backward within a chapter or track
R2	Search forward within a chapter or track
L3 Analog Stick	Cycle through subtitle options
R3 Analog Stick	Cycle through audio options
Select	Access the Control Panel
Start	Play or pause the disc

General PlayStation 2 Tips

✔ Don't change the PlayStation 2 from horizontal to vertical position while it's turned on, as this may damage the disc spinning inside. If no disc is inside, you can change positions safely.

✔ Digital surround-sound works only if you're using an optical cable.

✔ The Dual Shock 2 controller is fairly sturdy, but you should avoid throwing it, stepping on it, or spilling liquids into it.

✔ The X button is almost always the Enter button for game, movie, and system menus.

✔ Always plug your PlayStation 2 into a surge protector of some kind.

Web Sites to Check Out

✔ Sony's official PlayStation 2 site:
www.playstation.com

✔ *GamePro* (news, reviews, cheats, and chat):
www.gamepro.com

✔ Game release calendar:
www.gameweek.com/release_dates/index.asp

✔ DVD Demystified:
www.dvddemystified.com

✔ Hidden features on DVD movies:
www.dvdreview.com/html/hidden_features.shtml

Hungry Minds™

For Dummies®: Bestselling Book Series for Beginners

PlayStation® 2
FOR
DUMMIES®

PlayStation® 2
FOR
DUMMIES®

by Dan Amrich, *GamePro* magazine

Hungry Minds™

HUNGRY MINDS, INC.

New York, NY ◆ Cleveland, OH ◆ Indianapolis, IN

PlayStation® 2 For Dummies®

Published by
Hungry Minds, Inc.
909 Third Avenue
New York, NY 10022
www.hungryminds.com
www.dummies.com

Library of Congress Control Number: 00-112149

ISBN: 0-7645-0833-4

Printed in the United States of America

10 9 8 7 6 5 4 3 2 1

1B/RZ/QT/QR/IN

Distributed in the United States by Hungry Minds, Inc.

Distributed by CDG Books Canada Inc. for Canada; by Transworld Publishers Limited in the United Kingdom; by IDG Norge Books for Norway; by IDG Sweden Books for Sweden; by IDG Books Australia Publishing Corporation Pty. Ltd. for Australia and New Zealand; by TransQuest Publishers Pte Ltd. for Singapore, Malaysia, Thailand, Indonesia, and Hong Kong; by Gotop Information Inc. for Taiwan; by ICG Muse, Inc. for Japan; by Intersoft for South Africa; by Eyrolles for France; by International Thomson Publishing for Germany, Austria and Switzerland; by Distribuidora Cuspide for Argentina; by LR International for Brazil; by Galileo Libros for Chile; by Ediciones ZETA S.C.R. Ltda. for Peru; by WS Computer Publishing Corporation, Inc., for the Philippines; by Contemporanea de Ediciones for Venezuela; by Express Computer Distributors for the Caribbean and West Indies; by Micronesia Media Distributor, Inc. for Micronesia; by Chips Computadoras S.A. de C.V. for Mexico; by Editorial Norma de Panama S.A. for Panama; by American Bookshops for Finland.

For general information on Hungry Minds' products and services please contact our Customer Care Department within the U.S. at 800-762-2974, outside the U.S. at 317-572-3993 or fax 317-572-4002.

For sales inquiries and reseller information, including discounts, premium and bulk quantity sales, and foreign-language translations, please contact our Customer Care Department at 800-434-3422, fax 317-572-4002, or write to Hungry Minds, Inc., Attn: Customer Care Department, 10475 Crosspoint Boulevard, Indianapolis, IN 46256.

For information on licensing foreign or domestic rights, please contact our Sub-Rights Customer Care Department at 650-653-7098.

For information on using Hungry Minds' products and services in the classroom or for ordering examination copies, please contact our Educational Sales Department at 800-434-2086 or fax 317-572-4005.

Please contact our Public Relations Department at 212-884-5163 for press review copies or 212-884-5000 for author interviews and other publicity information or fax 212-884-5400.

For authorization to photocopy items for corporate, personal, or educational use, please contact Copyright Clearance Center, 222 Rosewood Drive, Danvers, MA 01923, or fax 978-750-4470.

Hungry Minds™ is a trademark of Hungry Minds, Inc.

About the Author

Dan Amrich has Pac-Man Fever, and it's driving him crazy. A child of the '80s, Dan has been writing about PC and video games since 1993 and playing them for well over 20 years. Since 1997, as a Senior Editor for *GamePro* magazine — the world's largest multiplatform video game magazine in America — Dan is currently in charge of features, news, letters, and departments. Before *GamePro*, he held such positions as Executive Editor of Internet lifestyle magazine *Digital Diner* and sports video game magazine *GameSport*, Managing Editor of the gaming/comics/teen lifestyle magazine *Flux*, and Senior Games Editor for the online entertainment publication *Critics' Choice* (way before online was cool). Dan has written articles for *Wired, NBA Inside Stuff, Slam, Guitar World, Family PC* and *Time Out New York*, among others.

When he's not playing video games, Dan enjoys playing rock guitar and drums, much to the dismay of his neighbors. He's also a rabid Knicks fan, juggles fire, and enjoys walking around town in his Ghostbusters uniform, complete with proton pack. One day he hopes to become a real live boy. Contact Dan at damrich@gamepro.com or through his personal Web site, www.bunnyears.net.

Dedication

This book is dedicated to Katrin Auch — my best friend, my wife, and my first choice for Player Two. Not only is she a constant inspiration, but if you had to endure all the stuff that she had to endure during the writing of this book, you'd deserve a dedication too.

Author's Acknowledgments

No man is an island — except for Marlon Brando, I guess — so I would like to thank all the folks who backed me up on this crazy thing. First and foremost, this book would not have been created without the efforts of the tireless, but exhausted, Jonathan Rinzler. Jonathan bridged the gap between *GamePro* style and Dummies style to create an all-new breed of writing, which, for lack of a better term, is now known as the Gummies style. I know, it's a bad name. Jonathan didn't edit this part.

This book would not exist without the assistance of the *GamePro* creative staff. They are, in alphabetical order: Kat Auch, Jake Blackford, Jennifer Cotton, Paul Curthoys, Nate Denver, Mike Kim, Danny Lam, Justin Lambros, Francis Mao, Wataru Maruyama, John Marrin, Ryan Meith, Sean Molloy, Wes Nihei, Shelly Reimer, Michele Thomas, Mike Weigand, and Lindsay Young. Not only do I appreciate their incredible talents and devotion to producing the best game mag on the market, many of them also generated Part III of this book (see Part III for details). Plus, they laugh politely at my jokes. You, the reader, can shut me up any time by simply closing the cover. They're locked up with me five days a week for hours at a time with *no hope of escape*.

Special credit and thanks to Francis Mao for Part III's icon illustrations and chapter opener art and Michele Thomas for all the original photographs that appear in this book.

Props to John F. Rousseau, who green-lighted the project and trusted me to do the mag proud; Jodi Jensen, a soft sweetheart in a crunchy editor shell; Sandy Rodrigues, Mary Jane Auch, and "The" Andy Eddy for their professional advice; Barbara Adams for showing me the writer within the smart-aleck; my parents Richard and Delores, who didn't yell too much when I wanted to stay inside on gorgeous summer days and play Atari in the '80s; and everybody who put up with me through this exciting, difficult project.

Publisher's Acknowledgments

We're proud of this book; please send us your comments through our Online Registration Form located at www.dummies.com.

Some of the people who helped bring this book to market include the following:

Acquisitions, Editorial, and Media Development

Senior Project Editor: Jodi Jensen

Senior Acquisitions Editor: Steven H. Hayes

Copy Editor: Jeremy Zucker

Proof Editor: Sarah Shupert

Technical Editor: John Kaufeld

Permissions Editors: Carmen Krikorian, Laura Moss

Editorial Manager: Kyle Looper

Editorial Assistant: Jean Rogers

Production

Project Coordinator: Emily Wichlinski

Layout and Graphics: Amy Adrian, Angela F. Hunckler, Clint Lahnen, Barry Offringa, Brent Savage, Jacque Schneider, Rashell Smith

Proofreaders: Andy Hollandbeck, Murray Montague

Indexer: Maro Riofrancos

Special Help
Janet Seib

General and Administrative

Hungry Minds, Inc.: John Kilcullen, CEO; Bill Barry, President and COO; John Ball, Executive VP, Operations & Administration; John Harris, CFO

Hungry Minds Technology Publishing Group: Richard Swadley, Senior Vice President and Publisher; Mary Bednarek, Vice President and Publisher, Networking and Certification; Walter R. Bruce III, Vice President and Publisher, General User and Design Professional; Joseph Wikert, Vice President and Publisher, Programming; Mary C. Corder, Editorial Director, Branded Technology Editorial; Andy Cummings, Publishing Director, General User and Design Professional; Barry Pruett, Publishing Director, Visual

Hungry Minds Manufacturing: Ivor Parker, Vice President, Manufacturing

Hungry Minds Marketing: John Helmus, Assistant Vice President, Director of Marketing

Hungry Minds Online Management: Brenda McLaughlin, Executive Vice President, Chief Internet Officer

Hungry Minds Production for Branded Press: Debbie Stailey, Production Director

Hungry Minds Sales: Roland Elgey, Senior Vice President, Sales and Marketing; Michael Violano, Vice President, International Sales and Sub Rights

◆

The publisher would like to give special thanks to Patrick J. McGovern, without whom this book would not have been possible.

◆

Contents at a Glance

Cartoons at a Glance

By Rich Tennant

"I don't get it. The PlayStation2 plays games, CDs, DVDs... Well, you keep looking for the tone arm and needle, and I'll page through the manual again."

page 5

Gerry and Mel Weintraub enjoy playing "Madden NFL Accountant" on their PlayStation 2.

Quick Gerry—defer the Signing Bonus! Watch the agent! Watch the agent!

page 77

"There's a slight pause here where the PS2 sequences your DNA to determine your preferences."

page 47

"Wait a minute... This is a movie, not a game?! I thought I was the one making Keanu Reeves jump kick in slow motion."

page 245

"Oh... you mean the controller is supposed to shake like this? I kept stopping the game to see who was paging me!"

page 273

Cartoon Information:
Fax: 978-546-7747
E-Mail: richtennant@the5thwave.com
World Wide Web: www.the5thwave.com

Table of Contents

Introduction

• •

*V*ideo games as we know them began in 1972 when Nolan Bushnell and Al Alcorn built the first successful coin-operated video game in a tiny office in California. They installed *Pong,* a crude version of video tennis, in a bar in Sunnyvale, California, but the machine broke down in just two weeks. When Alcorn went to inspect the damage, he couldn't believe what he saw. Their creation had short-circuited not because of faulty workmanship, but because too many quarters were inside. The *Pong* arcade game had broken because it was insanely popular.

The popularity of video games has grown exponentially since then, and *Pong* — with its black-and-white screen, simplistic controls, and one-line instruction ("Avoid missing ball for high score") — isn't even 30 years old. It seems like video games have been around forever, but they're still in their infancy compared to books, movies, or even television. I'd argue that video games have come farther faster than any other form of entertainment you can name.

The pinnacle of that lightning-paced evolution is Sony's PlayStation 2, a console that not only plays hundreds of video games but also doubles as a digital movie player. The machine's arrival has been anything but quiet. Some would say that you couldn't escape the deafening hype surrounding the launch of the PlayStation 2. In this book, I separate the fact from the fiction and define what the PlayStation 2 is, what it really can do, and how you can get the most out of yours. And, for history's sake, I have some advice on how to keep your own game machine from short-circuiting. (*One hint:* Don't put any quarters in it.)

About This Book

Rule #1: There are no rules! If you want to read this book cover to cover, I'd be terribly flattered, but I don't really expect that. Use it for reference, for starting up — whatever you like. The only suggestion I make is that you read the chapter on installation completely in one sitting because you'll find specific instructions there that should be followed in order. Otherwise, it's your book.

Conventions Used in This Book

Sometimes I introduce you to technical terms or concepts specific to the world of video games. If the term refers to something that's not common knowledge, like, say, *texture smoothing,* or other phrases that will make you sound really smart, I show it as *italicized* text.

I don't use them often, but when I reference a URL (Web address) within a paragraph, it will look like this: www.gamepro.com.

Foolish Assumptions

I don't know you, but I'm going to try to figure you out. I'm receiving vibes just from you holding the book, and my eerie psychic powers tell me that you're probably at least one of the following people:

 ✔ **The Serious Gamer.** You've just bought a PlayStation 2 and want to know how to get the most out of it. Show me the games! Show me the power!

 ✔ **The Serious Gamer on a Budget.** You've been saving up your cash to buy a PlayStation 2 and want to know all you can about it before actually purchasing one. Show me the games! Show me the power! Show me I'm not making a mistake! And show me how much I should expect to pay!

 ✔ **The Movie Buff.** You've wanted to buy a DVD player for a while now, and because the PlayStation 2 can also play games, you feel like you'll be getting two machines for the price of one. You may be a casual gamer, too, but digital movies are the main draw. You're already making popcorn for the big show.

 ✔ **The Hassled Parent.** Your kids have been bugging you to buy them a PlayStation 2, and you just want some straight answers before taking the plunge. Is this a toy or a computer? What control will I have over what my kids do with it? And show me how much I should expect to pay!

While writing this book, I had you — all of you — in mind. I'm also assuming that you aren't particularly fond of messing around with the wires behind your television set and would rather go slowly and hook up your PS2 right the first time. If so, I have three comforting words: Plenty of diagrams!

How This Book Is Organized

I divided this book into five parts, one of which is flat-out enormous. Read them in any order you like. The parts are self-contained and make sense on their own.

Part I: Open the Box, Already!

Part I starts at the very beginning — the moment you come home from the store with that heavier-than-expected blue box containing a PlayStation 2. The first chapter covers the console and its capabilities and progresses to detailed connection instructions and a guided tour of the machine's basic menus. By the time you finish reading Part I, you'll know the machine inside and out. Mostly out, though.

Part II: The Play's the Thing

It looks cool on its own, but the PlayStation 2 is a lot more exciting when you feed it games and movies. Whether you want to run PlayStation 2 games, load up some old favorites from the original PlayStation, pump up the jams from an audio CD, or kick back with a DVD movie, you'll find all the instructions you need in Part II. Because the DVD menu can be pretty confusing, I've broken it down, one icon at a time, so that you'll never feel flummoxed again.

Part III: Let the Games Begin!

Been to the store lately? There are just under a bazillion games there that run on your PlayStation 2. With the help of my fellow editors at *GamePro* magazine, I whittled the pack down to just under 200 of the best games and then separated them into logical categories based on interest. Looking for the thrill of driving 200 miles per hour? Are you aching for an epic role-playing quest? Ready to tackle your favorite sport? This part has dozens and dozens of quick game summaries for you to browse, plus a few cheat codes and bits of trivia thrown in.

Part IV: The Part of Tens

Say the name with reverence — the Part of Tens is a beloved tradition when it comes to *For Dummies* books. Here's where you'll find PlayStation 2 myths exposed, some DVD movie suggestions, a peek at what video games are like in Japan, and a list of cool toys you can buy to pamper your PS2.

Part V: Appendix

For some game fans, it's all about the numbers. How fast? How many? How strong? How long before it's obsolete? I can't answer that last question, but I do give you whatever information I can. If you've wondered how the

PlayStation 2 compares to other game machines on the market — as well as the ones that are about to come out — this section will let you wonder no more.

Icons Used in This Book

Whenever something of special note appears in the text, it's denoted with an icon in the margins. When you see an icon, you know that the text next to it is just a little bit more important or specialized than the rest.

At its core, the PlayStation 2 is a computer, and computers are technical beasts. On the few occasions when I delve into the science and geek-speak behind the PS2, you'll see this icon, so you can avoid the accompanying text if you like.

Because the PlayStation 2 is self-contained and fairly easy to use, there aren't many things that can go wrong with it. Nevertheless, I'm a professional at making things go wrong with my PlayStation 2, and I've found a few things that you should be aware of. If text is marked with a Warning icon, it's for a good reason. You should read it if you don't want to put your machine at risk.

This is my catch-all for useful advice. Whenever I have a helpful suggestion that you may not have considered yet, I flag that text as a Tip.

Where to Go from Here

Only one way to go, friend — forward! You may want to check out the table of contents now and see what looks interesting to you and then be a rebel and skip right to it. Get some software suggestions, see how the DVD player works, double-check your connection instructions, and — above all — have fun.

Good luck and happy gaming!

Part I

Open the Box, Already!

The 5th Wave By Rich Tennant

"I don't get it. The PlayStation 2 plays games, CDs, DVDs... Well, you keep looking for the tone arm and needle, and I'll page through the manual again."

In this part . . .

When Sony got into the video game market in 1995, nobody could have predicted that its first game machine would quickly take over the industry. But that's exactly what the PlayStation did. After selling more than 70 million machines, the PlayStation has spawned a sequel: the PlayStation 2.

In this part, I go over what makes the PlayStation 2 different — and better — than its earlier relatives. I also tell you the best (and safest) ways to hook the machine up to your TV, and I explain how to use your brand-new PlayStation 2 games as well as your favorite old PlayStation games with this new machine. I also tackle those labyrinthine menus and show you how to tweak the PS2's performance to your personal preferences.

Chapter 1

PlayStation 2: Play Harder

• •

In This Chapter

▶ All the cool things that PlayStation 2 can do

▶ A look at the Emotion Engine

▶ What the numbers mean

▶ PlayStation 2 and the Internet

• •

"That's an expensive toy" is the reaction I sometimes get from non-gameplaying friends when I tell them about my PlayStation 2. From Atari to Nintendo to Sega and on through to Sony, the last 25 years or so have spawned some great video games — some of which, it has been argued, approach legitimate art — but usually, the sum product of the interactive entertainment industry is boiled down to that one phrase: "That's an expensive toy."

Yet if calling video games *toys* sold the old systems short, calling the PlayStation 2 a *plaything* is downright ridiculous. Sure, it can play awesome games, suck you into its virtual worlds, and make you forget about . . . well, everything else. But the PlayStation 2 has much more power and potential than any game machine that came before it, and, by all indications, the PlayStation 2 — PS2 for short — is well on its way to setting a new standard. And it won't be a standard in toys.

What Can It Do?

Actually, the question is more like, "What *can't* it do?" The PlayStation 2 is the Swiss Army knife of the video game world. Among the discs it can happily accept are the following:

✔ **PlayStation 2 software.** SSX, Madden NFL 2001, and Tekken Tag Tournament are just a few of the new software titles that run exclusively on Sony's newest machine.

✔ **PlayStation games.** If you're not quite willing to give up all your old PlayStation favorites, like Crash Bandicoot, Hot Shots Golf, and Tony Hawk's Pro Skater 2, fear not — the PlayStation 2 plays original PlayStation games without a hitch.

✔ **DVD movies.** For the first time, a video game console can play full-length feature films in the form of Digital Video Discs, complete with all the extras and bonus material those discs offer.

✔ **Audio CDs.** By also handling digital music playback, the PS2 essentially takes the place of three different entertainment machines.

I go into detail about each of the above capabilities as the book goes on. For now, know that the PlayStation 2 is probably going to be the heart of your home entertainment center.

A brief history of the PlayStation

Sony's quest to enter the video game market actually started all the way back in 1988. That's when the company planned to create a CD-ROM drive that would work in conjunction with Nintendo's 16-bit Super Nintendo Entertainment System (SNES). But as Sony was developing that peripheral, engineers also came up with the idea for a stand-alone game machine that would play both SNES cartridges and Sony's own CD-ROM software, called Super Discs. Three years later, Sony named the machine the Play Station (two words!) and announced it at the 1991 Summer Consumer Electronics Show — much to the surprise of Nintendo, which still hadn't received its add-on drive yet. The next day, Nintendo announced a new deal with Philips, and the Sony partnership dissolved — rather unpleasantly. Plans for the Play Station were scrapped and the machine never made it to store shelves.

But that didn't stop Sony; the events only gave it more time to prepare. As the company published largely mediocre games for Sega and Nintendo machines under the Sony Imagesoft brand, Sony engineers set about creating the "Play Station X" (an internal development codename which, to Sony's disappointment, later leaked to the public. This leak is why you'll sometimes see hardcore gamers abbreviate the machine as PSX).

After major retooling and a commitment to CD-based games exclusively, Sony released a completely redesigned PlayStation (now one word) in Japan in December of 1994, for 370,000 yen (just under $400). It was an instant hit, selling 300,000 machines in its first month of release, with the millionth machine milestone coming just six months later. The U.S. release would follow in September of 1995 with a price tag of $299 . . . and the rest, as they say, is history. To date, over 75 million PlayStation and PlayStation 2 consoles have been shipped worldwide.

Playing with Your Emotions

The heart of the PlayStation 2 is a custom-built 128-bit processor nicknamed the Emotion Engine. It earned that title because Sony believes the Emotion Engine has the power to take games out of the realm of mere diversion and deliver deep, affecting entertainment — stuff so impressive and engrossing that you won't merely play it, you'll feel it. Marketing hype or major leap forward? You be the judge. Yet it sure will be cool if Sony makes it happen.

The Emotion Engine itself is quite a piece of work. While other game systems have had custom central processing units (CPU) — most do, really — this is the first one that's been designed to do such a wide array of tasks and have this much horsepower. For one, it's the first true 128-bit CPU in the world (more bits generally means faster calculations) and it features really tiny construction — no, um, small feat. The memory that this chip uses is roughly four times faster than the current standard used in the PC world, so images and sounds can be loaded super-quick. And the raw computing power of the Emotion Engine is so awesome that it technically classifies as a supercomputer — those room-filling machines that were once the exclusive playthings of governments and scientists. Now you're using one to play video football and to watch *The Sixth Sense* over and over again. Go figure.

If you want to know a little bit more about what makes the PS2 tick — so that you can sound *really* smart at your next party — check out Table 1-1.

Table 1-1	PlayStation 2: By the Numbers
Component	*Specification*
CPU	**128-bit Emotion Engine**
System Clock Frequency	294.912 MHz
Cache Memory Instruction	16K, Data: 8K + 16K (ScrP)
Main Memory	Direct Rambus (Direct RDRAM)
Memory Size	32MB
Memory Bus Bandwidth	3.2GB per second
Co-processor	FPU (Floating Point Unit; Floating Point Multiply Accumulator x1, Floating Point Divider x1)
Vector Units	VU0 and VU1 (Floating Point Multiply Accumulator x9, Floating Point Divider x3)

(continued)

Table 1-1 *(continued)*

Component	Specification
CPU	**128-bit Emotion Engine**
Floating Point Performance	6.2 GFLOPS
3-D CG Geometric Transformation	66 million polygons per second
Compressed Image Decoder	MPEG2
Graphics	**Graphics Synthesizer**
Clock Frequency	147.456 MHz
Embedded DRAM	4MB
DRAM Bus Bandwidth	48GB per second
DRAM Bus Width	2560 Bits
Pixel Configuration	RGB: Alpha:Z Buffer (24:8:32)
Polygon Drawing Rate	75 million polygons per second
Screen Resolution	Variable from 256 x 224 to 1280 x 1024
Sound	**SPU2+CPU**
Number of Voices	ADPCM: 48ch on SPU2 plus definable, software programmable voices
Sound Memory	2MB
Output Frequency	Variable up to 48 kHz (DAT quality)
IOP	**I/O Processor**
CPU Core	PlayStation (current): CPU
Clock Frequency	33.8688 MHz or 36.864 MHz (selectable)
IOP Memory	2MB
Sub Bus	32-bit
Interface Types	IEEE1394 i.Link, Universal Serial Bus (USB) x2, Controller Port x2, Memory Card x2
Disc Device	**CD-ROM and DVD-ROM**
Device Speed	CD-ROM speed: 24 times speed/ DVD-ROM speed: 4 times speed

The North American model includes these new features: Drive bay (for 3.5-inch hard disk drive); DVD-video playback built into the hardware, no memory card required.

Can I Have That in English, Please?

Baffled by the geekspeak overload? Not to worry. The following bulleted list breaks down some of the more important numbers into things normal humans can understand:

- **System Clock Frequency:** More commonly referred to as *clock speed*. You may have a Pentium III 500 or a Macintosh G3 400 at home — and that last number is the clock speed in megahertz (MHz), a rough determination of how fast the computer runs. The PS2's 300 MHz clock speed may not sound that fast, but there's more to it. A PC's processor has to do any number of tasks, but because the PS2 is dedicated solely to playing games and handling 3-D objects, that means you'll get streamlined performance.

- **Floating Point Performance:** A measurement of how many advanced calculations the chip can do, especially when those numbers apply to graphics. Every internal calculation is based on a complex algorithm (a mathematical formula) — you can't tear around a hairpin turn in a racing game without a truckload of the suckers crunching numbers inside your console system. The best way to express those really long numbers then is to encode them as floating point operations, or FLOPS. The PS2 can do 6.2 GFLOPS — that is, 6.2 gigaflops or 6,200,000,000 floating-point operations per second. The very respectable Pentium III 450 MHz computer chip can perform a bit over 500 million FLOPS. That's 0.5 GFLOPS — and that means the PS2 is very powerful indeed. Suddenly, the clock speed doesn't sound so important, huh?

- **3-D CG Geometric Transformation:** A measurement that tells how many triangles the machine can create. Most graphic images in modern video games are made out of polygonal shapes composed of triangles (see Figure 1-1) — the more triangles, the more detailed the graphics. The original PlayStation produced 1.5 million polygons a second, so the PS2's 66 million per second is obscene.

- **The Compressed Image Decoder:** This chip takes digital data and turns it into DVD video. That's essentially all you need to know.

- **Screen Resolution:** A pretty big deal — literally. It determines how large and detailed the graphics can be. For example, 1280 pixels by 1024 pixels is a high resolution; most computer games run at 640 x 480 or 800 x 600. Most PS2 games should run around there as well because the higher the resolution, the more screen the computer has to draw, which can slow things down. Plus, televisions can't handle resolutions much higher than 640 x 480 (but it's nice to know the potential for prettier pictures is there for high-definition TV).

✔ **Number of Voices:** A specification that determines how many sounds the PS2 can play at once; in this case, 48 channels. Each of those channels could be a sound effect, some music, a voice, an explosion, whatever. The 48 kHz output frequency is actually higher quality than CD audio (a mere 44.1 kHz).

✔ **The I/O Processor:** The processor handles input and output signals — things like interpreting button presses on the controllers and sending video signals to your TV screen. What's amusing is that the chip being used for I/O in the PS2 is the same one that ran everything in the original PlayStation (which is why the PS2 will be able to play regular PlayStation games too, but more about that in Chapter 4). Maybe Sony just had a bunch of them lying around.

Figure 1-1:
Even the most complex 3-D PlayStation 2 environments — like this level in Time-Splitters — are comprised of millions of little polygons.

In addition to the controller ports and memory card slots, the PS2 features two *Universal Serial Bus (USB)* jacks — for things like keyboards, speakers, mice, joysticks, and other peripherals — and an IEEE 1394 port, better known by its Apple brand name, FireWire (which Sony has dubbed i.Link for its own products). The 1394 port is sort of a goosed version of USB that's currently popular for transferring digital video from camcorders to computers. Sony hasn't gone into much detail about what exactly the company plans to do with these doodads, but one launch game *(Unreal Tournament)* allows gamers to connect a generic USB keyboard and mouse in addition to a standard game controller. Rumors of an official PS2 keyboard, mouse, digital camera, and even a voice-recognition system are swirling, but Sony's not confirming anything yet.

The Hard Drive and the Internet

One word you may find conspicuously absent from the list of PS2 features is *Internet*. The PlayStation 2 will definitely have online capabilities . . . eventually. Right now, Sony is building a new, high-speed computer network exclusively for the PS2. When the network is ready, you'll be able to buy an add-on that will let you connect a cable modem or a DSL line (the so-called "broadband" Internet connections) to your console and hit the Net. Sounds great, doesn't it? The only problem is that it's going to take some time. After all, Internet connectivity is a pretty big undertaking, and because the network will be broadband-only, the rest of the computing world will need time to catch up.

An Internet connection isn't much good if you can't save the stuff you download, so the PS2 Internet peripheral will come out around the same time as the PS2 hard drive. Yep, a hard drive — another gaming console first. As with the Net connector, Sony plans to release a simple plug-and-play upgrade that slides into the back of the PlayStation 2 to boost the machine's storage capacity. (In Japan, the hard drive is already out, but it doesn't fit inside the PlayStation 2. Instead, it's an external unit connected to the PS2 with a cable.) With a hard drive installed, you could surf the Web, download game upgrades, customize parts of your favorite games, and who knows what else. Sony has dropped hints about future possibilities like downloading TV shows or even renting movies on demand, but nothing has been finalized yet. Just know this: Sony is a big company that thinks equally big, and it's very serious about making the PlayStation 2 the greatest game machine on the market.

What's this PS one thing?

It almost sounds like a bad joke: If there's a PlayStation 2, where's the PlayStation 1? Sony seized the opportunity of the PS2's launch to overhaul and redesign the original PlayStation, and, yes, renamed the old console so that it had a number in the name. The PS one (note the number spelled out with a lowercase *o* in the figure) is about ⅔ the size of the original PlayStation, but it still uses all the same games, controllers, memory cards, and accessories. Sony just found a way to build it cheaper and update the PlayStation's design, so it did.

Since the PS one is smaller, it's easier to take with you on the road. And although the new model doesn't run on batteries like a true portable system, Sony and several third-party companies are planning to create a four-inch LCD screen for the PS one so that the machine can be self-contained. In other words, don't expect to see the PS2 render the original PlayStation obsolete — the PS one represents a more affordable option for gamers who aren't quite ready to make the jump to the PlayStation 2 just yet.

Chapter 2

No Assembly Required —
Well, Okay, a Little

*O*kay, so you've done the impossible — you've actually gotten your hands on a PlayStation 2, fresh in its factory carton. Pretty color blue, huh? Yeah, and the machine isn't too ugly either. If you cut through that white PlayStation sticker seal and open the box, you should find the following:

- ✔ A PlayStation 2 console

- ✔ One black Dual Shock 2 controller

- ✔ One AC power cord

- ✔ One audio/video connection cable

- ✔ Pages of printed material, most of which is the system manual

Unpacking the Pieces

If you're missing any of the items I just listed, double-check that you're the first person to have broken the little white sticker on the box flap. If it's already been broken, someone may have tampered with your new toy. If that's the case, contact the store where you bought your game system immediately.

On the other hand, if your box came factory-sealed with more than one of anything, congratulations — Sony goofed in your favor. Because you can't use your PlayStation 2 without all the above, it's important to know which is which and what they all do (see Figure 2-1).

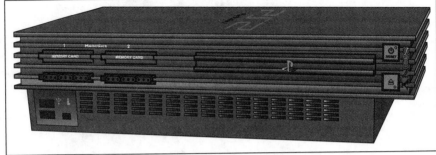

Figure 2-1:
Sony's
PlayStation
2 looks
unlike any
game
console
before it.

PlayStation 2 console

Good things come in sleek, black packages. The PlayStation 2 itself doesn't really need much explanation; you'll deal with it more after you have it all hooked up. For now, it's a good idea to become familiar with its parts (as shown in Figures 2-2 through 2-6). Go ahead and remove the Styrofoam bumpers and put the machine in a safe place.

Dual Shock 2 controller

Sony includes one Dual Shock 2 controller with every console (see Figure 2-2); you may want to buy a second or even more later on, but this one will suffice for the time being. Nearly all your interaction with the PlayStation 2 takes place through this device.

AC power cord

In the wise words of *Back to the Future*'s Doc Brown, "This sucker's electrical." You don't need 1.21 gigawatts here, though; a simple 120 volts out of your standard household electrical outlet will do. This plug will look familiar if you have other electronic appliances (and you probably do) like VCRs or CD players connected to your home entertainment center; it's an industry standard cable (see Figure 2-3).

Audio/Video connection cable

Officially, Sony calls this cord the AV cable, so I will too (see Figure 2-4). You hook up the cable directly to your TV; its wires carry the audio and video signals to the television's speakers and picture tube, respectively. The AV cable isn't the only way to connect things, though; if you'd like some information on advanced methods, skip ahead in the chapter to "Advanced Connection Options."

Figure 2-2:
Your PS2 comes equipped with one Dual Shock 2 controller.

Figure 2-3:
Now you're playing with power! A standard power cable gives your PS2 some juice.

Printed material

I don't think you need an illustration of what the written words look like, yet it's a good idea to verify the contents. You should have a plastic bag with a staple-bound instruction manual, a flyer with Sony's technical support phone number, a guide to the Entertainment Software Rating Board (ESRB) software rating system, and at least one advertisement from Sony. This list is subject to change, but whatever comes in this packet, keep it all (at least for now) — especially that owner's booklet.

Figure 2-4:
The AV cable delivers audio and video signals to your TV.

Even if you skip over everything else in the instruction manual, take the time to read pages two through five, which detail safety precautions, as well as installation tips, advice on antenna interference, and other basic information that every PS2 owner should know.

Before you start plugging things in, now is an excellent opportunity to write down your PS2's serial number. There's a small space for you to write it on page 2 of the instruction manual, but I suggest being a rebel — scrawl it large and legibly on the back cover of your manual. It's the eight-digit number starting with the letter *U* on the back-left side of the PS2. You need this number if you ever call Sony with a technical or warranty question.

Striking Some Familiar Cords (Or, Wire We Doing This Again?)

Now that you have everything laid out and unwrapped, it's time to start connecting the cables. If you've ever built a computer, this will be easy; if you've ever turned on a television, this will be only slightly trickier.

Connecting the AV cable

There's no real right or wrong order to plugging things in, but the path I show you offers the least opportunity for doing something wrong or dangerous.

The first cord to connect is the AV cable (see Figure 2-5). The rectangular end plugs into the rear of the PlayStation 2, in the lower-right corner where it says AV Multi Out. Because you want to send multiple audio and video signals out of the PlayStation 2 and into your TV, this must be the right place. Sony has shaped the plug so that there's only one way that it can fit in correctly; to make it even easier, the cable itself has an arrow, the PlayStation logo, and the Sony name — all of which should be facing up when you plug it in. Slide the cable into the PS2's port gently so as not to bend the silver sleeve.

The other end of the AV cable ends in three-colored plugs (refer to Figure 2-4) commonly called *RCA plugs* — yellow for the video signal, red and white for the stereo audio signals. Again, if you've connected a VCR before, this plug should look familiar. Depending on your television, you should see three input jacks for audio and video that match these three plugs. Your TV's ports may be color-coded to match these cables or they may not; the ports may be in the front or in the back (or both!). In all cases, your ports should be labeled in tiny letters as to what they do: Video 1, Input 1, and so on — it depends on your TV. But however your ports are labeled, that's the channel you'll be watching through. Plug the yellow cord into the video jack, the red cord into the right audio jack, and the white cord into the left audio jack. If you don't have a stereo television and therefore don't have two audio jacks, connect only the white plug to your TV. You won't hear PS2 games and movies in stereo, but you will hear all the audio from both channels squished into one.

If you've already got a VCR or a CD player hooked up through your home theater system, chances are you've got a receiver as the main hub of your entertainment system. The connection is the same to a receiver as it is to a television; the only difference is that you should hook up the red, white, and yellow cables to the back of your receiver on one of the video inputs. Most receivers have at least two video inputs, often cleverly titled Video 1 and Video 2. Either will do; just make sure that you select the proper video input when you want to use the PS2. And if you're out of available video inputs, fear not — a solution is just a paragraph away.

One thing you may be tempted to do is connect your PlayStation 2 to your TV through your VCR's input jacks, using the VCR as a middleman. Don't! The PlayStation 2 plays DVD movies (more on that in Chapter 5) and, consequently, a copy-protection scheme has been built into both the movie discs and the VCR to stop people from simply copying DVD movies to VHS tapes. Because that copy protection is encoded into the video signal, your VCR may know when it's being fed an illegal signal from a DVD player (your PS2), and it will intentionally sabotage your viewing experience. The result is noticeably bad video — the screen may switch between too bright and too dark every few seconds, or distort the picture, or it may choose to do something entirely different but really annoying. If you do notice 1950s-style picture quality, don't panic — there's nothing wrong with your games, your movies, your TV, or even your PlayStation 2. You've just hooked the system up in a way you shouldn't have.

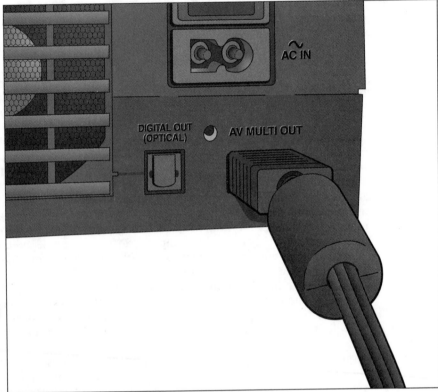

Figure 2-5:
The rectangular AV cable plugs into the AV Multi Out port on the rear of the console.

If you have only one set of input jacks on your TV, and you already have something plugged in there, you either have to swap the cables every time you want to use the other device, or you can get a multiple input-output box — commonly called an A/B switcher, A/V switcher, or just switcher — so that you can have several devices connected to your TV at once. A switcher enables you to choose between your VCR, PS2, or whatever at the touch of a button. Sony makes one such switcher — but so do a lot of other companies. Check your local electronics store or the TV/games department of stores like Wal-Mart or Target. For more information on advanced connection options and high-end cables, zip forward to "Advanced Connection Options" near the end of the chapter.

Hey, these cables don't fit my TV!

If your TV set is a bit elderly, you may run into an entirely different problem at this stage — your TV may not have input jacks at all. If your set has a little silver-threaded barrel connector in the back, but no other obvious inputs, you're going to need a different cable than the one that came with your PlayStation 2. It's called an *RFU adapter* (Sony's part number is SCPH-10071, but plenty of third-party companies make similar cables for a little bit less), and it slides over that silver barrel in the back of your TV. Choose a channel (three or four) on the RFU adapter, and when you change the TV to that channel and turn the PS2 on, you see the PS2's output on that channel. Unfortunately, the image isn't quite as crisp as it is with the AV cable, and the sound isn't in stereo, but the RFU adapter does get the job done.

But if many people have little silver barrels on the back of their TVs, why do you have to buy the RFU cable separately? Most modern TV sets have input jacks, so Sony chose the connection method that offered the best quality and that would be the most popular with their expected audience. If your old set conks out and you buy a new TV, you'll be able to use the cable that came in the PS2 box, and you'll notice an improvement in the quality of both the audio and video when you play games or watch DVDs.

Connecting the controller and power cord

The Dual Shock 2 controller is up next. Plug it into the nine-hole, three-segment slot on the front-left portion of the PS2, just below the small door that says *Memory Card* and the number *1* (see Figure 2-6). Like the AV cable, the Dual Shock connector is shaped so that there's only one way that it can go in — with the Sony logo and the small silver square on top. You don't hear a clicking noise or anything, but the controller should fit snugly into the PS2.

For the purposes of setting up the machine, you could technically plug it into port 2 and still be okay — menus can be navigated and DVDs can be played using controllers in either port 1 or 2. But when it comes time to play a game, the difference matters much more.

In addition to the four main action buttons and the four shoulder buttons, the Dual Shock has two directional controllers: a digital thumbpad and an analog joystick. In the menus, they work interchangeably; in a game, if the software supports it, the analog stick offers smoother, more precise movement (kind of like in a car, when you want more steering accuracy while turning a corner). Some older PlayStation games don't support the analog stick, but you'll find that most newer games (and their menus) do.

You should plug the controller into the machine before you power it up, just to make sure it's completely calibrated and ready to go. But it's okay to shove one in with the power on, too. For example, if you're playing a single-player game and want a friend to join in, you don't have to power the console down just to add a second Dual Shock.

Finally, take the remaining cable — the AC power cord — and plug it into the back of the PS2, just below the power switch (see Figure 2-7). Again, the plug is shaped in such a way that there's only one way to connect it to the PlayStation 2. The other end goes into the wall, of course, unless you'd like to use a surge-protecting power strip (see sidebar).

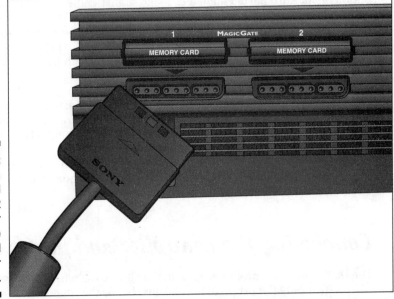

Figure 2-6:
Plug
your Dual
Shock 2
controller
into the
left-hand
controller
port.

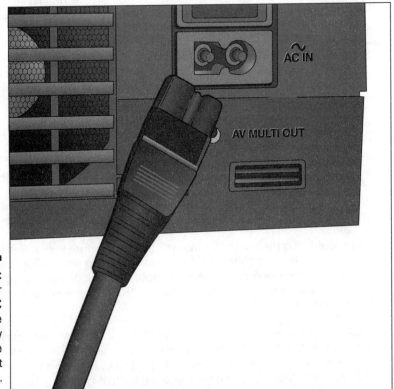

Figure 2-7:
The port for
the AC
power cable
is slightly
above the
AV Multi Out
jack.

USB and i.Link: The funky jacks

Aside from all the obvious connectors, a few more small jacks may become very important before long (although they're not necessary for your initial installation). On the front-left area of the PS2, just below player one's controller port, look for a gradient blue panel with two wide rectangular openings and one small, almost square, hole (see the following figure).

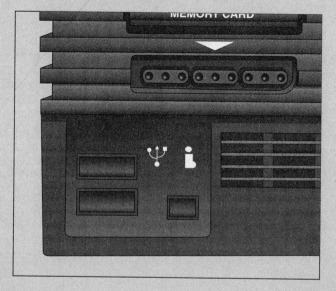

The larger rectangles are Universal Serial Bus (USB) connectors; they're denoted by the small three-pronged icon, which is supposed to represent easy connectivity of multiple devices; instead, it comes off looking like a bent pitchfork. USB is a big deal in the Windows and Macintosh communities because the technology allows different peripherals and accessories — such as mice, keyboards, scanners, disk drives, joysticks, and other neat stuff — to be connected easily for instant use. As soon as you plug in a USB device, the computer recognizes it and knows how the device should be used.

Right now, the PlayStation 2 doesn't use the USB ports for anything official, but a few games from independent programmers — namely, *Unreal Tournament* and *Half-Life* — already support USB keyboards and mice, the input devices of choice for skilled players of both games. When the PS2 gets its Internet act together, you'll probably need those peripherals for Web surfing, too.

The smaller hole is for the i.Link cable, which is Sony's name for a scary-sounding technology called IEEE-1394. Most of the world, however, currently knows this cable by its Apple brand name, FireWire. The i.Link port is similar to the USB port, but the cable that can be inserted there will move much more data, making it perfect for such things as digital video cameras, CD-ROM burners, and very fast hard drives. Will that stuff actually come out for the PlayStation 2? Maybe, maybe not — of all the doohickeys on the PS2, Sony's said the least about the i.Link port. In Japan, the company did demonstrate a digital camera, the Cyber Shot P1, but whether that will appear on American shores is a matter of time and speculation.

You Control the Horizontal, You Control the Vertical

One of the coolest things you can do with the PlayStation 2, without even turning it on, is to stand it on its end, vertically (see Figure 2-8). The standard way to run the PS2 is laid flat (horizontally) like a VCR. But if you look carefully, you'll notice little rubber feet on the left face of the machine (near the power and controller jacks). It's not only okay to stand the PS2 up on its end, it's actually intended to operate that way. In the horizontal position, the PlayStation 2 looks and functions like a normal CD player; when it's balanced vertically, a little lip in the CD tray keeps the game or movie disc from falling out when you load it. Whichever angle you prefer can be complemented by an optional stand specifically designed for that position. The stand's gradient blue fade looks pretty, and the stand costs only $10 to $15. But the little rubber feet that come installed on the PS2 will do just as good a job.

Don't put the PlayStation 2 in any position other than horizontal or vertical. In horizontal mode, the printing on the memory card doors should be legible; when the machine is vertical, you should see the shining, silver Sony logo at the top and the PS2 logo on the side is right-side up. Any position where you see text upside down is wrong! Besides, two orientations should be plenty.

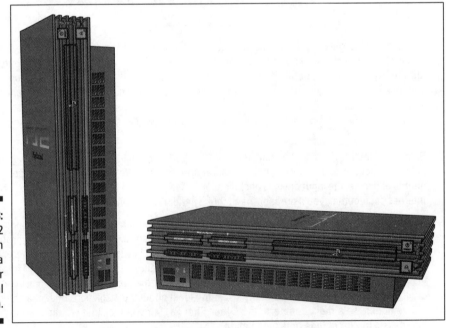

Figure 2-8:
The PS2
runs in
either a
horizontal or
vertical
position.

Another thing — figure out which way you want to run the machine and leave it that way as long as it's turned on. If you start playing a game with the PS2 in the horizontal position and then change your mind and want to go vertical, you could damage the disc that's currently trapped inside if you change the machine's orientation. Take the disc out, turn the machine off, and then realign the machine to your preference.

One of the niftiest, silliest aesthetic details on the PlayStation 2 is that the small, colorful logo on the CD drive door rotates (see Figure 2-9)! If you like to keep your PS2 in horizontal mode, the logo is already in the right position; if you prefer vertical, twist the logo gently to the right, and it snaps into place so that it's right side up even when the machine is up on its end. You can switch it back and forth at will. It makes no difference and serves no purpose. It's just cool.

Figure 2-9:
The drive door's PS2 logo rotates manually left and right to match horizontal or vertical mode.

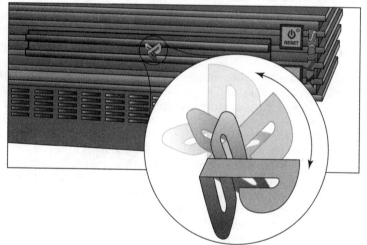

Advanced Connection Options

Now all the elements are in place for you to use your PlayStation 2. But if you want to get optimum performance out of your new machine, and if your television and sound system are relatively new, you can buy a few special cables that dramatically improve your sound and pictures. Better still, you may already have the jacks you need for those special cables — ready and waiting to be used — and not even know it.

Will using non-Sony cables break my PS2?

If you call Sony tech support, they will tell you that using third-party peripherals of any kind can damage your PlayStation 2 and invalidate the warranty. Most of the time, that's sound advice — Sony can't control how other companies make peripherals, and a few of the cheaper ones either break real fast or, on occasion, have damaged the console they're plugged into. Time and again, Sony's own controllers and memory cards have proven themselves, outlasting and outperforming the competition. But when it comes to video cables, it's not a major deal. Sure, Sony doesn't want you using third-party cables when you could be buying its own brand. But the fact is that Monster Cable's S-video cord (detailed in "S-video and why you want it") is far superior to Sony's own, and it's non-licensed third-party stuff — supposedly taboo! Other than "if it's cheap, maybe it was cheaply made," there's no reason not to buy whatever cable fits your budget.

S-video and why you want it

For the best possible video connection, you may want to consider replacing your standard AV cable with an *S-video cable* (see Figure 2-10). The cable for S-video — short for super video — replaces the yellow RCA-style video plug with a five-pin barrel connector. The S-video cable has been a standard for high-end video for a number of years now, so the input jack may be built into your television without you realizing it. S-video lives up to its heroic name — with it, you'll notice sharper images and richer colors. If your television does have an S-video input jack in the back, connecting the cable to your PlayStation 2 is the same as before — just plug the rectangular end into the AV Multi Out port and the other end into the appropriate jack on your television. Sony makes an S-video AV cable, and so do many other companies. The cable will run you between $10 for a bare-bones wire from InterAct and $40 for Monster Cable's awesome gold-plated GameLink 300 S-Video AV Cable. Bottom line: If you can connect your PS2 via S-video, do it. The improved quality during both gaming and movies is worth the extra expense.

The light sounds of optical audio

The equivalent technology to S-video — *optical audio* — is a little newer. As with S-video, you'll notice the difference immediately if you opt for optical audio. Fiber optic technology is what telephone and Internet companies now use to improve speed and quality — literally moving digital data at the speed of light. Your PlayStation 2 comes ready to take advantage of optical audio, but you need a special cable (which usually costs about $30, depending on the brand) and an optical audio receiver (quite a bit more). An optical audio receiver is merely one that features an optical audio jack on the back panel. If yours doesn't have a small port that says "Optical In" or something similar, you aren't ready for this step.

Figure 2-10: S-video connectors feature five pins tucked inside a silver barrel.

On the PS2, the jack for the optical audio cable is in the back, just to the left of the AV Multi Out port; it's labeled *Digital Out (Optical)*, and is covered by a small spring-loaded door. You can insert one of the optical cable's ends into the jack, noting that there's only one way to insert it correctly (the rounded end goes on the bottom — see Figure 2-11). With the optical connector attached, you don't need to use the red and white plugs from your AV cable. You can leave them disconnected if you want.

Most optical audio cables come with small plastic sleeves on the tips so that the connector isn't damaged in transit. Remember to remove that guard, though, before you plug the cable into anything, or you'll get the cable jammed in the jack.

The hard part of enhancing the sound is finding something to plug the other end of the cable into. Fiber optic audio is a new enough technology that there's a good chance you're not set up for it — unless you've bought a new, high-end stereo setup in the last two or three years. Luckily, a number of companies have started to produce stand-alone speaker systems for computers, DVDs, and, yes, PlayStation 2s that take advantage of optical audio. The speakers start as low as $200 (for one that emulates surround sound with just three compact speakers) and go as high as $500 (for a full six-speaker setup that delivers a full Dolby Surround home-theater experience). The speakers represent a sizeable investment, but they'll make a huge difference. Digital audio is much crisper through optical cables than it is via RCA-plug analog wires. If you're in the market for a new speaker system and you want to take advantage of digital audio, check out Chapter 13 for some suggestions.

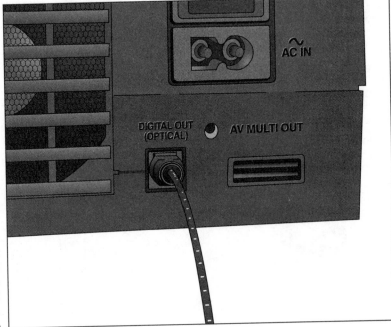

Figure 2-11:
The optical
audio output
is located
right next to
the AV Multi
Out port.

One drawback to the PlayStation 2's audio offerings is that you can't obtain
true Dolby Surround — the five-channel, all-encompassing, bowel-shaking
sound you hear in real movie theaters — without using an optical cable. If
you hook up the PS2 with the regular AV cable, you get only normal stereo.
It's an unfortunate all-or-nothing scenario, but Sony is betting that optical will
become a standard (especially for DVD enthusiasts) over the next five years.
Sony is planning for the future by making the PS2 fully capable of generating
great sound quality.

The shocking truth about surge protection

Accidents happen, so it pays to be prepared. If (heaven forbid) your house is hit by lightning, or the power company experiences problems and pushes too much juice through your electrical outlets, that extra energy has to go somewhere. Where you don't want it going is into your precious PlayStation 2, which will promptly fry if it gets too much of a good thing. The best protection against such power surges is an aptly named *surge protector*. The concept behind the surge protector is simple: If too much electricity is sent through the wires, the surge protector shuts it out, turns itself off, and refuses to let any power get through to your electronic components. Surge protectors should be a part of every household, and they're even more important when you're defending delicate computer equipment like the PlayStation 2.

All surge protectors are rated in *joules*, a basic unit of electrical energy measurement. The higher the joule rating, the more excess power the protector can ward off. Depending on what else you plan to plug into it, you should go with a power strip rated for at least 500 joules. Check the outside of the package before you buy. If you can't find a joule rating, don't buy it.

Surge protectors are available at hardware, office supply, and department stores as both small single-plug adapters or full six-plug power strips. It's important to note that all power strips are *not* surge protectors — make sure surge protection is explicitly stated on the packaging before you pick one up. Price varies from $10 on up to $60, depending on the quality of the components used. In theory, however, you don't have to pay top dollar because the joules rating is your real guide to the amount of protection. Shop around, and you'll be surprised.

That said, one of the nicer options for gamers is Monster Game's PowerStation 600, a colorful six-outlet power strip rated at 555 joules, which features wide-spaced slots for those space-hogging "wall-wart" power supplies (the big cube things, especially popular on older video game systems), lockable outlets (for safety, so metal objects or water won't fall in when nothing's connected), additional surge protection for your phone line, and a flat-face, gold-tipped connector. It costs about $30.

Chapter 3

Power On — Now What?

*B*y now, you've probably curtailed your giddy joy long enough to connect all the parts that need connecting. If not, go back one chapter and make sure that you have all the cables in all the right jacks. Now it's time for the biggest step of all: Turning the PS2 on. Go ahead. You've earned it.

Playing with Power (The Right Way)

No doubt, as you were messing around in the back of the machine as you hooked things up, your fingers stumbled on a rocker switched (just above the AC power cord) marked with an *I* and an *O* (see Figure 3-1). This is the main power switch — although it may seem that one of those huge metal switches with a big wooden handle out of an old horror movie would be more appropriate. Nah, all you need is this little black switch that you can flip with one finger. Oh well.

Figure 3-1:
The main power switch is located at the rear corner of the PS2.

Assuming that you turn on the machine correctly, two small, colored lights — green and blue — light up on the Reset and Open buttons, respectively (see Figure 3-2). That's a good thing. And, for what it's worth, that blue light is rather unusual. Most of the little lights you see in electronic components are LEDs (light emitting diodes) and they're red. Red LEDs are easy to make and therefore cheap. Yellow and green are fairly common, too. But blue . . . blue was the Holy Grail of little, colored lights until a few years ago. The fact that Sony used one here has (believe it or not) been the topic of much discussion and excitement because the technology, no matter how basic it may seem, is fairly new — and the blue LED looks cool. So if you hear geeks joking about the blue light in the PS2, you'll know why.

Figure 3-2:
When the PlayStation 2 is powered on, you'll see a green light and a blue light on the Reset and Open buttons.

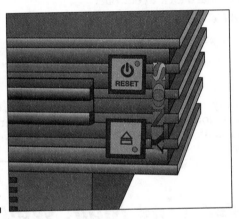

You may be wondering why I call this section, "Playing with Power (The Right Way)." Flipping the little rocker switch won't put you at any great risk — it's kind of hard to do it wrong, really — but the PlayStation 2 has more power modes than merely On and Off. A third mode, *Standby*, is new to the console world. PC and laptop computer users may already be familiar with something similar. Standby is sometimes known as *Sleep mode*. In Standby or Sleep mode, the power is on, but the machine is dormant. This mode saves power and wear and tear on the machine (computer equipment generates heat — the longer it's on, the hotter it gets), while the machine is still ready to spring to life at a moment's notice. Standby mode is handy when you're going out for only a few hours, say to buy some new PS2 games or the new issue of *GamePro* magazine (hint hint), and you know you'll be back to play soon.

To put the PS2 into Standby mode, simply press and hold the Reset button for about a second and a half. A light tap to the Reset button (as its name suggests) resets the machine. But if you hold it in a bit, the green light changes to red and the blue light goes out altogether. That's it — the red light means you've got power and the machine is on, but resting. To wake the machine up again, simply press and release the Reset button quickly. The green and blue lights return, and things should start jumpin' again.

How do you know when to put the machine into Standby mode and when to turn it off? Use your discretion. Turning the power off overnight is a good idea; if you're going to use the PS2 multiple times over the course of a single day, however, Standby mode should be fine. As a rule, it's better to power down completely if you're going to be away from your PS2 for six hours or longer.

After you have the PlayStation 2 running, don't move it around. You want to avoid yanking any live cables out of their sockets and messing up your software. When the PS2 gets a disc spinning at a few hundred miles an hour, the last thing you want to do is mess up its balance. If you want to change the machine's orientation from horizontal to vertical, power it down and remove any disc that's inside first; then move the machine to your preferred position.

Taking Control of the Controller

Before you dive into the menus, make sure that your controller is connected. You should only have one hooked up, in the first (left-hand) controller slot for single-player games, and a controller in each slot for two-player games. If you accidentally plug a controller into port 2 for a single-player game, you won't have much luck when the game loads; just unplug the controller and move it to port 1. You can use the black Dual Shock 2 (see Figure 3-3) controller that came with the machine, or you can just as easily use an original Dual Shock or any other PlayStation controller. That's great news if you're moving up from an original PlayStation because it means you already have some spare controllers for multiplayer games. Dual Shock 2 controllers have an advantage over the older models in some games (check out the sidebar in this chapter), but for the menu navigation you're about to do, there's no difference between the old and new Dual Shock.

Before using the Dual Shock 2, Sony recommends that you place your thumbs on the analog sticks and rotate them once to calibrate them and ensure that they're not off-kilter when you start a game. To be honest, as long as the sticks are centered before you start, you shouldn't need to recalibrate them manually. Treat them nicely and don't move them around while the machine is starting up, and you'll be fine.

Figure 3-3:
The Dual
Shock 2
controller
is your
interface to
everything
the
PlayStation
2 offers.

Dual Shock 2: The sequel

PlayStation 2 controllers look and feel just like original PlayStation controllers. Inside, however, they're different in a key way that affects how you use them. The difference is the new analog buttons. Yes, just the buttons. No, wait, I know you care — let me explain.

Traditional buttons on a gamepad (including the original Dual Shock) are digital in that they have two stages: on and off. When you press a button, you complete a small electrical circuit inside; when you let go, you disconnect it again. Simple, right? In the original *Ridge Racer,* pressing a button either stomps on a car's accelerator or slams on the brake. With *Ridge Racer V*'s

support of analog buttons, however, how hard you press determines how far down the gas pedal goes. This pressure sensitivity gives you the same kind of a-little-is-enough control over your acceleration and braking that you have in a real vehicle. Consequently, you can ease off the gas going around a turn or lightly apply the brakes in heavy traffic, which makes a big difference in your game strategy and affects the realism of the action.

This analog-button innovation could open the door to new types of PS2 games, depending on how programmers choose to implement it.

Browsing Through Your Memories

After turning the power on, but before you load a game or movie disc, you see a short animation and land at the PlayStation 2's main menu (see Figure 3-4). Besides the pretty swirling lights, you have two main options here: *Browser* or *System Configuration*. (I cover those smaller icons at the bottom of the screen shortly.) You can access this menu only when there's no disc inside the machine. (You'll want to visit this screen every so often, for reasons that will become clear shortly.) Highlight the word Browser on the menu (it becomes blue when selected) and press the ✖ button on your controller.

Throughout the PlayStation 2 menus, the ✖ and ● buttons are constants. The ✖ is always *Enter*, which selects an option, and the ● is always *Back*, which returns you to the previous menu. Pressing ▲ calls up *Options* for more information or access to things you can change, but the triangle is not used quite as often as the other two buttons. For basic navigation, mind your ✖'s and ●'s.

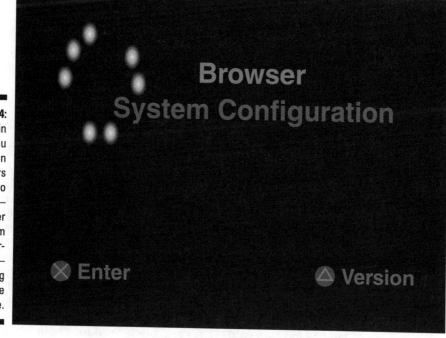

Figure 3-4:
The main menu screen offers only two options — Browser and System Configuration — keeping things nice and simple.

Browser
System Configuration

✖ Enter   △ Version

Navigating the Browser

The Browser is a visual menu of whatever memory cards or disc-based software you have plugged into the PS2. (If you have nothing loaded, which is likely at this stage, you'll see the matter-of-fact summary, No Data, instead.) Assuming that you have a memory card of some kind, go ahead and plug it into one of the two small doors marked Memory Card, if you haven't tried to do so already. As you may have guessed, they slide in with the label/writing facing up (see Figure 3-5).

Figure 3-5: Insert the memory card face up, just above the controller port.

Memory card management

There are two types of memory cards: PlayStation and PlayStation 2. If you plug in an original PlayStation card, you see a gray memory card icon with rounded bottom edges appear on the screen; if you insert a PS2 memory card, the icon is black and has sharper corners on its bottom edges (see Figure 3-6). In truth, the icons look a little too similar, but they're very different in terms of size and application. An original PlayStation memory card can hold 120K of data; a PS2 card can hold 8MB — over 66 times more. If you were hoping to sell all your old memory cards on eBay thanks to all that extra space, don't. Original PlayStation games still need to save their data to original PlayStation memory cards, and PS2 games can't save games to anything but PS2 memory cards. The PlayStation 2 can read both types of cards, but it uses each for a different purpose and it can't bend those rules. So even though you can copy original PlayStation game data to a PS2 memory card, you can't access that data from within the game. Sorry.

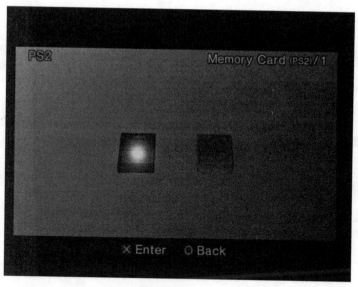

Figure 3-6:
Gray
memory
card
icons are
PlayStation
cards, while
black
ones are
PlayStation
2 format
memory
cards.

To see what's saved on the memory card, whether an old or new one, use the directional pad or analog stick to position the glowing white dot over the memory card icon; then press the ✖ button. You should see . . . nothing. That's right — you haven't put any data on the card yet (unless you put an old card in, in which case you'll see your old saved files). Later, after having saved some high scores, settings, records, or custom elements in a game, you'll see small 3-D icons for each title. The data for the Electronic Arts (EA) snowboarding game *SSX,* for example, is represented by a small animated 3-D snowboard; the off-road racing game *Smuggler's Run* generates a little red truck on the screen when it saves your progress through the game's missions. Here's a look at my current memory card (see Figure 3-7):

Four of the six icons in Figure 3-7 are for PlayStation 2 *game saves* (the files that keep track of how far you've progressed in a game). The one in the center of the top row — the uncanny, tiny reproduction of the PS2 console itself — is the PlayStation 2's own system settings. That's where the console keeps things like your clock choices, your viewing preferences, and other preferences you'll set up shortly. The remaining icon is for an original PlayStation saved game from *Tony Hawk's Pro Skater 2,* which I've copied from an original PlayStation memory card as a backup. Icons for original PlayStation game saves are simple 2-D squares. The PlayStation 2 keeps the old icon intact but presents it as a floating 3-D tile. All original PlayStation saves appear this way when you view them on a PS2.

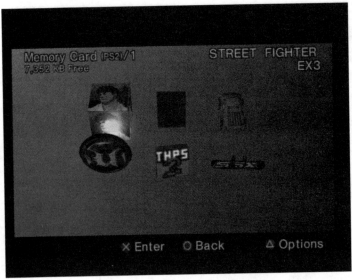

Figure 3-7:
Each game's
saved
data is
represented
by an
appropriate,
often
entertaining,
icon.

Moving the white glowing cursor around with the analog stick always selects a file. The description of that file appears in yellow in the upper-right corner of the Browser screen. The description is usually just the name of the game that the data belongs to. Other times, the description may be more specific and state whether the saved file is a record of your personal preferences for that game or an instant replay of a cool moment in the game you wanted to keep. Either way, if you forget that, for example, the little cube with Ryu's face on it is saved data for *Street Fighter EX3,* just highlight the icon with the cursor and you find out immediately what the icon represents. If you want even more information about a file, press the ▲ button while the file is highlighted to activate the Options menu. You don't really get options, but you do get details, such as what type of data it is, exactly how much space on the card the saved file takes up, when the file was last accessed, and whether or not there's any file protection on it.

Some of you may be asking about file protection. What do you need to protect a game file from? Well, some games lock the saved information to one card and one card only. You can delete it, but you can't copy it to another memory card. This is a drag if you're paranoid and like to have your data backed up, but it's meant to discourage people from sharing things like secret characters with friends who didn't put in the effort to earn those goodies. Whether or not a game save is automatically protected depends on the programmers and their intent, but if it's locked the first time you see it, there's nothing you can do to change that. You've gotta play the games by their rules!

Copying and deleting saved data

If a saved file isn't locked to one memory card, copying is not only possible, but easy, and a pretty good idea. No memory card is foolproof, not even the ones made by Sony. Sometimes, saved games (your place in the game) get lost or corrupted — a little unexpected static charge, an accidental trip through the washer, who knows? It's not a bad idea to be prepared, so back up your saves every week or so.

To copy a saved file, follow these steps:

1. **Make sure that you have two memory cards plugged in — your *source* card that you're copying data from, and the *destination* card that you want to copy the data to. If you don't, it's safe to insert them now.**

2. **Highlight a saved file with the cursor and press ✖.**

   A second menu appears with basic details and two options: *Copy* and *Delete* (see Figure 3-8).

3. **Select Copy with the ✖ button.**

   You're then asked where to copy the file. The name of your destination card should come up automatically.

4. **Press ✖ again and the file copies to the second memory card.**

   When it finishes, a message appears on the screen telling you that the job is done.

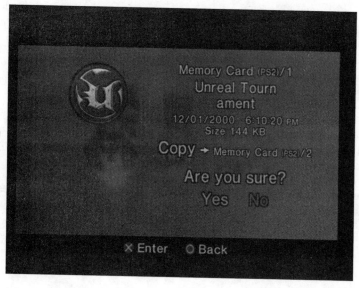

Figure 3-8: Copying and deleting data are best managed from the Browser.

When copying data to or from a memory card, keep your hands off! If you yank out the card too soon, you stand a good chance of wiping out or corrupting the very information you're trying to preserve. Wait until the screen says it's okay to remove a card before doing so.

Remember: If you copy original PlayStation game data over to a PlayStation 2 memory card for safe keeping, you can't access that data from within the game. You have to move that data over to a regular PlayStation memory card before you load that file to play that game. And because original PlayStation cards don't have enough space for PS2 saves, you can't copy the newer saves to an older format card.

A similar procedure applies when you want to delete data. If you have unwanted data, for example, from a rented game that you know you'll never play again, or you have an outdated or redundant backup saved game, follow these steps:

1. **Highlight a saved file with the cursor and press ✖.**

2. **When the second menu featuring Copy and Delete appears, select Delete and press ✖.**

3. **To make sure that you haven't reached this menu by mistake and are about to make a huge error, your ultra-polite PS2 asks, "Are you sure?" If you are, press left on the control pad to highlight Yes in blue, and press ✖.**

Poof — a digital disappearing act.

After you delete a saved game from a memory card, there's no Undo — it's gone for good. Be sure that the data you choose to delete is stuff you're never going to want again, because you can't get it back — ever.

Tweaking Your PS2 to Your Tastes

In addition to the Browser, the PS2's main menu also offers an option named System Configuration. If you don't have a wristwatch or clock handy, now is a good time to get one.

The System Configuration menu is broken down into five categories (see Figure 3-9). Each one is easy enough to set correctly, as long as you know what they all do.

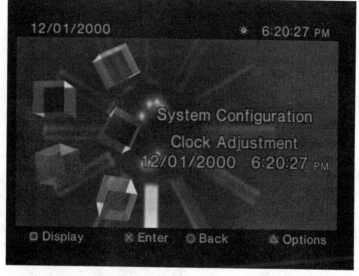

Figure 3-9:
The System
Configura-
tion menu:
boring
information,
pretty
packaging.

Clock Adjustment

The first thing to configure is the clock. Check the date and time. If they're not right, make them so. Press ✖, and you can monkey around with chronology. Sorta. Setting this information correctly is important because games time-stamp their saved files, and some even incorporate this data into the game-play itself. For instance, *Madden NFL 2001* makes note of special holidays like Thanksgiving if you play the game on the appropriate Thursday. Neat.

You can make four more adjustments here by pressing the ▲ button. You can choose a 12-hour or 24-hour clock, the format for the date, your proper time zone, and whether or not you're currently observing Daylight Saving Time. Scroll up and down within the Clock Adjustment Options menu and press ✖ when you find something you want to modify. Tap ● to go back when you're done.

Screen Size

Do you want to get rid of those black bars at the top and bottom of the screen in your menus? The 4:3 setting is the default for normal TVs and owners who don't mind the letterbox look. If you prefer a full screen, though, you can switch it here. If you have a widescreen television, choose the 16:9 option for best viewing.

Digital Out (Optical)

This one's easy: If you have an optical audio cable connected (see Chapter 2 for details on why you'd want one in the first place), select On. If you're just using the wires that came in the box, set this to Off. It's worth noting that the only way to get full Dolby Digital sound — and all the cool surround effects it creates — is through the use of an optical cable. If you don't have the hardware for it, this option is a moot point.

Component Video Out

Believe it or not, the confusing, seemingly random string of letters found here doesn't matter. Both Y Cb/Pb Cr/Pr and RGB apply only to people with really high-end video cables, and folks with that level of expertise are probably not you. (If, however, you are using component cables for your system, set this to Y Cb/Pb Cr/Pr, and check out page 7 of the manual for more details.) If you're using an AV cable that ends in a standard RCA video plug or an S-Video plug (for more info on these wiring choices, see Chapter 2), you don't even have to worry about this setting. Speaking words of wisdom, let it be.

Language

If you'd rather read *Configurazione di Sistema* or *Systeemconfiguratie* than *System Configuration*, by all means, play around here! The PlayStation 2 is multilingual and can display its core menus in seven languages: English, French, Spanish, German, Italian, Dutch, or Portuguese. (What, no Latin? Plebians!) See? It's fun *and* educational.

You can also hit the pink ■ button at any time in this menu to make all those distracting words go away; then you can just stare hypnotically at the transparent geometric shapes floating in the background. Whatever makes you happy.

Delving Deeper and Deeper into System Configuration

You're more than ready to actually pop in a game and begin having some real fun. But some of you may have noticed one more icon on the main menu — a green triangle with the word Version next to it — and you want to know what this icon does. I'm so glad you asked. Press that ▲ button at the main menu, and you shall be rewarded.

After pressing the ▲ button, you see a menu (see Figure 3-10) that offers version numbers for the PlayStation 2's *firmware* — the software that's physically inside the machine, loaded into the computer chips. In time, Sony will likely create CDs with updates to the firmware to fix bugs or extend its capabilities. It's almost a certainty that a firmware upgrade will come with the planned hard drive and Internet port, given that the machine will have to know how to run the new bits you'll be adding to it. Out of the five items listed on this menu, you can only interact with two of them: DVD Diagnosis and PlayStation Driver, as displayed in Figure 3-10.

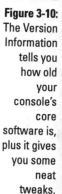

Figure 3-10:
The Version Information tells you how old your console's core software is, plus it gives you some neat tweaks.

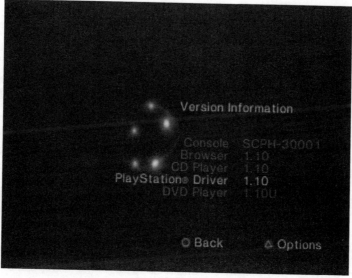

DVD Diagnosis

DVDs are sensitive animals. If for any reason your PS2 is not playing DVDs to your satisfaction, you can come to this menu, highlight the word Console, and press ▲. Then set *Diagnosis* to On and pop in the DVD video that's giving you trouble. The PS2 automatically analyzes it for a few seconds and temporarily adjusts its settings to match the DVD as best it can. If you still experience poor performance, you may have a defective disc. But at least the PS2 has a function built-in to let you know that it's not a hardware problem.

The next time you press the Reset button or load game software, this setting reverts back to its normal state, where it doesn't assume the DVD you've loaded needs any extra help to play. (In truth, you're not likely to use this tweak often.) If you have trouble with that same disc again, just remember to run the Diagnosis before you watch the flick.

The PlayStation driver

The original PlayStation featured a double-speed CD-ROM drive and some of the best 3-D graphics of its day. The PlayStation 2 features a CD drive roughly 12 times faster than its predecessor and 3-D graphics that make the old games look like the technological baby steps that they were. Shouldn't the new technology give a boost to the old software? It can and does. If you press ▲ while highlighting *PlayStation Driver* from the Version menu, you bring up a small menu of those boosts.

If you're planning on playing an original PlayStation game, you can tweak two important settings: *Disc Speed* and *Texture Mapping*. Disc Speed, as the name implies, can be set from Standard to Fast for quicker loading of game data. Depending on the game, you may find that the little Loading progress bar you're accustomed to seeing crawl across the screen (with the first PlayStation) now makes it only halfway there before popping straight to the finish line. Yes, this is what you bought a new game system for — speed, and plenty of it.

The other option is Texture Mapping, which you can set from Standard to Smooth in an effort to make your old games look prettier. One of the necessary by-products of original PlayStation games was giant pixels whenever you got too close to an object like a wall or a tree. If you set Texture Mapping to Smooth, the textures painted on those walls and trees will have a slightly blurry, but altogether less distracting look. Different games react in different ways to this boost: Some will look better, others will look worse, and some may not show any appreciable change (see Figure 3-11). A few games may even freak out — because you're monkeying with the speed of their data and the quality of their textures — and lock up on you, causing you to reset the machine (don't worry, no permanent damage). It's for you to experiment with if you have the patience and desire. The only drag is that, like the Diagnosis option, Texture Mapping reverts back to its Standard state every time you reset the machine — this is not a setting you can save. If you enjoy having faster loading times and smoother graphics, you will need to set this manually every time before you load an original PlayStation game. But hey, if you want to run your games like a power user on the bleeding edge of technology, by golly, you've got to accept the occasional inconvenience.

You're now done with the boring setup, and I hope you're wiser for the experience. Shall we play a game?

Before

Figure 3-11:
An example
of how
game
images look
just a little
bit sweeter
with Texture
Mapping set
to Smooth,
as it is in the
After shot.

After

Part II

Games, Movies, and Music: That's Entertainment!

The 5th Wave
By Rich Tennant

©RICHTENNANT

"There's a slight pause here where the PS2 sequences your DNA to determine your preferences."

In this part . . .

Some say that razor companies don't make money on razors, so much as on razor blades; after they hook you on the base model, it's the accessories that keep bringing your business back. If you stick with that analogy, the PlayStation 2's razor blades are game discs, DVD videos, and audio CDs — the core elements of a modern home entertainment library.

Running games and audio CDs shouldn't pose too much of a problem for most users, but the DVD functions of the PS2 can be a bit tricky, especially if this is your first DVD player. Fear not! In this part, I break down all the options, commands, and menus so that you'll never feel like the PlayStation 2 is out of your control.

Chapter 4

Running Games

*Y*ou'll probably be relieved to know that running games on the PlayStation 2 is pretty darned easy. You could say that it's similar to operating a toaster: You put the bread (game disc) in, push the button, wait for the bread to become brown (the game to start), and *ta da* — instant breakfast (or instant gaming fun). I don't recommend shoving bread into your PlayStation 2 any more than I suggest slapping a copy of *NHL 2001* into your Sunbeam 4-slicer, but you get the idea.

You can't do much wrong when it comes to getting a game up and running. As long as the disc you're trying to play is a PlayStation game, it's made for the country in which your PS2 was intended to be sold, and it's a legitimate piece of Sony-approved software and not some cheesy knockoff, you should be fine.

Discs of Many Colors

The easy way to distinguish a PlayStation or PlayStation 2 game from other formats — aside from the obvious appearance of the PlayStation logo on the box and the disc label — is the color of the disc. Original PlayStation/PS one CD-ROMs feature a shiny black layer on the underside of the disc; this black layer is partly for copy protection and partly, according to a Sony spokesman, because it looks cool. If you access the PS2's Browser from the console's main menu (see Chapter 3 for detailed instructions on where you find the Browser and how to use it) and insert a PlayStation disc, you see a black CD icon representing the game. Another identifier is the PlayStation's packaging (see Figure 4-1). Most PlayStation games ship in standard CD jewel cases, though some of the older games come in larger plastic or cardboard boxes that are about eight inches long and five inches wide. The thought was that the bigger the box, the more shelf space the game would take up in stores and the more attention it would draw. But when it became clear how wasteful this was, Sony decided to use traditional CD cases instead. Sales didn't suffer one bit.

Figure 4-1:
PlayStation games have been shipped in normal audio-style jewel cases as well as in extra-large custom boxes.

Photo courtesy of Michele Thomas

PlayStation 2 games come in two varieties: CD-ROM or DVD-ROM. CD-based software is colored a brilliant blue and holds about 650MB of data. Most of the PS2 launch games (*Tekken Tag Tournament, Ready 2 Rumble Boxing: Round 2, Silent Scope*) shipped on CD simply because these games didn't need tons of extra disc space. Additionally, DVD-ROM discs are bit pricey and manufacturing cost is always a factor for game companies. DVD-based games, including *Kessen* and *Rayman 2 Revolution,* ship on silver, higher-density discs that can hold over 4GB of game data. All PS2 games ship in DVD-style plastic cases (see Figure 4-2).

Figure 4-2:
PlayStation 2 software comes in locking, plastic DVD-style cases.

Photo courtesy of Michele Thomas

As for installing the game, I'll say it only once: label side up (see Figure 4-3). Putting it in the wrong way won't do anything bad, but it won't do anything particularly good either because you can't play the game that way. Everyone does it the wrong way at least once and feels silly, but as with every other CD-based software, the label faces up and the side lacking printing faces down. If you're running your PS2 in the horizontal position, just place the disc on the tray — there's no locking mechanism to keep it in place — and press the Open/Close button.

Figure 4-3:
Place the game disc in the PS2 label side up when loading.

Photo courtesy of Michele Thomas

If you opt to put the machine up on its end in the vertical position, inserting a game disc isn't much harder. A small lip on the tray loosely and carefully cradles the disc (see Figure 4-4). Slide the disc into that lip, and it will stay there on its own. Again, no tabs keep the disc in place; as soon as you hit the Open/Close button, the PS2 will pop the CD or DVD onto the spindle and start reading.

If you have a memory card with relevant data plugged in when you start a game, the PS2 usually loads that info automatically, depending on which game you're running.

If you're trying to run game software that's any color but silver, black, or blue, it probably won't work. And even if it is correctly colored, a few things can still keep the game from working, so read on.

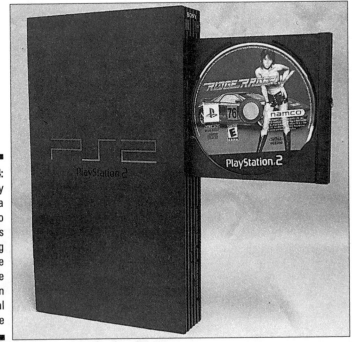

Figure 4-4:
The tray
features a
small lip to
keep discs
from falling
out of place
when the
unit is in
vertical
mode

Photo courtesy of Michele Thomas

Old dogs, new tricks, and backward compatibility

The PlayStation 2 runs games designed for the original PlayStation as well as the new software built for its own unique capabilities. Don't take that perk — called *backward compatibility* — for granted. No other game system has made it a standard feature before. Historically, game systems haven't had much respect for the machines they're replacing. Even in the old days of home gaming — you know, way back in 1986 or so — playing old games on your new system usually involved buying an expensive or hard-to-find converter. The PS2, however, makes backward compatibility not only possible, but easy.

If you can play PlayStation games on your PS2, can you also play PS2 games on your original PlayStation? Sorry, no. It doesn't work that way. The PlayStation 2 uses the original PlayStation's main chip as a supplementary processor, so when you drop in an old game, the PS2 welcomes the old game like a family friend. That's the secret to the magic. The reverse situation — playing a game for the PS2 like *SSX* on an old PlayStation — would be *forward compatibility*, and that's a magic trick that nobody in gaming has been able to pull off.

Imports of Importance

Some serious (or just seriously impatient) gamers like to play games imported from Japan, and maybe you'll want to do so, too. Japanese games are usually very different from the ones found in the U.S. for various cultural reasons. (For some shining and amusing examples of those differences, check out Chapter 15.) But different certainly doesn't mean bad, and because many PS2 games are born in the Land of the Rising Sun, being aware of what's going on in that market can give you clues as to what games may come out in your local stores.

So the big question is: Can you run Japanese games on an American PlayStation 2? And the big answer is: No. You can't run Japanese games on the original PlayStation either. In fact, no U.S. console has ever been able to play software from across the Pacific. Because few stores in America carry Japanese import games, it's kind of hard to buy the wrong kind of game by accident. Yet, with online shopping and Internet auctions so popular, you could conceivably wind up purchasing the wrong game. And because games from both countries are kept in DVD-style cases, and the PlayStation 2 logo appears in the same place on both boxes, the Japanese packages don't look dramatically dissimilar to the American ones. Sometimes they even share the same cover art, as in the case of *Ridge Racer V* and *Gradius III* and *IV.* Nevertheless, the tons of Japanese text on the front and back covers as well as on the box spine should be a dead giveaway (see Figure 4-5). If you're buying a game sight-unseen over the Internet or through a classified ad, it's best to ask first to make sure it's an American game disc.

Figure 4-5:
You tell
U.S. and
Japanese
games apart
by all that
foreign text.

Photo courtesy of Michele Thomas

Chips Ahoy

An American PlayStation 2, as it comes in the box, will not play Japanese games. But if you choose to modify your American PlayStation 2 — that is, open it up, void the warranty, and add a few chips and wires — it is technically and technologically possible to trick your machine into playing imported games. It's both risky and potentially expensive, but it can be done.

The next section describes unspeakable acts of electronic surgery and technological manipulation. In addition to putting your shiny new PS2 in serious peril, the activities below also put your Sony warranty on a one-way trip to Guarantee Heaven. I only included this stuff in case one of your modification-minded friends suggests playing digital doctor and using your PS2 as the patient. Make your own decisions; but if your PS2 ends up in a coma from the gentle doctor's "attention," don't say that I didn't warn you.

As the PlayStation gained in popularity over the years, enterprising amateur engineers began taking the covers off their consoles and adding custom components to Sony's design. With a couple of wires and a computer chip, these folks found a way to make their machines gleefully accept any PlayStation game it was fed, whether it was American or Japanese. This procedure, known as *chipping* or *modding*, became remarkably popular in some circles, and a similar method was devised for Sega's Dreamcast within a few months of its release in 1999.

There's just one problem: You're not supposed to do that! At least, not if you want your consumer agreement with Sony to stay intact. The moment you crack open the cover of your console, you've voided the warranty. Chipping is the kind of homegrown hot-rodding that Sony frowns upon. So if you go messing around with the innards of the console, you're on your own. Sony won't answer questions or honor the warranty. That said, many daring gamers have taken the risk and led long, happy lives with their customized game consoles.

It should come as no surprise that, yes, a mod chip is already available for the PlayStation 2. It enables your system to play PS2 games from either America or Japan, and it unlocks original PlayStation games from either territory, plus Europe (if you have the appropriate television to interpret those PAL signals). A chip will run you about $40, but you have to install it yourself or hire someone else to do it. Chipping is a difficult procedure involving precise soldering in tiny spaces and a bit of electronics knowledge. Plus, you run the risk of frying your $300 machine faster than you can say, "But-all-I-wanted-to-do-was-be-the-first-one-on-my-block-to-own-the-latest-games."

As you may have assumed by now, my advice is to leave your U.S. PS2 alone. Use it for its intended purposes and don't risk destroying it just to feel like you're on the cutting edge of gaming. If you're serious about playing Japanese games, consider buying a Japanese PS2. It will probably cost you around $500, but you'll have the peace of mind that comes with knowing you haven't screwed up your American investment. If that doesn't sound like a viable option, be patient! Most Japanese games with cross-cultural genres, such as driving, fighting, and role-playing, are translated and surface in America eventually.

Bootleg Software is Bad, Mmmkay?

Some people don't want to chip their consoles to play imports as much as to play bootleg copies of games. That's a nifty side effect of PS2 modification — not only does it fool the PS2 into ignoring the territorial lockout, but it also circumvents the copy protection schemes built into the games as well. And, unfortunately, a disturbing number of people will rent a game, create a copy of it on their home computer's CD burner, and then run the copy on a chipped system. The copies go by several names — gold discs, CD-Rs, backups, burns, or whatever the cool hacker term of the day may be — but it all boils down to one word: Theft. Playing bootleg games reminds me of what Ian Malcolm says in *Jurassic Park*: "Your scientists were so preoccupied with whether or not they could, they didn't stop to think if they should." Just because it's technologically possible to do something doesn't mean it's necessarily a good or ethical idea to do it. Illegal copies of games take money out of the pockets of the creators. If you like a game, why not reward the people who made it by paying for it so that they'll have the resources to make more games? It's an old argument, but it makes sense in respect to the PlayStation 2.

The first telltale sign of a bootleg game disc is that it won't run. If you happen to pop one into your PS2, you'll be greeted with a screen telling you that the game is not valid software. On the disc itself, most enterprising thieves will use the PlayStation logo and make the discs look very official. But if it's not black, blue, or silver on the underside, you'll know it's not for real. Green and gold are not valid colors for PlayStation games. Of course, if someone has gone so far as to scrawl *Bootleg Copy of NBA Live 2001* across the top of the disc with a permanent marker, that's something of an obvious flag, too.

The chances that you'll unknowingly buy an illegal copy of a game are slim. Beware of game dealers who operate on street corners, out of the trunks of their cars, or through Web sites you've never heard of, selling games at prices that sound too good to be true — they probably are.

Chapter 5

Movies and Music Made Easy

As three-letter abbreviations go, DVD wields a lot of power. Few acronyms have created more excitement (well, maybe MTV) and fear (okay, *definitely* IRS) in the minds of Americans. DVD is a technology with massive potential — and potential for mass confusion. Like all buzzwords, DVD gets thrown around a lot, whether or not the people who do the throwing truly know what they're talking about. It's high time the topic was demystified!

DVD and How It Got Here

DVD stands for Digital Video Disc or Digital Versatile Disc, depending on who you talk to. Truth is, nobody is really sure, and it doesn't much matter anyway. DVDs are 5-inch optical discs that can store anywhere from 4.7 to 17 gigabytes (GB) of digital information, depending on how it's compressed. (Sticklers for detail may remind you that it's actually 4.7 billion bytes, and because computer bytes are measured in multiples of 1024 instead of an even 1000, DVDs can store only between 4.3 and 15.8 *true* gigabytes. They're right, but tell them to be quiet anyway. They're not helping.) Even if you take the low end of that range, 4.7 gigs is a bit over seven compact discs, or somewhere in the neighborhood of 3 billion floppy diskettes. Because you don't watch movies on floppies, however, you probably don't care; knowing that a single DVD can hold up to eight hours of high-quality video probably makes more sense.

In addition to packing an entire workday's worth of visual entertainment, DVD can do a lot more:

- ✔ Skip directly to a scene when you punch in the track number on your remote

- ✔ Hold up to eight tracks of digital audio (foreign languages, director's commentaries, isolated musical scores, and more)

- ✔ Store up to 32 subtitle/captioning tracks, including lyrics for karaoke sing-alongs

- ✔ Execute seamless *branching* of video so that manufacturers can store two versions of the same film on one disc (say, a PG-rated edit and an R-rated cut)

- ✔ Show up to nine angles of the same scene, which is especially cool with DVDs of musical concerts or behind-the-scenes looks at movies

Branching video is particularly interesting. If a disc offers two differently rated versions of the same movie on the same disc, you can watch whichever version you want, have the player branch off to insert the appropriately rated version of the footage at the appropriate time, and then return to the main content stream — invisibly to you. The *Terminator 2: Judgement Day* DVD offers branching playback between the edit shown in theaters and the director's cut; similarly, the DVD for *The Rocky Horror Picture Show* can branch to show either the American or British versions of the film. Videotape *definitely* can't do that.

DVD: The standard that almost wasn't

DVD is a unified standard. You don't have to decide between DVD and a similar competing technology — as people had to decide, for a while, between VHS and Betamax — or like you may have just done with PlayStation 2 versus every other cool game console on the market. But when DVD all started, it, too, was set up to be another two-horse race.

When the next generation of high-capacity video storage was being developed in the early 1990s, two standards were proposed: the MMCD format, which had Sony and Philips in its corner, and the SD standard, backed by equally big names like Toshiba and Time Warner. It took the influence of yet another corporate giant, IBM, to force the two sides to find a common ground. As a result, the DVD we know and love was announced to the public in September of 1995 — the same month Sony released the original PlayStation. Over 200 corporations make up the DVD Forum, which was established in 1997 to oversee the format. The Forum also controls the trademark (since Time Warner was nice enough to give it up) and ensures that everybody who makes discs has the information they need to make DVDs that are compatible and unified (for a surprisingly low fee). As a result, no single company actually owns DVD technology the way Sony owns the PlayStation or Microsoft owns Windows. So you can watch movies safe in the knowledge that the DVD Forum is watching out for you.

The stuff I mention in the preceding list is just a smidgen of the DVD's capability, but that's some of the neatest stuff you'll likely encounter. Not every movie supports all those doodads, either; you can check the back of the movie's box for its particular special features. Other positives are that DVDs don't wear out like videotapes, and DVD players are fairly sturdy, without a lot of moving parts that can malfunction.

Regional Encoding

One aspect unique to DVD movies is *regional encoding*. In an effort to thwart global piracy and give the movie studios some control over where their films are shown and when, most discs are encoded with a signal that allows them to be played only on machines sold in a specific country. (Some Hollywood products aren't released in theaters in other parts of the world for months or years after they've had their theatrical run in the States.) To that end, the whole world is split up into eight regions:

- ✔ **Region 1:** U.S., Canada, and the U.S. Territories (Guam and whatnot)
- ✔ **Region 2:** Japan, Europe, South Africa, and the Middle East (including Egypt)
- ✔ **Region 3:** Southeast Asia and East Asia (including Hong Kong)
- ✔ **Region 4:** Australia, New Zealand, Pacific Islands, Central America, Mexico, South America, and the Caribbean (however you want to pronounce it)
- ✔ **Region 5:** Eastern Europe (the former Soviet Union), Indian subcontinent, Africa, North Korea, and Mongolia
- ✔ **Region 6:** China
- ✔ **Region 7:** Reserved (for whom, Martians? Ooh, spooky)
- ✔ **Region 8:** Special international venues (like international flights)

Then there's Region 0, which doesn't really exist, but it's an unofficial way of referring to discs without any regional encoding. Regional encoding is entirely voluntary, so some smaller companies looking to save money on manufacturing costs will leave out the region code and sell the same DVD worldwide. Digital Leisure usually eschews regional encoding on their DVD versions of classic arcade games like *Dragon's Lair, Space Ace,* and *Hologram Time Traveler.* They all play fine in a PS2, wherever it is.

The shakeout is that movies intended for sale in England or Japan won't play on your U.S. PlayStation 2, so DVDs bought overseas make lousy souvenirs. Similarly, Japanese PS2's can't play American movies because the machine is set up for a different region. Regional encoding is usually noted on the back of the DVD's case, either in the fine print at the bottom or as a logo (usually a picture of a globe with a number in the middle of it). You won't have any trouble if you buy your DVDs at your local mall, but if you're buying from a small store or an individual online, make sure that you're purchasing discs with the correct region code for your PlayStation.

Open Wide! Or, Do You Feel Full?

Some DVDs feature content on both sides of the disc, usually when the disc contains two versions of the same film: full screen and widescreen. Full-screen formatting (sometimes called *pan-and-scan*) zooms in on widescreen movies so that the film can use all the TV screen space available, just like broadcast TV does. Widescreen (or *letterbox*) films, on the other hand, are presented in the same scale that they were shown in theaters (see Figure 5.1). A small set of numbers called the *aspect ratio* will tell you just how wide that wide screen really is: 1.33 to 1 letterboxing (that is, the screen is one and one-third times as wide as it is tall) isn't too distracting, but 1.66 to 1 gives you pretty decent sized bars at the top and bottom of the screen. Movies shot in super-wide aspect ratios like 2.35 to 1 include the classic James Bond movies and Cinemascope epics. Full screen, by contrast, is 4:3.

The important thing to remember is that there's no way to make the black bars go away if the disc offers only widescreen. If letterboxed films irritate you — and they do annoy a lot of people, especially those with smaller television sets — double-check the disc before you buy it. Most DVDs are available only in widescreen, and most have it on the cover as a selling point. The serious film buffs who helped establish DVD as a viable consumer format don't mind the black bars. You can talk with your local store salesperson to find out which screen formats your favorite film comes in.

One word you'll see thrown around quite a bit in regard to widescreen movies is *anamorphic*. When a disc is encoded for anamorphic widescreen (sometimes labeled as "optimized for 16:9 televisions"), that means it's ready to deliver a high-definition picture on a widescreen television. The image will still be fine in regular letterbox mode on your TV, but if and when you upgrade to a wider television screen (which most of the TVs of the future are expected to be), your movie will be ready to strut in its originally intended aspect ratio without losing any quality. Anamorphic encoding is nice to have if you're looking to upgrade the rest of your gear in a few years because you won't have to worry about buying that movie a second time. Plus, your PS2 can be set to display anamorphic films in 16:9 (check out Chapter 3 for details). For now, however, anamorphic doesn't do anything for or against your current setup.

Full screen

Figure 5-1:
Different
DVDs offer
films in
different
screen
formats,
from full to
extreme
widescreen.

Widescreen

Because there's always at least one exception to every rule, here are a few exceptions for DVD movies. Some films, such as the Limited Edition of *Men in Black,* have both widescreen and full-screen versions on one side of the disc. Other films may be widescreen only but still take up both sides of the disc, as does *Amadeus*. Still others, like *It's A Wonderful Life,* feature the complete movie on one side and supplementary material like documentaries on the other. More recently, DVD manufacturers have found a way to put two layers of data on the same side of the disc — imagine two independent grooves on the same side of a 33 rpm record — so you won't find many more discs that require you to get up and flip the DVD yourself.

Many DVDs also come with DVD-ROM material embedded on the disc, offering things such as interactive games, links to a movie's Web site, or the complete screenplay for you to browse or print out. You aren't able to see these elements on your PS2; you can only access them by using a home computer with a DVD-ROM drive. What's more, most DVD videos with ROM materials require a Windows-based PC (sorry, Mac owners) in order to see those computer goodies. If a movie features DVD-ROM extras, you'll see it listed on the back of the box.

Firing Up a Flick

As with games and audio CDs, you should insert the label side of a DVD face up; if it's a dual-sided disc without large printing on one side, the inner ring of the disc will tell you (in tiny writing) which version or half of the film you're loading. Whichever text you can read when you put the disc in the tray is the info that will load. The PS2 automatically recognizes and plays the disc; if you're in the Browser screen, move the glowing cursor to the picture of the compact disc and press ✖.

If you're not already at the Browser screen — for example, you're playing a game but want to stop and watch a movie — it's just as easy. Remove the game disc by pressing the Eject button, load the movie into the tray, and press Reset. The disc tray retreats into the PS2 and your movie loads in a few seconds.

The Control Panel (and Controller Shortcuts)

After placing a disc in the drive, you're ready to kick back and relax. Just one thing is standing in your way: You have no concept of how to control the keener functions of the DVD player, such as skipping directly to a chapter or activating extra audio tracks.

All DVDs have an internal menu, which is usually a simple list of features like Play Movie, Scene Selection, and sometimes Bonus Features. These features vary and depend on the disc you're playing, but the PlayStation 2 has its own interface. You can access the content on a DVD through your PS2 in two ways: memorize the dozen-plus default commands assigned to your controller or navigate the confusing jumble of numbers and icons masquerading as the on-screen Control Panel (see Figure 5-2). Both interfaces are just tricky enough to make at least one thing leak out of your brain at the exact moment you need to recall it. Because the Control Panel gives you a visual reference, I'll tackle its commands and note the gamepad shortcut for each function as I go.

Figure 5-2:
This slightly cryptic Control Panel can be tamed for your viewing pleasure!

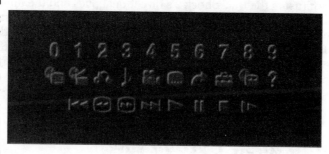

Just to keep things consistent, I use the phrase *DVD menu* to refer to the disc's own interface, and the phrase *Control Panel* when I'm talking about the PS2's interface.

Display the Control Panel

Press Select on your controller, and you see the Control Panel come up in translucent characters, superimposed on top of the film. Press Select again, and the Panel repositions itself a few inches down, in case the film you're watching has a busy background. Press it a third time, and it disappears altogether.

The Control Panel looks terribly imposing, which is kind of ironic because icons like these are supposed to be instant visual shortcuts to let you know what the heck you're doing *without* unnecessary confusion. But, take heart, a closer look reveals that the Panel is more familiar than you might think.

No matter how confusing things become, whenever you need to select something from a menu, the "enter" key is always ✖. If you highlight something and it doesn't work, press ✖ and it probably will. The literature that comes with some DVDs may tell you to press Enter or Select to access a part of the disc, but because your controller's Select button does something different, ignore that instruction. What they mean is press ✖.

Many of the commands on the Control Panel also have corresponding shortcut buttons on the Dual Shock controller. When the Panel is displayed on-screen, however, you can't use these shortcut buttons; to use them, you have to close the Panel by pressing Select. Or, you can just use the Control Panel and find the icon for the task you want to complete. Either way you're golden — you just can't have it both ways at once.

Control Panel: Top row

The top row of characters is a string of numbers. Highlight any of them with your cursor (using the Dual Shock 2's directional pad) and the numbers not only turn blue, but they also are joined by a little message at the bottom of the menu that says, Go to Chapter. If you want to skip ahead in the movie and you know the number of the scene you want to view (usually the chapter stops are printed on a card inside the DVD case), just punch it in by moving the cursor to the number you want and pressing the ✖ button. For two-digit numbers, press ✖ after each digit.

Control Panel: Bottom row

Skip down to the bottom row of eight Control Panel icons, which should look pretty familiar if you've used a CD player before. These icons correspond to the DVD player's most basic functions.

Previous and Next

The first icon on the left side is the Previous Track icon; it corresponds to the L1 button on your controller. Select Previous or press L1 while a movie is playing, and you skip backward to the previous chapter stop or sometimes to the beginning of the current chapter you're watching. If it keeps taking you back to the start of the current track instead of to the beginning of the chapter, simply hold down the L1 button a little longer, and the player will get the hint. Likewise, the R1 button matches the fourth icon in the row, which is marked Next. It skips you forward one chapter. If you're trying to go from the beginning of the film to the final scene, you'll want to use the Control Panel because it's just more efficient. The L1 and R1 buttons are good for jumping short distances.

Search

The second and third icons in the row are the Search icons. They enable you to rewind or fast forward through a chapter so that you can find the specific scene, frame, or piece of dialogue you want. The audio mutes while you do this, so all you have to go by is the jerky every-few-frames video. The L2 and R2 buttons on your Dual Shock match up with these functions. In case you hadn't guessed, L2 searches backward and R2 searches forward.

Play and Pause

The fifth icon in the bottom row is probably the most recognizable: a right-facing isosceles triangle (remember those from high school geometry?), which is now pretty much the international icon for Play. Without getting too fancy, when you select this, the movie starts to play. Honest. Unsurprisingly, the Start button on your Dual Shock shares that triangular shape and handles the shortcut function. To the right of the on-screen triangle is the Pause icon, and you can guess what that does. The Pause function is also handled by the Dual Shock's Start button. If a movie is playing, press Start to pause or un-pause it. When the movie is paused, you can't change things like subtitles or audio; the disc must be playing or stopped for those functions to be available. (You'll receive a little on-screen reminder if you try to do something that you can't while the film is paused.)

Stop and Slow

The last two icons in the row are Stop (the square) and Slow (the segmented triangle). Stop corresponds to the ● button on the controller. Any time you want to, well, *stop*, press, um, the Stop button. One cool thing about DVDs is that the PS2 resumes playing the movie where you stopped it, as long as you don't take the disc out. So if you're watching something late and have to go to bed, press Stop, go to sleep, come back later and press Play. You'll pick up right where you left off. Of course, if you do take the disc out or turn off the machine, the save point is lost.

If you stop the movie and you *don't* want to pick up where you left off, press Stop a second time to clear that short-term memory. When you press Play again, you start at the beginning of the movie.

The Slow function is sort of the Play button's evil twin. It plays the movie, but, as its name indicates, it plays it v-e-e-e-r-y s-l-o-o-o-o-o-w-l-y. At this speed, you can see all the hidden jokes in the *Toy Story* movies. Or, pop in *Reservoir Dogs* to see who really did what and when in the final scene. Because this is a feature you wouldn't want to activate by accident (and because it mutes the sound), the controller has no shortcut button that corresponds to Slow. To access it, you have to open the Control Panel with the Select button. To return to normal speed again, just press the Start button or choose Play from the Control Panel.

Control Panel: Middle row

I'm sure that for many of you, the top and bottom rows were no big shockers; you'd seen those icons before on CD players, VCRs, tape decks, and stuff like that. The middle row, however, is a little unusual because that's where all the DVD-specific functions are located.

DVD menu

The first icon calls up the DVD menu. As I mentioned before, DVDs have their own internal menu to help you play the movie, see the special features like outtakes and making-of documentaries, set your preferences for what sound-track and subtitle will accompany the film, and so on. Every disc menu is different, and many of the fancier ones have animated menus. In any case, one thing does remain standard: You use the directional pad on your controller to move around these menus. If you want to return to square one of the movie you're watching, the DVD menu icon is what you'll want. You can press the ▲ button to go straight to this menu without going through the Control Panel.

Title menu

A related icon sits next to the DVD menu icon: the Title menu icon. In theory, the Title menu icon should take you to a list of titles — yet another way to segment a film on a disc for quicker navigation — but I haven't found a lot of DVDs that support it. The titles are more of a behind-the-scenes feature for use by the DVD player itself; the Title menu has a more useful role when I discuss Parental Controls later in this chapter. If you do select this icon, you'll probably see a brief message on the screen saying, The operation you have chosen cannot be performed on this disc. This is the PS2's polite way of saying, "No dice, Jack." Go ahead and try its shortcut button — ■ — on the next DVD you play, and see if anything happens. If nothing does, it's no big deal; the disc simply wasn't mastered with that option in mind. You can still go to the DVD menu or access a track number directly with the Control Panel.

Return

The third icon represents Return, which is purely a menu navigation helper. If you've started to explore a menu and want to go one menu back, highlight Return and press ✖. Again, you'll find that this icon doesn't work with all discs; the DVD's own internal menu may override this function with its on-screen Back or Main Menu selections. As with the Title menu icon, try it out. There is, however, no shortcut button for it.

Audio settings

The musical note — fourth from the left — is for your Audio settings. Many discs come with multiple language soundtracks so that you can watch the movie with dialogue in French, Spanish, Japanese, or some other tongue. One popular DVD option that you'll often find on the audio track is a running commentary on the making of the film by people such as the director, the writer(s), or some of the actors. Some movies have multiple commentary tracks; some have none. Another popular DVD option is music-only tracks, the kind that *Camelot* and *The Matrix* offer so that you can hear the film's orchestration without the film's dialogue. This all depends on the disc publisher, and you'll usually see its languages, commentary, and music options listed on the back cover.

The shortcut button for the audio track is a little unusual: the R3 button. R1 and R2 are marked, so they're easy to find, but R3 is actually the right analog stick. If you press it down, you'll hear a faint clicking noise. It's a joystick and a button at the same time! Very few games take advantage of this feature, but because DVDs offer so many user options, Sony crammed special commands into every button on the Dual Shock controller. So press R3 to cycle through the disc's options. The current audio track will appear in the upper-left corner of the screen briefly and then disappear.

Angle

The fifth icon, a mini movie camera, changes the angle on your DVD visuals. Angle is another feature that few mainstream discs currently support. Imagine a rock concert on DVD where you can choose which of five cameras you want to watch at any given time just by activating the Angle feature. Presto — the view changes. King Crimson's *Deja Vroom* DVD is often mentioned as one of the better examples of the Angle technology. Some movies (such as *Fight Club* and the three-disc *Toy Story* boxed set) also use this option to show behind the scenes footage or rough takes, so you can swap between the real scene and the rough cut at will. Because this isn't a feature that many discs support, the controller has no shortcut key for it.

Subtitles

Subtitles are another neat DVD trick, and the screen-shaped icon sixth from the left on the Control Panel handles this feature. Whether you're hard of hearing, watching a film late at night with the sound down, prefer your discs in a different language, or are trying to learn a new one, most discs support at least English as a subtitle, with many offering other languages as well. (For example, *The Craft: Special Edition* offers no less than *seven* subtitle tracks, including Portuguese and Thai.) *Ghostbusters* takes unique advantage of the subtitle technology, offering tracks that reveal making-of notes as the film progresses and one subtitle track that isn't a subtitle at all, but the moving silhouettes of the writer, director, and producer as if they were sitting in front of you in a theater; they'll even point at things on the screen as they talk about the film on one of the alternate audio tracks! This particular *Ghostbusters* option is pretty cool, and while you're watching, you can easily switch to it on the fly with the L3 button (press down on the left analog stick).

One weird behavior you should be aware of is that some discs load up with English subtitles turned on by default. Nothing you can do can prevent that from happening, and there's no user preference that you can adjust to stop it before it starts. If the disc wants to do that, it will tell the PS2 to turn the subtitles on and the PS2 will comply. To remove them from the screen, just turn them off manually by tapping L3. It's a minor annoyance but an easily solvable one.

If you look very closely at your owner's manual, on page 15, you'll find Sony's warning in tiny little print that says even if a DVD does support multiple angles, subtitles, and various audio tracks, you may not be able to switch between them using your PlayStation 2! No reasons, theories, warning signs, or clues are provided. This warning is just put out there like, "Cough cough, stuff might not work, cough cough." An undeniably lame cop-out, but at the same time, Sony has no way to ensure that all DVD manufacturers are following the same rules. Other DVD players sometimes run into problems like this, too, so it's not Sony alone who needs to put microscopic warnings in its instruction manual. But if you do try to access these fancier functions and they don't work, consider yourself warned — quietly.

Go to Title

Seven from the left (or four from the right, if you prefer), you'll find a right-turn arrow that says Go to Title when you highlight it. This icon is related to the Title menu icon. If your disc supports titling and you know the number of the title marker you want to view, this icon enables you to enter it. Select the Go to Title icon, and then use the numbers to select your destination. As with the Title menu icon, there's a good chance Go to Title won't do squat. Additionally, the controller has no button shortcut for it, so you probably shouldn't worry too much about it.

Chapter Setting

The ninth icon from the left is the cleverly titled, Chapter Setting icon. (Yes, I skipped the eighth; it's a biggie and requires more space to explain. To see what's so special, check out "The DVD Setup Submenu" section later in this chapter.) Selecting this icon causes the Title and Chapter to appear on-screen and keeps it there until you tell the player to cut it out, already. When you select it, the words Chapter Setting On or Chapter Setting Off appear on-screen briefly. Is this handy? Maybe — if you really want to see how the film is divided up on your disc, you can play with this one.

Help

The right-most icon in the middle row — icon 10, phew! — is a big ol' question mark for the Help menu. Selecting this icon brings up a list of all the commands your Dual Shock controller can handle so that you don't have to run to the instruction manual (or even this book) to remember them. Because that's all the Help icon does, I'll make it even easier for you — this same information is included on the Cheat Sheet tear-out card at the front of this book.

The DVD Setup Submenu

In the preceding section, I skipped over the eighth icon in the middle row of the Control Panel. You'll be pleased to know that it actually does something worthwhile. The eighth icon, known as the Setup icon, is pretty important, and it's a shame that it's practically hidden in that middle row. Pick it, and you'll see a whole new Setup submenu pop up on the screen, with four new trees of stuff to worry about! Chances are, you'll need to go here only once — it's a set-it-and-forget-it kind of menu. Still, you should consult Setup, establish everything to your liking, and then get back to enjoying your movie.

The Setup menu is divided into four sections: Language Setup, Screen Setup, Custom Setup, and Audio Setup. You'll find a little map of these menus on page 17 of the instruction manual, and some items on the map will look similar to the stuff covered in Chapter 3. But those settings were for the PlayStation 2 overall, while these options pertain solely to DVD playback.

You can change options only for elements that glow blue when you highlight them; if the text appears in standard white, you can't monkey with it here. You can probably monkey with it somewhere else, though. See Chapter 3 for details about navigating the other big setup menu.

Language Setup

This setting is pretty self-explanatory. The four options are OSD (for on-screen display), the DVD Menu, the default Audio track, and Subtitles (see Figure 5-3); you can choose one of an impressive number of languages for each element. If you set Subtitle to Audio Follow, the subtitles (assuming the DVD you play contains subtitles in multiple languages) will automatically appear in the same language you select for the main audio soundtrack if that subtitle language is available. For example, if you choose the Spanish soundtrack of a movie and then turn on the subtitles, Audio Follow will make those subtitles appear in Spanish (if the disc contains Spanish subtitles). Sorry, the PS2 can't translate languages!

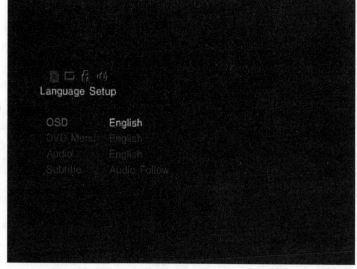

Figure 5-3: Check out the Language Setup menu to see what languages your PS2 is fluent in.

Screen Setup

If you read the "Open Wide! Or, Do You Feel Full?" section earlier in this chapter, you may remember all that stuff about aspect ratios, 4:3, 16:9, widescreen, and full screen. Well, that information is back with a vengeance (see Figure 5-4).

You can modify the visual details of your PS2 by using the Screen Setup menu. The TV Type shows the setting you chose in the System Configuration menu (if you aren't sure what that setting is, check out Chapter 3). DNR stands for Digital Noise Reduction. If you're getting a poor picture and you know it's not your cables (for instance, it looks poor only on one or two discs), you can turn this on to minimize the problem. Press Right on the directional pad when you have DNR highlighted, and you'll find two levels to choose from: DNR1 offers a more subtle effect than DNR2, and it may or may not actually help the problem, depending on the disc. But it can't hurt to try because you can always turn off DNR.

Similarly, Outline Sharpening makes the images more or less blurry; press Right when it's highlighted to make edges stand out more (+1 and +2) or blur more (–1 and –2), depending on your tastes. Finally, the Display option lets you choose whether or not you want to see the little Play and Pause icons in the upper-right corner of the screen when you press a button during DVD viewing. For now, you'll want to leave Display on until you become comfortable with the player.

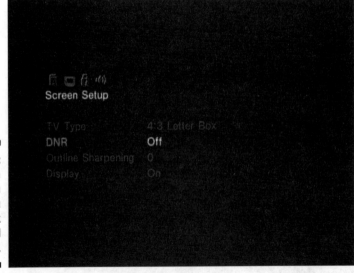

Figure 5-4:
The Screen
Setup menu
enables you
to tweak
your visual
details.

Custom Setup

Now it's time to assert your individuality by maximizing your PS2 through customization. Thankfully, the machine enables you to express yourself in at least two important ways, so read on.

Pause Mode

Pause is such a basic function that you may not have thought that you could set any options for it. Amazingly, you can. Your options are Auto and Frame and the difference between the two is minimal (the Frame option means slightly higher resolution). Consequently, unless you're planning to painstakingly examine the film when it's paused, leave Pause Mode on Auto.

Parental Control

Parental Control is helpful if you have kids in the house and want to restrict what they're able to see, to an extent. Some DVDs can play back under an eight-point rating system. This means, for example, that you can program the player not to show any type of flick except G- or PG-rated films. Your password would unlock this restriction. Figure 5-5 shows the screen that you see if you're using Parental Control and a disallowed disc is loaded into the machine.

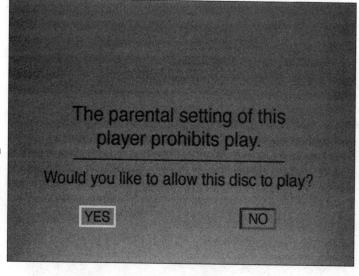

Figure 5-5:
The
Parental
Control
prohibit
screen.

The parental setting of this player prohibits play.

Would you like to allow this disc to play?

YES   NO

Because the technology exists to have multiple ratings of the same movie on one disc, a Parental Control code can tell the disc to substitute the R-rated parts of the film with G or PG versions (or just to skip them), and then rejoin the main film when the questionable stuff has passed. (This is an example of branching video as explained in the "DVD and How It Got Here" section at the beginning of this chapter.) Very few DVDs support this multiple-ratings feature because it's a lot of work and hassle for the studios. Still, a few big movies, such as *Crash* and *Poison Ivy*, do support it.

You should also remember that the Parental Control returns to whatever default you've set it at when the disc you're watching is stopped. That way, a younger viewer can't swap discs and watch some film you may not want them to see simply because you entered the code for one specific play of one disc.

Setting the Parental Control password

To set the Parental Control password (see Figure 5-6), press Right at the Parental Control option to choose and set a four-digit password; then set the Region and the level at which you want to restrict material. If you're a consenting adult and you know your DVD is safe from prying eyes, set this to Off to ensure that your player shows you everything that every disc offers. If you want to change your password, there's an option for that, too.

Resetting your Parental Control password if you forget it

If you forget your password and want to reset it, a built-in code will erase the existing one and enter a new one. That code is 7444, and is standard across all PlayStation 2 consoles.

Figure 5-6:
The all-
important
Parental
Control
setup menu.

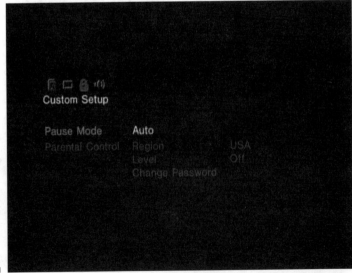

Audio Setup

Another way to customize the DVD setup of your PS2 is by delving into the intricacies of sound. While this may seem esoteric, some of the Audio Setup options are integral to your listening pleasure (see Figure 5-7).

Digital Out/Optical

This menu (and therefore this portion of the book) is of great interest only if you're using the optical output cable for digital sound. But there's one important option that applies to everybody else.

The Digital Out/Optical menu tells the machine what types of signals it should deal with. If the PS2 doesn't have to send information to the optical port, it doesn't really want to; if you are using the optical output cable, turn Digital Out/Optical to On and choose whether you want it to play back signals intended for Dolby Digital, DTS, or both. Dolby Digital and DTS are two competing surround sound formats. They do nearly the same thing, but because they do it differently, the PS2 has to know which standard it should cater to at any given time. Your home theater/speaker system will determine this preference, and most DVDs are Dolby Digital, though some DVDs are encoded specifically for DTS.

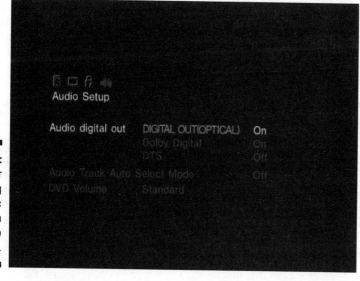

Figure 5-7: Adjust your DVD dialog and music options in the Audio Setup menu.

You should note that if you turn Digital Out/Optical to Off, you won't be able to obtain full, five-channel surround sound from the PS2. If you're not using an optical cable — if you're just hooked up to the TV with the cables that came with your PlayStation 2 — you're not getting full surround-sound anyway. Don't turn Digital Out/Optical to On if you don't have it, or you could hurt your equipment and/or your ears. In any case, if you play around with this, you probably know what you're doing, and the rest of us can leave it be.

Audio Track Auto Select Mode

When the Audio Track Auto Select Mode is set to On, it automatically picks the best-sounding audio track based on the rest of the system settings. For example, if you've told your PS2 that you have a DTS decoder hooked up, it will give DTS signals priority. Because foreign language tracks are usually not encoded in Dolby Digital or DTS, however, that means the PS2 will play English first, when you may prefer to hear your movies in French or Spanish. If you're multilingual, set Auto Track Auto Select Mode to Off and choose your soundtracks manually. Otherwise, this setting will override what you chose in the Language Setup.

DVD Volume

The DVD Volume option is a neat tweak that everybody can use. DVDs have a tendency to sound softer than games and audio CDs you play in the PlayStation 2. As usual (say it with me!): It all depends on the individual disc and the way it was created or mastered by the company that made it! If that's a problem, you can boost the setting to +1 or +2 here, but be wary of distortion — you don't want to amplify the signal so much that it damages your speakers. If you're using an optical cable for your PS2 sound, you probably won't be able to select this option. But DVD Volume is handy for folks using the standard A/V cable.

Using the CD Player

Playing regular compact discs is a lot easier than DVDs because there's less to worry about. All that jargon concerning the middle row of the Control Panel? It doesn't apply here. You won't have to worry about the top and bottom rows, either — the chapter numbers become track numbers, and the track skip, search, play, stop, and pause features all do exactly what they say. That Slow icon on the far right of the bottom row doesn't do anything with regular audio CDs, so if you're a guitar hero trying to learn the lead licks of your favorite players, sorry; that won't work here.

Play Mode

Head to the Browser screen and insert an audio CD into the PlayStation 2. (If you're not sure how to get to the Browser screen, take the easy way out —

remove the disc currently in the PS2, replace it with an audio CD, and hit the Reset button.) When you highlight the CD's icon with the cursor, you see a green triangle and the word Options appears at the bottom of the screen. Press ▲ and take a look at what you can do.

Play Mode offers three modes: Normal, where the disc's songs are played in numerical order; Program, where you choose a specific order in which the tracks will be played; and Shuffle, which lets the PS2 cut loose and choose the song order at random. See Figure 5-8 for an example of what a CD's tracks might look like after they're programmed or shuffled.

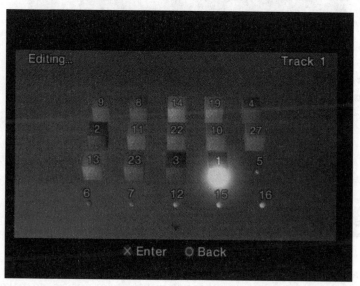

Figure 5-8: After you load a CD into your PS2, you can choose the order in which the songs are played in the Options section via the Program and Shuffle modes.

Repeat

The other element to this menu is Repeat, which is similarly straightforward. If Repeat is set to Off, the PS2 plays all the way through once (and plays whatever order you've chosen from the Play Mode menu) and then stops. If Repeat is set to All, the machine plays all the tracks in that order over and over again until you intervene. Set to 1, the PS2 plays a single song on the disc over and over again until your mind melts and you descend slowly into madness.

Just play that funky music, already!

You don't have to play with those options if you don't want to. To cut to the quick, highlight the disc in the Browser and press ✖ to see the CD tracks, which are represented as textured, colored cubes floating in space. Pretty.

Move the cursor over the track you want to play and press ✖ for instant music. A colored cube slowly rotates on the playback screen, and the Play or Pause icon (third and second from the right, respectively) flashes if the player is in either of those modes (see Figure 5-9); otherwise, there ain't much to see here. If you were looking for a cool lightshow like the one the original PlayStation offered, too bad. After all, the PS2 is just behaving like a regular CD player now. You do, however, get to stare at that cube . . . .

Figure 5-9: The PlayStation 2 doesn't provide a cool lightshow with audio CDs, but it does provide great digital music.

That's it. You now know everything your PlayStation 2 can do when it comes to movies and music — whether you wanted to or not. So, go make some popcorn, kick back, and watch a flick without worrying about how it works!

Part III
Let the Games Begin!

The 5th Wave   By Rich Tennant

Gerry and Mel Weintraub enjoy playing "Madden NFL Accountant" on their PlayStation 2.

Quick Gerry—defer the Signing Bonus! Watch the agent! Watch the agent!

In this part . . .

A game system isn't much without games, is it? Because the PlayStation 2 doesn't come with so much as a demo disc, you're left on your own to forage for games. And if you've walked into a software, toy, or department store lately to check out what's for sale, you've probably learned the answer — too much!

This is where *GamePro* comes in. The editors of that particularly popular, multiplatform video game magazine have culled all the necessary information on the current crop of PlayStation 2 games, as well as the best offerings for the original PlayStation (and its redesigned-but-entirely-compatible clone, the PS one; see Chapter 1 for more info on the clone). No matter what kind of game you enjoy playing — sports, action, racing, role-playing, or something else entirely — this part will offer some helpful information, including game descriptions, prices, ESRB ratings (for concerned parents), Fun Facts, and even S.W.A.T.Pro codes (the term "S.W.A.T.Pro" comes from the codes section of *GamePro* magazine). These codes concern special button presses that get you ahead in the games by opening up levels, making you invincible, invisible, and so on. So read on to discover the best PlayStation gaming out there.

How to Use This Games Directory

Welcome to the Part That Is Not Like the Other Parts. Any book about video games wouldn't be complete if it didn't recommend a few titles. Because over 800 games run on the PlayStation 2, this book can't even hope to be comprehensive. I've therefore attempted to be authoritative instead, choosing close to 200 games that matter most. This number includes just about all of the newest games, some of which weren't even on store shelves at the time of this writing (but will be by the time you read this). The rest of the games consist of the most influential and most enjoyable games that were originally released for the first PlayStation console — and which are, of course, compatible with the PS2. In other words, if you don't know what games to buy, this book has nearly 200 suggestions!

Icons Used in This Part

Since Part III is a bit specialized, I've come up with three icons that pertain only to these game summaries. If you're just browsing through this section, the icons can provide you with quick information about the category of the game.

Like any other form of entertainment, some games are more appropriate for adults and some are more appropriate for children. While the ESRB (Entertainment Software Rating Board) ratings work great, I figure there's no substitute for first-hand experience. Therefore, when I list a game that's particularly appropriate for younger gamers — that is, low on the scary imagery and content, but high on the fun factor — you'll see the Family Friendly icon.

When the going gets tough, the tough . . . cheat! Programmers like to hide tricks and options in the video games they create, and once you know the secret code (usually a specific sequence of button presses), you can access all kinds of things. For example, you can find special sports teams, secret levels, extra characters, or hidden elements. Every month, *GamePro* magazine corrals these cheats into a special section called S.W.A.T.Pro (Strategies, Weapons, and Tactics). I've searched these S.W.A.T.Pro archives for particularly cool secret tricks; to signal a successful find, I've added the S.W.A.T.Pro icon next to the pertinent text.

I'm a sucker for trivia, so if I know about a cool, behind-the-scenes story or a weird little tidbit of info that I think you might find entertaining, I've added it as a Fun Fact. They were fun for me to write, at any rate!

The ESRB and Its Ratings

Ten years ago, video games were seen as toys for kids. But as the gaming audience slowly aged, so did the subject matter of the software. People started to worry that the younger gamers were playing titles intended for older gamers, and sometimes parents would unwittingly buy their kids games with scary imagery, violent gameplay, or mature plot lines. In an effort to educate consumers before they went to the cash register, the Entertainment Software Rating Board began rating games in 1994 with a simple labeling system that now appears on the outer packaging of almost every game sold in America. Every game receives one of the following designations.

Early Childhood

If you're looking for the safest of the safe, here it is. Early Childhood (EC) games feature "content suitable for children ages three and older and do not contain any material that parents would find inappropriate." As you may expect, EC is used on a lot of educational software and is good for teaching kids basic motor skills, logic, and developmental stuff.

Kids to Adults

If you're six or older, chances are that you can handle any game rated Kids to Adults (K-A). The ESRB says K-A games "may contain minimal violence," "some comic mischief" (like cartoon-style blows to the head), or "some crude language" — which is no worse than the mildest four-letter words you'll hear on TV.

Everyone

Same rating as Kids to Adults, but a different icon. On January 1, 1998, the ESRB swapped K-A with the Everyone designation. The span of possible content is the same as Kids to Adults, too. Most sports, puzzle, racing, and character-based platform games are rated K-A or E.

Teen

True to its name, the Teen (T) rated games have content suitable for persons ages 13 and older. The ESRB says Teen titles "may contain violent content, mild or strong language, and/or suggestive themes." In real life, that means action/adventure games, many role-playing quests, outer-space shooting games, and some one-on-one fighting games.

Mature

Mature (M) rated games are intended for players 17 and older. Mature games are usually a bit more graphic than the Teen games. The ESRB says an M rating can also denote "mature sexual themes," but American games that explore sexually mature territory are rare. More often than not, an M rating in the U.S. means blood, guts, and/or guns. First-person shooters, gory fighting games, horror adventures, and anything that shows characters dying in a messy way will almost always receive an M. While many popular games have earned the Mature rating (and many more will continue to do so), some major stores, including Sears, Wards, and Kmart, no longer carry M-rated software.

Adults Only

Too hot to handle! Adults Only (AO) products contain content suitable only for adults. These games "may include graphic depictions of sex and/or violence." Not only are AO games intended for sale only to persons over the age of 18, but they're also nearly impossible to find on store shelves. I can't think of a single AO game, and there aren't any represented in this book.

Rating Pending

This isn't a rating you'll see on actual boxes, but you will see it in ads, previews, and in a few of the summaries in this directory. Rating Pending (RP) simply means that the ESRB hasn't yet received a finished version of the game, so it can't make a definitive call (or it's in the process of making one). No game hits store shelves with an RP icon. The ESRB always makes a decision before the game company prints the final packaging.

In addition to the basic categories, games also have a content descriptor phrase listed on the back of the box that tries to pinpoint just why the game earned its rating; these descriptors will say things like, "comic mischief" or "animated blood and gore." Ultimately, if you're a parent buying software for your children, the final decision is yours. The ESRB ratings are there to help you make your choice. If you ever have any questions about a particular game's rating, you can call the ESRB's hotline at (800) 771-3772 or visit its Web site at www.esrb.org, which contains a searchable database of every game ever rated.

And I'd Like to Thank . . .

Two hundred games is, well, a lot. When it came time to compiling all this info, I turned to the experts — my colleagues at *GamePro* magazine — and credit is definitely due. The pages in Part III were written by (alphabetically) Katrin Auch, Jake Blackford, Paul Curthoys, Justin Lambros, Francis Mao, John Marrin, Wataru Maruyama, Sean Molloy, Wes Nihei, Jonathan Rinzler, Mike Weigand, and Lindsay Young. I helped a little, too, but the praise for this part really goes to them. I hope that our combined strengths will supply you with the information you need to make the right buying and renting decisions.

Chapter 6

Action Games

*N*o lights, no camera — just action! The word *action* covers a lot of ground in gaming — from cute-and-cuddly platform style games to side-scrolling shooting games filled with nasty aliens to a few classic arcade reissues thrown in for good measure. A lot of good action games are available for the PlayStation 2. This chapter introduces you to some of the best.

In This Chapter . . .

Ape Escape

In *Ape Escape,* a scientific experiment goes awry and threatens to tip the evolutionary scales in favor of the apes. Consequently, Specter, a super intelligent monkey, outfits an army of simians with "smart-hats" and sends them back in time to turn the tables on mankind. Your job is to trip through history and mop up the monkeys! *Ape Escape* features an interface that relies entirely on the two analog joysticks of the PlayStation controller. You use them to wield all sorts of ape-catching gear — ranging from a Jedi lightsaber copycat to a trusty net — to defuse traps and snag your prey. *Ape Escape* is an action-packed, challenging game that could make a monkey out of you. The only thing missing is a cameo by Charlton Heston.

99 Explosive Bullets — You need ammo to fight off some of the more vicious creatures. To gather 99 slugs, pause the game and press

> R2, Down, L2, Up, Right, Down, Right, Left

Platform:
PlayStation/PS one
Publisher: Sony
Price: $39.99
ESRB: Everyone

Armored Core 2

Giant robots blasting each other is a sure recipe for high-octane action on your PS2, and *Armored Core 2* delivers with awesome sound and visuals and deep gameplay. Set on an earth decimated by war and controlled by corporations, *AC2* allows you to jump right into the mission-based action or to customize your robot — called an Armored Core — with a staggering 10 billion combinations of parts and weapons. It may take a while for you to master moving and targeting (controlling a giant robot isn't easy, especially without a license), but AC2 offers plenty of topnotch action for newcomers and hardcore gamers.

Did You Know? — *Armored Core 2* is actually the third *Armored Core* game. Agetec made *Armored Core: Project Phantasma* and *Armored Core: Master of Arena* for the original PlayStation.

Platform:
PlayStation 2
Publisher: Agetec
Price: $49.99
ESRB: Teen

Army Men: Air Attack 2

Platform:
PlayStation 2

Publisher: 3DO

Price: $49.99

ESRB: Rating pending

What if those little green and tan plastic soldiers from your childhood really did wage war on each other? That's the setup for 3DO's hugely popular *Army Men* series — sentient toys manning the controls of toy helicopters that spew deadly bullets, missiles, and rockets. In this sequel to *Army Men: Air Attack* for the original PlayStation, you pilot several types of helicopters as you do battle with the evil Tan Army. You fight through 26 missions in 10 environments, including a Japanese Garden, the Wild West, and Halloween Night. An addition to the original *Air Attack* game is that you can now use your helicopter's winch to swing objects as if they were wrecking balls and to toss items at your enemies.

Army Men: Sarge's Heroes 2

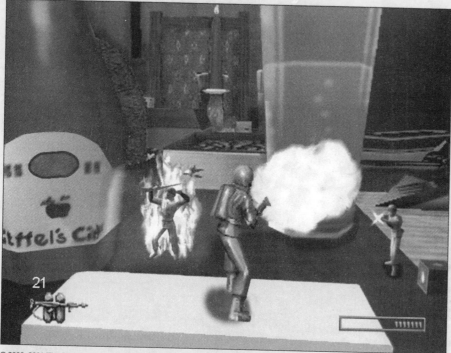

Platform:
PlayStation 2
Publisher: 3DO
Price: $49.99
ESRB: Teen

The eternal struggle between Green and Tan plastic soldiers continues on the PlayStation 2 in this silly, kids-oriented action game inspired by generic, dime-store plastic soldiers. You control Sarge, hero of the Green Army, from a third-person view in his war against the Tan Army's General Plastro. Sarge and his girlfriend Vikki fight through 14 missions, including a freezer, a bedroom, and the innards of a pinball machine, all while being attacked by Tan troops and tanks. Luckily, Sarge is armed with some serious weaponry, including a shotgun, bazooka, and flamethrower. *Sarge's Heroes 2* is a good game for kids who like to play soldier, but aren't old enough for more realistic shooting games.

Did You Know? — 3DO has published 12 *Army Men* titles for five gaming platforms (PlayStation, PlayStation 2, Nintendo 64, PC, and Game Boy Color), for a total of 21 *Army Men* releases.

Bomberman Party Edition

Platform:
PlayStation/PS one

Publisher: Vatical

Price: $14.99

ESRB: Everyone

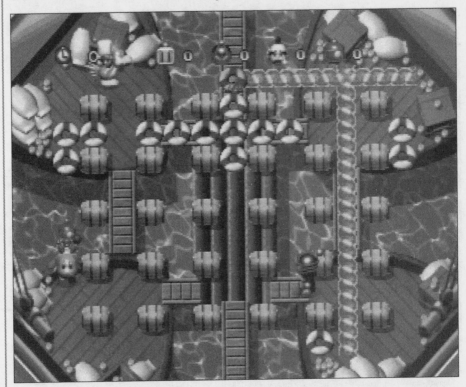

Here's the PlayStation take on a classic multiplayer game that totally redefines the idea of getting bombed. One to five people (with the multitap peripheral) can play this game. After each player picks out a differently colored Bomberman, they find themselves transported into a giant maze. Then you attempt to eliminate your pals by moving around the maze and dropping time bombs that hopefully go "boom" on your unwary opponents. Last man standing wins! *Bomberman* is famous for its myriad power-ups that can produce humongous, maze-filling explosions. But the game also includes creatures you can ride and skill icons that enable you to do things like kick bombs or move more quickly. Sorry, but there's no other way to say it: *Bomberman* is a blast!

The Bouncer

Platform:
PlayStation 2

Publisher:
Square EA

Price: $49.99

ESRB: Rating
Pending

The Bouncer is for people who like the idea of fighting games, but are usually left feeling numb by the mindless button-mashing and obscure move combinations. Set in a futuristic city, the plot revolves around a huge corporation that kidnaps a girl whose friends just happen to be bouncers at a nearby bar. The standard action, 3-D rescue mission is complemented by role-playing elements. (Square is the undisputed champion of console-based role-playing games and the maker of the hugely popular *Final Fantasy* series, which you find in Chapter 11.) You roam 3-D environments in which you can use or break many objects that you see among the scenery, such as tables or street signs. The story unfolds via both in-game events and gorgeous computer-generated cinemas. The developed story and diverse gameplay complements the two-fisted action nicely.

Platform:
PlayStation/PS one

Publisher: Sony

Price: $19.99

ESRB: Everyone

Crash Bandicoot: Warped

Warped is the third in a series of PlayStation games starring Crash Bandicoot, the fleet-footed marsupial you've probably seen in TV ads. Naughty Dog, the company that developed all the *Crash* games, has all the elements together for a truly enjoyable package. *Crash* busts out with non-stop, insanely addictive run-and-jump gameplay as well as eye-blasting graphics and an amazing assortment of moves. The game's story line involves the evil Uka Uka and his henchman Dr. N. Tropy, who use a time machine to zip through history stealing precious energy gems and magic crystals that will enable them to rule the world. Crash and his sister, Coco, really have to move to catch the diabolical duo. In fact, *Warped* requires a whole lotta running as Crash races through 30+ levels to beat Uka to the treasures. For the price, this game is a can't-miss must-buy.

Hidden Level — In Road Crash (level 14), you can drive your motorcycle into the yellow alien-crossing sign on the left side of the road to warp to a hidden level.

Platform:
PlayStation/PS one

Publisher: Sony

Price: $39.99

ESRB: Everyone

Crash Bash

In a departure from other *Crash* games, *Crash Bash* contains 28 mini-games that feature varying types of gameplay and levels of fun. Using the PlayStation's multitap peripheral, up to four players can compete in free-for-all action-oriented contests that generally involve collecting as many objects as possible, knocking objects into goals, or trying to blow each other up. You can also play in an adventure mode that ties together different arenas in a loose story line and adds boss characters whom Crash must . . . well, bash. Considering all the game challenges offered, you're bound to find several that will make you and your pals come back for more.

Did you know? — Part of the fun of *Crash Bash* is trying to identify the classic games that many of this disc's mini-games mimic. Depending on your video game experience level, you may recognize *Tank, Pong, Warlords, Poy Poy,* and others.

Dave Mirra Freestyle BMX

Ready to do stunts on a bicycle you'd never, ever try in real life? That's what BMX stunt master Dave Mirra does for a living — and what his game lets you experience for yourself. You can find out how to bust a bunch of cool two-wheeler moves and pull gravity-defying aerial tricks with relative ease. You can also pump pedals with eight real-life X sport pros. As your bike-busting proficiency improves, you take on 12 arenas ranging from a dirt lot behind Mr. Mirra's house to bigger and more challenging venues. BMX fans will recognize the San Jose Ramp Club and Camp Woodward's famous Lot 8. Even more gamers will recognize the laid-back grunge tunes featuring big-name bands like Sublime, Cypress Hill, Pennywise, and others. *Freestyle BMX* is a safe and sane way to let your bike-riding fantasies run wild.

Unlock All the Bikes — At the bike selection screen press

> Up, Left, Up, Down, Up, Right, Left, Right, ●

If you enter this code correctly, you'll hear a sound.

Platform:
PlayStation/PS one

Publisher: Acclaim

Price: $39.99

ESRB: Everyone

Frogger

Frogger is one of those simple digital diversions that proves the old video-game adage: Fun is fun. This version is a remake of the classic arcade game that challenged you to guide a frog past all manner of amphibian-squashing dangers, both amphibious and automotive (as seen on an episode of *Seinfeld*). This disc comes with the retro levels plus brand-new areas and multiplayer games. The game's 3-D graphics are uncomplicated and downright funny at times, while the controls are straightforward and easy to master. *Frogger* is a great trip down memory lane for those familiar with the original arcade machine, and it's a relaxing challenge for first-timers, too. Hardcore gamers would rather eat a fly than admit that this is one of the most popular games ever. Your goal is simple — just don't croak.

Platform:
PlayStation/PS one

Publisher: Hasbro Interactive

Price: $19.99

ESRB: Everyone

Die Hard Trilogy

Platform:
PlayStation/PS one

Publisher:
Fox Interactive

Price: $44.99

ESRB: Mature

The big screen flows nicely into the little screen as *Die Hard Trilogy* accurately captures the run-and-gun style of its cinematic brethren. This disc presents a unique value in that it combines three styles of gameplay. The first game, *Die Hard,* serves up third-person combat action in which you guide John McClane as he battles terrorists inside the Nakatomi Building. The second game, *Die Harder,* takes place at Dulles Airport where you use a first-person, target shooting view to take out more terrorists and save some hostages. In the third game, *Die Hard with a Vengeance,* you drive a cab through New York City in a wild race against time to defuse time bombs. If you're a fan of the films, *Die Hard Trilogy* offers a challenging way to triple your fun.

Good-Cop Bonus — At the beginning of Level 1-1 of the *Die Hard 2: Die Harder* game, don't shoot any civilians or blow up any cars. When the game takes you inside the airport, take care of the terrorist with the hostage behind the counter, and you will be rewarded with a Good Cop Bonus. When you're back outside with several metal containers, look inside them for better weapons and power-ups.

Donald Duck: Goin' Quackers

Platform:
PlayStation 2
Publisher: Ubi Soft
Price: $49.99
ESRB: Everyone

When it comes to family fun, it's hard to beat the characters of Walt Disney. World-famous reporter Daisy Duck is kidnapped while on special assignment trying to find out what's happening inside Merlock's Ancient Temple. And guess who must rescue her? Donald, of course. You control Donald as he attempts to hold his temper through four 3-D environments comprising 20 levels. His explosive personality ranges from determined to hyperactive, all the way to berserk. Gameplay includes chases, boss battles, and bonus levels. For gamers who aren't yet old enough to enjoy the more lifelike PS2 games, *Donald Duck: Goin' Quackers* may fit the bill. Ha!

Did You Know? — Donald Duck first appeared in 1934 in the Silly Symphonies short *The Wise Little Hen*.

Einhänder

Platform:
PlayStation/PS one

Publisher:
Square EA

Price: $19.99

ESRB: Everyone

Here's an excellent example of the side-scrolling shooter, enhanced for the newer generation of game machines. You pilot a spaceship against an increasingly powerful armada of enemy vessels backed by huge boss ships. While the game starts from the side-scrolling perspective, the view changes as the game progresses, taking full advantage of the PlayStation's 3-D power. *Einhänder* is twitch-action gameplay at its best — you slide up and down the screen to avoid enemy blasts while blasting adversaries by rapidly pushing the fire button. You can choose from three ships with varying arsenals and grab weapons from the spacecraft you destroy to build up big-time firepower. If you're looking for a non-stop workout, this gorgeous game is a winner (even though nobody knows what *Einhänder* actually means).

A Secret Area — In Stage 1, you can access a hidden level if you do all the following: Obliterate the weapons carriers, shoot all the neon signs, and destroy only the bottom section of the flying robot mid-level boss.

Gauntlet: Dark Legacy

Gauntlet is perhaps the most effective coin-slurping arcade game ever. If your medieval adventurer was about to collapse in the 2-D dungeon, you just slid in a few more quarters, and he would keep hacking or your archer would keep shooting . . . for a few more minutes anyway. Well, on your PS2, you don't need quarters to keep up with your comrades in this third title of the classic multiplayer arcade series. Besides the warrior, wizard, archer, and valkyrie, you can now play as a hammer-flinging dwarf, bomb-throwing jester, knight, or sorceress. In addition to updates of the Mountain, Desert, Forest, and Castle realms, *Dark Legacy* has four new realms: Ice, Town, Sky, and Dream. If you're looking for a fast-paced, arcade-style alternative to fantasy role-playing games, *Gauntlet: Dark Legacy* is for you.

Did You Know? — The original *Gauntlet* arcade game was made by Atari and was released in 1985. *Dark Legacy* is actually the fourth game in the *Gauntlet* series, an expansion of Midway's modern update, *Gauntlet Legends*.

Platform:
PlayStation 2

Publisher:
Midway Home
Entertainment

Price: $49.99

ESRB: Rating
pending

MDK2 Armageddon

In this gritty yet cartoonish game with a dark sense of humor, you lead a trio of reluctant heroes as they try to prevent aliens from strip-mining the earth. You control all three characters: Max, the wacky six-legged dog/action hero; Kurt, the stealthy sniper with the ribbon parachute; and Dr. Hawkins, the brainy mad scientist who combines household objects into lethal weapons of destruction. The slapstick humor nicely meshes with the colorful graphics, brain-bending puzzles, and twitchy combat. *MDK2* was first released for the Sega Dreamcast and was plagued by poor controls and a steep difficulty curve. The PS2 version will likely address those problems.

Platform:
PlayStation 2

Publisher:
Interplay

Price: $49.99

ESRB: Rating
pending

Gex 3: Deep Cover Gecko

Platform:
PlayStation/PS one
Publisher:
Eidos Interactive
Price: $19.99
ESRB: Teen

Gex 3 represents the apex of this popular game series about a smart-aleck gecko lizard and his further adventures in the Media Dimension: a world drawn from the pop-culture of movies and TV. This premise enables the game to present seemingly endless parodies of diverse topics such as Greek myths, Christmas TV specials, war films, Clint Eastwood, superheroes, Mafia movies, Sherlock Holmes, pro wrestling, and even *The Wizard of Oz*. Comedian Dana Gould supplies the voice for Gex, and he drops some sidesplitting (and sometimes obscure) one-liners. The platform-style gameplay has Gex climbing up and down walls, hopping around obstacles and traps, and tail-whipping adversaries through 34 tough levels. This well-constructed action game could make a lounge lizard out of you.

Super Gex — To make Gex invincible, pause the game, press and hold L2, and then press

Up, ●, Right, Up, Left, Right, Down

If you entered the code correctly, you should hear a confirming sound effect. Unpause the game, and Gex cannot be hurt.

Gradius III and IV

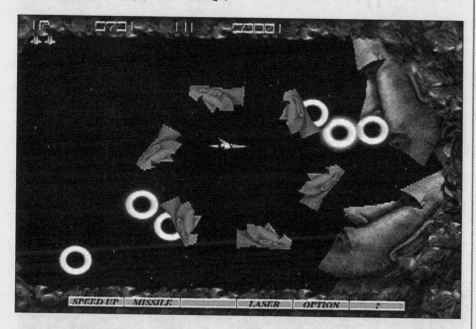

Platform:
PlayStation 2
Publisher: Konami
Price: $49.99
ESRB: Everyone

Gradius III and IV hardly pushes the technological limits of the PS2, but there's probably no better choice for mindless, old-fashioned space-shooting fun. Your job is to pilot a spaceship through several levels while collecting weapon boosts and blasting tough enemy bosses. While *Gradius IV* has slick sounds and graphics, *Gradius III* really shows its age: It was originally released for the 16-bit Super Nintendo, and the antiquated graphics and tinny sound haven't been improved. The only new additions to the PS2 versions of these game are a few rendered cinemas; otherwise, these are the original classic games, warts and all. Still, *Gradius III and IV* is a good value for fans of classic shooting games. Just don't expect any mind-blowing PS2 graphics.

Did You Know? — The first *Gradius,* considered by many as the *original* 2-D side-scrolling shooting game, was released in arcades in 1985 and was called *Nemesis.*

GunGriffon Blaze

Platform:
PlayStation 2

Publisher:
Working Designs

Price: $49.99

ESRB: Teen

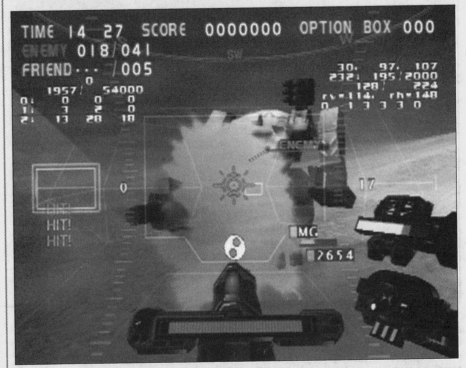

It's 2020, and you're at the controls of a giant robot — a *mech* in the game's lingo — keeping the peace in a post-apocalyptic world. From a first-person view inside your mech, you perform missions in colorful environments such as Guam, Tibet, and Greece, each filled with details such as roads, trees, and buildings in the local style. The environments are interactive, and you leave behind a swath of damage after you cruise through with your guns blazing. You use different tactics and weapons as you fight enemy mechs, tanks, and helicopters, including jumping behind your enemies or hiding behind obstacles. You're also able to upgrade your mech or even obtain a new one as you progress in the game.

Did You Know? — The original *GunGriffon* was released in 1996 for the Sega Saturn.

Half-Life

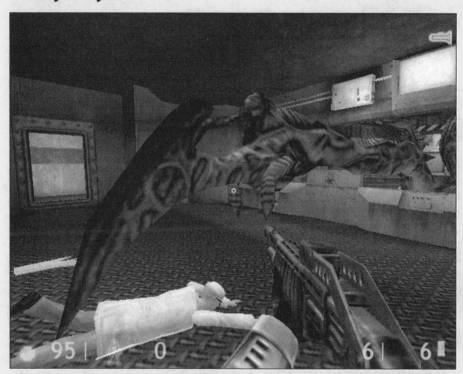

Platform: PlayStation 2
Publisher: Sierra
Price: $49.99
ESRB: Rating pending

When it came out for the PC several years ago, *Half-Life* broke new ground by combining first-person style action and shooting with a gripping science-fiction story. The result was a title lauded by many as one one of the best first-person shooters to date, and quite possibly one of the best games ever. The game takes place in the near future, and you're mild-mannered scientist Gordon Freeman, who works at the fictional Black Mesa Research Facility under the desert of New Mexico. When a risky interdimensional experiment goes horribly wrong, you must fight your way out of the massive underground compound, past terrible alien monsters, only to find the Marines have been called in to wipe out any evidence of the project. Who's behind the conspiracy, and will you live to find out? If you want a gripping story to go with your first-person action, don't miss *Half-Life*.

Did You Know? — The PC version of *Half-Life* was named game of the year by more than 50 publications in 1998.

Herdy Gerdy

Platform:
PlayStation 2

Publisher: Eidos

Price: $49.99

ESRB: Rating
pending

This fairy-tale-style game takes place on imaginary Balley Island, an isolated, magical land whose culture focuses on natural harmony. The herders who care for the island's creatures are the most respected citizens. You play as young Gerdy, who hopes to be such a herder, as he sets off to compete in the annual herder tournament in Mudland Wallow, home turf of the reigning (evil) herder, Drego. This 3-D action/adventure game promises to be nonlinear — players can take Gerdy wherever they want. As he makes his way across the island, Gerdy has to herd various creatures, improving his skills in the process. The graphical capabilities of the PS2 guarantee that *Herdy Gerdy* is a beautiful adventure for younger gamers.

Medal of Honor Underground

Medal of Honor Underground is a World War II combat action game that drops you behind enemy lines . . . and you may not want to come back! The game takes up where the equally impressive *Medal of Honor* left off. You embark on your campaign as a female member of the French Resistance, who's been recruited by the American O.S.S. (Office of Strategic Services) to work espionage missions in North Africa, Crete, Italy, and France. The first-person perspective combat enables you to lock-and-load an impressive arsenal of historical military firearms, but you also have to use your brains as you don disguises, outwit Nazi guards, and sabotage heavily guarded military facilities. Excellent animation and extraordinary audio effects inject a massive dose of realism into the adventure. With *Medal of Honor Underground,* war is swell.

Did You Know? — *Medal of Honor Underground* and its predecessor *Medal of Honor* were inspired by the movie *Saving Private Ryan* and created by DreamWorks Interactive. In fact, Steven Spielberg was the driving force behind the game, which he created for his son, Max. Spielberg based *Medal of Honor* on the real-life exploits of the O.S.S. and the French Resistance, the Maquis.

Platform:
PlayStation/PS one
Publisher:
Electronic Arts
Price: $39.99
ESRB: Teen

No One Lives Forever

It's the swinging '60s in this Austin Powers-inspired spy shooter, and you're Cate Archer, female secret agent. No, James Bond has nothing to do with this one. This unusual spy-parody game combines over-the-top characters and tongue-in-cheek humor with intensely realistic first-person shooting action in espionage-rich environments such as East Germany and Morocco. Despite the lifelike weaponry — AK-47s, sniper rifles, and more — you need to rely on stealth and cool gadgets to get back to London alive. Your gadgets include exploding lipstick, a lock-picking barrette, and lots more. If you're the type of video-game hero who likes a little sweetness in your tea, *No One Lives Forever* could be your bag . . . baby.

Did You Know? — A James Bond novel titled *Nobody Lives Forever* by John Gardner — not Bond's creator, Ian Fleming — was published in 1986, but was never made into a movie.

Platform:
PlayStation 2
Publisher:
Fox Interactive
Price: $49.99
ESRB: Rating pending

Mega Man X5

Platform:
PlayStation/PS one

Publisher: Capcom

Price: $39.99

ESRB: Everyone

Mega Man, one of the all-time video-game heroes, first made the scene in cartridges for the old Nintendo Entertainment System (NES) in the late '80s. *Mega Man X5* harkens back to those thumb-bruising days with the sort of vicious, side-scrolling blast-and-dash action that made the *Man* famous. Evil robots called Reploids are threatening to plunge an asteroid into Earth, so you have to hunt them down across eight outer-space colonies. The colorful 2-D graphics look sharp and . . . well, like a high quality old-school video game. But don't drop your guard because of the cartoony visuals — aggressive robot bad guys, insane puzzles, diabolical traps, and methodically murderous end bosses will make fair-weather players cry for their Mega Mamas. You can't claim hardcore gamer status until you've mastered *Mega Man X5.*

Namco Museum: Volume 3

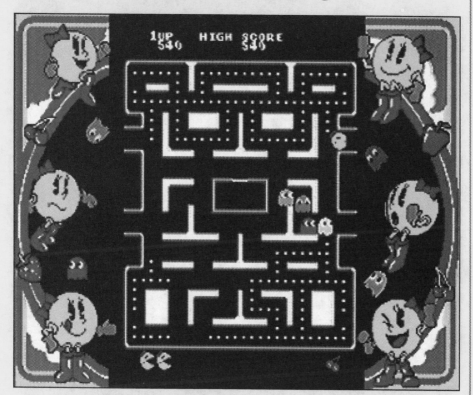

Platform:
PlayStation/PS one
Publisher: Namco
Price: $19.99
ESRB: Everyone

Namco Museum: Volume 3 contains some classic coin-crunchers from arcades past: *Pole Position II, Dig Dug, Galaxian, Ms. Pac-Man, Phozon,* and *The Tower of Druaga.* The graphics in these games are simple by today's standards, but the timeless gameplay these titles offer never gets old — it's perfectly preserved, just the way you remember them from the arcades of old. The PlayStation controller can't match the feel of an arcade-quality joystick or steering wheel, but the controls are on the money. As this disc's title implies, there are several more CDs in Namco's *Museum* series. Each of them presents rock-solid gameplay, and they're true enough to the originals to soften the heart of gamers. Now if you missed any of the video chestnuts in this series the first time around, you may want to educate yourself at the *Museum.*

Did You Know? — The five volumes in this series spell out *NAMCO* in big red letters with their covers! Silly but true.

Oni

Platform:
PlayStation 2

Publisher:
Rockstar Games

Price: $49.99

ESRB: Rating
pending

Oni should satisfy gamers who want varied action — shooting and fighting, together in a single game. This slick-looking game takes advantage of the PS2's powerful graphics engine to combine martial-arts action with fast-paced gunplay, all in an interactive 3-D environment. It's the future, and you're Konoko, a female police officer who fights high-tech crime. You fight multiple bad guys at once from a third-person perspective, using wild kicks and punches intermingled with automatic weapons that spray bullets all over the sharply designed levels, including cityscapes, office buildings, and factories. You can also take weapons from enemies and learn new moves as you go along. The deep fighting engine offers lots of attacks, special moves, and cool combinations.

Did You Know? — *Oni* means *devil* in Japanese.

Poy Poy

Platform:
PlayStation/PS one
Publisher: Konami
Price: $39.99
ESRB: Kids-to-
Adults

You know that feeling you get when you just want to throw something across the room? That's the basis for *Poy Poy,* a strategy/action game where the whole point is to knock your opponents out by lobbing things at them. Up to four players can participate in a series of game show–like stages, ranging from deserts with twisters to prehistoric jungles with famished dinosaurs (guess who's coming to dinner). You can play solo, but it's as a multiplayer game that *Poy Poy* shines. *Poy Poy*'s music, audio, and control are of excellent quality; the only hard part might be finding a copy of the game itself.

Did You Know? — Actually, I still don't know . . . what *Poy Poy* means. There's a rumor which claims that the game title most likely refers to a Japanese sound effect, the kind you may read in a comic, like "Blam!" My source is fairly reliable, so you may want to scream, "Poy," each time you outsmart someone during gameplay. If nothing else, this tactic will confuse your opponents.

Quake II

Platform:
PlayStation/PS one
Publisher:
Activision
Price: $19.99
ESRB: Mature

Quake II is a take-no-prisoners, first-person perspective, combat/action game that's an all-out blastfest. You play a space marine who crash-lands on a hostile, alien world, and you have to complete several mission objectives to survive. But really, this game is about shoot-first-ask-questions-later gun battles with hostile aliens, so you're armed to the teeth with super shotguns, rocket launchers, and more to battle militant mutants through 19 intense (gore-filled) levels. You can even engage your pals in four-player deathmatches in 12 multiplayer levels. If you're into this type of video game action, *Quake II* rocks with solid graphics, excellent sound effects, blazing metal tunes, and tight controls. Sure, this is the reason for Congressional investigations, but that's why *Quake II* is rated Mature. Adrenaline served here at a bargain price.

Did You Know? — *Quake II* is one of id Software's most successful titles, joining PC hits like *Wolfenstein 3-D* and the revolutionary *Doom* series. No mere quick cash-in, the PlayStation version of *Quake II* earned id's seal of approval.

R-Type Delta

Platform:
PlayStation/PS one
Publisher: Agetec
Price: $19.99
ESRB: Everyone

Oh, for the golden age of mind-numbing, thumb-burning, side-scrolling shooters! *R-Type Delta* is a 3-D upgrade of the classic space shooter, *R-Type,* and it manages to capture the same sort of rip-roaring, spaceship-soaring action of the original. The mysterious Bydo empire is back with its serpentine robotic bosses, gigantic motherships, and nightmarish techno-creatures spread across eight excruciatingly tough levels. The graphics are a psychedelic treat and the controls are excellent, but you need to put on your game face and generate intense concentration if your starfighter is going to make any headway here. The key to this type of game is figuring out the repeating attack patterns of your adversaries. If you have good reflexes and patience, you may be the type for *R-Type.*

Force Module Power-Ups — Start a game and collect a Laser Crystal; then grab the Force Module that appears. After you've found both items, pause the game and enter any of the following codes:

> Blue Power-Up: Press and hold L2; then press Left, Right, Up, Down, Right, Left, Up, Down, ✖

> Red Power-Up: Press and hold L2; then press Left, Right, Up, Down, Right, Left, Up, Down, ■

> Yellow Power-Up: Press and hold L2; then press Left, Right, Up, Down, Right, Left, Up, Down, ●

If you enter the code correctly, you'll hear a chime. Unpause the game, and your Force Module will have maximum power.

Rayman 2: Revolution

Platform:
PlayStation 2
Publisher: Ubi Soft
Price: $49.99
ESRB: Everyone

In this cute, cartoonish, 3-D adventure game, you play Rayman, a weird-looking long-eared creature with floating hands that aren't attached to its body. An evil pirate force is terrorizing Rayman's world, so Rayman must scour his massive world in search of shattered pieces of magic called Lums in order to defeat them. This huge quest takes you across 54 areas within 21 fantastically rendered worlds. To win, you not only have to run, jump, and fight, but ride rockets, water-skis, and lava waves. With movie-quality audio and perfect controls, *Rayman 2* offers an engrossing adventure for all gamers.

Did you Know? — *Rayman* was originally released as a PC game in 1996, but didn't come to consoles until 1999, when *Rayman 2: The Great Escape* was released for the Nintendo 64. (*Rayman 2* was released for the original PlayStation in 2000.)

Red Faction

Platform:
PlayStation 2
Publisher: THQ
Price: $49.99
ESRB: Rating
pending

Red Faction takes a revolutionary approach to first-person shooters, starting with walls that will no longer be invincible blockades that let you hide from your enemies. Rocket launchers can level small buildings and armor-piercing bullets can shoot through barriers. You play as Parker, a worker in the mines of Mars where colleagues suffer unbearable conditions at the hands of the Ultor Corporation. When a plague sweeps through the workers, you lead a revolution against the company as you search for the source of the disease. You're also able to pilot several vehicles as you go from the mines of Mars to the offices of the Ultor Corporation, the surface of the red planet, and even onto space satellites. Time will tell if *Red Faction* is the first of a new breed of shooter games.

Silent Scope

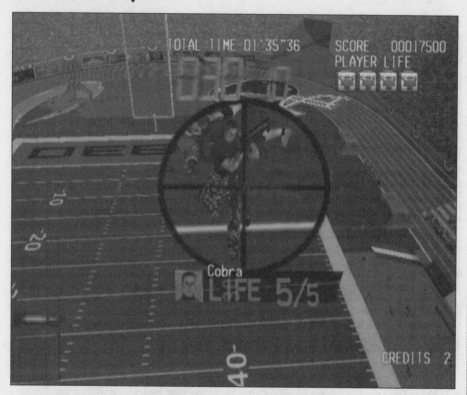

Platform:
PlayStation 2
Publisher: Konami
Price: $49.99
ESRB: Mature

This may be the perfect game for S.W.A.T. team wannabes who have a sense of humor (if such people exist). In this pixel-perfect translation of the great arcade shooter (minus the realistic rifle controller), you're a good-guy sniper who must save the president and his family from swarms of terrorists. You move your crosshairs across incredibly well-drawn backgrounds — city streets, a football stadium, a hotel, a mansion — and zoom in with your scope to zap bad guys. Though it sounds brutal, *Silent Scope* is not excessively bloody. And rather than being a true-to-life sniper simulation, it's actually a fast-paced, arcade-style game with plenty of tongue-in-cheek humor.

Did You Know? — The arcade version of *Silent Scope* has a life-sized sniper rifle with a small monitor inside its scope to give you a close-up view of the action.

Silpheed: The Lost Planet

Platform:
PlayStation 2

Publisher:
Working Designs

Price: $49.99

ESRB: Rating
pending

Silpheed: The Lost Planet is a classic shooting game that features updated graphics for the PlayStation 2. Though the visuals have been improved with 3-D polygonal objects and dazzling special effects, the gameplay remains true to the classic formula. You control your spaceship, the Silpheed fighter, as you blast enemies and pick up weapon boosts. But don't let the straightforward-sounding gameplay dissuade you. The game has many challenges and the graphics boast well-drawn levels and enemies. If you want an old-fashioned shooter with modern graphics, go back to the future with *Silpheed: The Lost Planet*.

Spyro: Year of the Dragon

He flies through the air with the greatest of ease . . . he's Spyro, a plucky little purple dragon, and one of Sony's most popular mascots. You won't find smoother flowing PlayStation gameplay anywhere. Spyro is the master of his environment, which is again the Forgotten World in this third installment of the franchise. Your mission is to find 148 stolen dragon eggs hidden across a humongous landscape. You fry bad guys with fiery dragon breath and ram 'em with head butts — all this between puzzles as you search for hidden pathways and beat mini-games that include hockey and skateboarding. You even have to play four other characters, too. Spyro handles it all with ease; you'll be amazed at how much fun this game packs in.

Platform:
PlayStation/PS one

Publisher: Sony

Price: $39.99

ESRB: Everyone

Tempest X3

In the modern age of video games, you must remember two important games: *Tetris* and *Tempest*. Although they sound alike, *Tetris'* brick-laying puzzle gameplay is nothing at all like the abstract psychedelic shooter that is *Tempest*. *Tempest's* famous gameplay view has you looking down into a virtual channel, sort of like staring down the edge of a tube. In this wormhole scenario, your task is to defend your end of the galaxy from an alien invasion (and the aliens look like little red bow ties — don't ask!). The adversaries attack you along the wall of the tube, and you sort of roll a battle station around the edge, firing blasts down the sides of the channel to intercept the oncoming assault. *Tempest X3* sports excellent graphics, two-player gameplay, and 99 adrenaline-charging levels. Few games offer the frenzied rush of *Tempest!*

Did You Know? — The arcade original *Tempest* was the first Atari game to feature color vector graphics. It's also one of the most sought-after arcade machines among coin-operated game collectors. The idea for the game came to its programmer in a nightmare about creatures or monsters crawling up from a hole in the ground.

Platform:
PlayStation/PS one

Publisher:
Interplay

Price: $29.99

ESRB: Everyone

Strider 2

Platform:
PlayStation/PS one
Publisher: Capcom
Price: $29.99
ESRB: Everyone

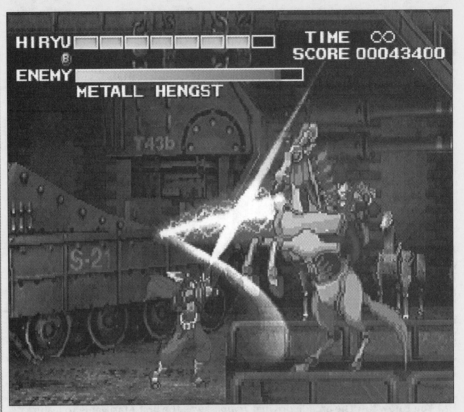

Strider is another famous video-game arcade hero who's making a return run on the latest game systems. This two-CD set features the two arcade originals, *Strider* and *Strider 2*, retooled for PlayStation duty. Strider, a futuristic ninja, swings a mean power sword and pulls a slick wall-climbing move to defeat robot assassins. This is old school, thumb-pumping, run-through-the-levels stuff, but it's undeniably enjoyable — while it lasts. The experience is a gas for old time's sake, but *Strider 2* has only five levels, and they go by fast after you get the hang of the gameplay. Fortunately, you can replay them as the more powerful Hien Strider (see the icon below). This set belongs in any serious video-game collection — it's a true piece of history.

Play as Hien — A slick, special character is hidden in *Strider 2*. To find him, finish the game on any skill setting and save the game to a memory card. Start a new game with the saved data and at the title screen, select Game Start. You'll find a new play option, Hien Mode, that enables you to play as Strider Hien.

Surfing H3O

Platform:
PlayStation 2
Publisher:
Rockstar Games
Price: $49.99
ESRB: Everyone

Cowabunga, dudes! Using the PS2's horsepower and a real-life physics model, *Surfing H3O* churns out spectacular waves that crash on six exotic beaches. The game's 11 surfers are equally good looking and can pull off more than a dozen aerial tricks, which can be linked together for virtually unlimited combinations. The coolest feature, however, is the miniature surfboard that comes with the game and slips over your PS2's analog controllers so that you can surf with your fingers. Unfortunately, the controls make it difficult to catch waves, with or without the special plastic mini-surfboard which clips on to your Dual Shock gamepad. Still, *Surfing H3O* is the PS2's only surfing game so far, so if that's your gig, you'd better catch this wave.

Time Crisis

Platform:
PlayStation/PS one

Publisher: Namco

Price: $49.99 (price includes Guncon)

ESRB: Teen

Time Crisis is the PlayStation version of Namco's popular arcade gun game. It comes as a set packaged with the Guncon, a special controller designed to look and work like a plastic pistol. If you have a problem with handling handgun hardware and taking care of video game bad guys with virtual bullets, this is not a game for you. If, on the other hand,you pencilled in John Woo as the next president of the N.R.A., you ought to get a kick out of the trigger punishing combat. Unlike any other gun game, *Time Crisis* (via the Guncon) enables you to duck behind cover to plan ammo-efficient strategy or do some last minute prep on your Clint Eastwood impression. You'll need a small converter to make the Guncon work with your PS2, but the so-called "Guncon converters" are cheap, easy to find, and worth tracking down for such a great game.

Cheat Menu — At the title screen, quickly shoot the hole in the letter *R* in the logo twice, and then shoot the center of the crosshair to the right of the word *Time*. If you did the trick correctly, a cheat menu will appear, which includes extra lives, unlimited continues, and removes the need to reload your gun during play.

TimeSplitters

RANK
1st

Green Zombie got the bag!

Platform: PlayStation 2

Publisher: Eidos

Price: $49.99

ESRB: Teen

If you like gun games, especially first-person shooters, *TimeSplitters* is a must-own title for the PS2. The TimeSplitters are an evil, extra-dimensional, alien race who control Earth, and it's up to you to stop them. You assume the role of several characters over 100 years spanning from 1935 to 2035, each period with its own unique weapons and enemies. Story aside, this game rocks because of its frenzied shooting action with lots of cool weapons — twin M-16s, shotgun, laser sniper-rifle, and even an antique blunderbuss — supported by sharp visuals and dominating sound effects. Unlike those of most first-person shooters for consoles, the controls in *TimeSplitters* are dead-on: logical, responsive, and totally configurable. When you conquer the single-player missions (which will take a long time), you can create your own levels and save them to a memory card. The four-player split-screen action (with no graphics slowdown) makes *TimeSplitters* a great party game, too. It's simply one of the best PS2 games out there.

Tony Hawk's Pro Skater 2

Platform:
PlayStation/PS one

Publisher:
Activision

Price: $39.99

ESRB: Teen

Tony Hawk's Pro Skater was easily the best skateboarding game ever created; with the sequel, The Birdman and friends actually kickflip it up a notch to reset the standard. Choose from 13 professional skaters (or create your own custom riders), and then bust wild skateboarding tricks through detailed levels, including schools, skateparks, and even a Mexican bullring. After you master those arenas, you can build your own custom levels with the alarmingly easy, built-in editor. If you don't know the difference between stunts like a stalefish and a benihana, fear not — the arcade-style gameplay is easy to pick up and requires no previous skating knowledge. This game is addictive, it's rewarding, and, unlike real skating, it's painless. Besides, you can't help but look cool doing wild 720-degree spins with your limbs akimbo.

Unlock Nearly Everything in the Game — While in career mode, pause the game, hold L1 and enter the following button presses:

✖, ✖, ✖, ■, ▲, Up, Down, Left, Up, ■, ▲, ✖, ▲, ●, ✖, ▲, ●

If you've done it right, the screen will shake. Select End Run and watch the fireworks. This will give all the skaters in your career file a completed career, tons of money . . . and basically ruin the whole game.

Unreal Tournament

Platform:
PlayStation 2

Publisher:
Infogrames

Price: $49.99

ESRB: Teen

On the PC, *Unreal Tournament* is the grand master of multiplayer, first-person shooting games. With its awesome levels and armory — sniper rifles, rocket launchers, plasma guns, and more — it's no surprise that it's come to the PS2. In a dark future, workers fight each other for sport — think *The Running Man*, but with more guns. The weapons and levels have a futuristic, gritty feel, like that of the *Alien* movies. Two- to four-player split-screen modes offer plenty of action, and the single-player mode delivers hours of fun as you blast hordes of smart, computer-controlled enemies. But the controls aren't totally configurable, and there's no online multiplayer action, which is the heart of the PC game. If you want only one first-person shooter, get *TimeSplitters* rather than *Unreal Tournament*.

Did You Know? — You can plug a USB keyboard and mouse into your PS2 to play *Unreal Tournament* the same way as PC gamers play *UT* on their computers.

WinBack: Covert Operations

Platform: PlayStation 2

Publisher: Koei

Price: $49.99

ESRB: Rating pending

Originally released for the Nintendo 64, *WinBack* offers a thrilling PS2 mission. Playing as Jean-Luc Cougar, you're tasked with infiltrating the base of terrorists who are threatening the world with satellite-based lasers. But when your squad's chopper comes apart before it reaches the drop zone, everyone parachutes in separately, leaving Cougar alone against the terrorists. Cougar occasionally pairs up with squad mates and takes on bosses. Fans of *Syphon Filter* will feel right at home with the third-person firefights, which should deliver plenty of action mixed with stealthy infiltration. WinBack offers four-player split-screen action. The game also promises an excellent targeting system that lets Cougar automatically take cover. Perfect for armchair commandos.

X Squad

Platform:
PlayStation 2

Publisher:
Electronic Arts

Price: $49.99

ESRB: Teen

X Squad is a typical example of a first-generation PS2 game — nice and shiny, but not very innovative or satisfying. It's 2037 and you're Ash, leader of *X Squad,* a band of four commandos who follow you around and respond to your orders (the corny dialogue and lame story are not even worthy of Saturday-morning cartoons). The game is played from a third-person view, and the controls make it easy to move and look around, but not to aim your weapons. Although the characters are smoothly drawn and look great, the environments are for the most part surprisingly bland corridors. The best part of the game is the cool semi-realistic weapons, but it takes a while to obtain good ones. If you're willing to put in the effort and overlook a few shortcomings, you'll enjoy *X Squad;* otherwise, take a pass.

Unlock All Weapons and Gadgets — At the main menu, press

> L1, L1, L2, L2, R1, R1, R2, R2

If you enter the code correctly, you'll hear a gunshot. All weapons and gadgets become unlocked, and there is no weight limit.

Xena: Warrior Princess

Platform:
PlayStation/PS one

Publisher:
Electronic Arts

Price: $39.99

ESRB: Teen

No one can control Xena the Warrior Princess in her TV fantasy land, but now you can run her through her paces with the PlayStation. This game is a fan's dream-come-true. Responsive controls enable you to execute Xena's signature fighting style, which is equal parts martial arts, acrobatics, and slapstick. You can even fling her famous Chakram — a sort of bladed Frisbee — and guide it in flight from a first-person perspective. Adding to the game's overall attention to detail are music and sound effects drawn straight from the TV show. Maybe the most intriguing thing about this game is that it follows the show's moral: Violence isn't always the answer (but without it, there'd be no show).

Super Xena — Here's how to make the Warrior Princess invincible. At the main menu, highlight New Game, and then press

> Up, Up, Up, ●, ■, Up, Right, Left

If you enter the code correctly, you'll hear a faint chime.

Chapter 7

Adventure Games

Creepy monsters, dismal dungeons, power-crazed madmen, scary situations — the PlayStation and PlayStation 2 have all your favorite adventure scenarios covered. You better start reading your mission briefings, however, because you have spy scenarios to complete, mysteries to solve, and zombies to obliterate. Oh, and since you're already up, the world could use saving.

In This Chapter . . .

Alone in the Dark: The New Nightmare

The originator of the survival/horror genre, *Alone in the Dark* returns with its fourth installment. You play as Edward Carnby, a supernatural private-eye who must identify and locate the murderer of a friend. The game is set on an island inhabited by other-worldly creatures. And did we mention the only weapons are light-based? *Alone in the Dark*'s visual scheme consists of gorgeous 3-D prerendered backgrounds with fixed camera angles, so you can't always see what's lurking nearby. Loaded with scary moments and a brooding atmosphere, this episode in detective work will keep gamers on the edge of their seats for days.

Platform:
PlayStation/PS one

Publisher:
Infogrames

Price: $39.99

ESRB: Rating pending

Did You Know? — The original *Alone in the Dark* put Infogrames on the map as a software developer; *Alone* was one of the first games to use polygons to create its characters.

Diablo

In *Diablo,* you play as one of three adventurers who have entered a cursed town. To survive the 16 levels of dungeons, catacombs, and — ultimately — regions of Hell, you need bravery, weapons, and some seriously powerful magic spells. Instead of plodding strategy, *Diablo* relies on fast-action gameplay, with lots of hacking and slashing of dungeon dwellers. The responsive directional pad does a good job of keeping the complex controls in check, and the randomly generated levels ensure replay value, as no two dungeons are alike. *Diablo* was a giant hit on the PC, and the PlayStation version delivers a devilishly good time, too.

Platform:
PlayStation/PS one

Publisher:
Electronic Arts

Price: $19.99

ESRB: Mature

Ye Olde Two-Player Cheat — If, as one character, you find something that would be valuable for another character — say, a sorcerer finds good bows that the rogue could use — save the sorcerer to a memory card, and then import him into a new two-player game with a rogue character. Give the bows to the rogue and save the rogue; then restart the game without saving the sorcerer after the transaction. When you restore the sorcerer's original game, he'll still have the bows, which he can then sell to Griswold for a profit!

Castlevania: Symphony of the Night

Platform:
PlayStation/PS one

Publisher: Konami

Price: $19.99

ESRB: Teen

Castlevania: Symphony of the Night is an excellent 2-D side-scrolling game that continues the *Castlevania* series, one of the longest running video-game narratives. But instead of playing the role of the hero (as was the case in other titles in the series), you assume the role of Alucard, a half-vampire descendant of the evil Count Dracula. *Symphony* is loaded with impressive elements like cool weapons, magical spells, and a gigantic castle complete with hidden areas ripe for exploration. Plus, *Symphony* has its own army of darkness — and just guess who they don't like? (That'd be you.) Fans agree that this is one of the best PlayStation games ever made.

Play as Richter Belmont — Finish the game and save the data to a memory card. Start a new game and enter the following password as your name: **RICHTER.** Start the game, and you can now play as Richter Belmont.

Dino Crisis 2

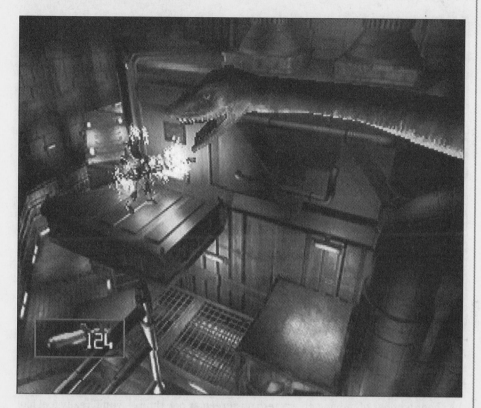

Platform:
PlayStation/PS one
Publisher: Capcom
Price: $39.99
ESRB: Mature

Gamers who want a *Jurassic Park*-esque experience should sink their teeth into *Dino Crisis 2,* an adventure game with a survival theme. Playing as one of two characters, you must endure a dangerous trip through the prehistoric era. Although several types of dinosaurs are trying to swallow you whole, you can purchase various exotic weapons and useful health items to help keep your prehistoric adversaries at bay. Using an over-the-shoulder camera view, you run and gun through dense jungle, solving puzzles and even donning scuba gear for battles with underwater dinos. *Dino Crisis 2* delivers plenty of intense action, but beware: This game's gory graphics are rated Mature for good reason.

Did you know? — Actress Stephanie Morgenstern, who voices the character of Regina, has appeared in several TV productions and motion pictures. One of her more high-profile roles was in the critically acclaimed 1997 drama, *The Sweet Hereafter*, in which she played Allison.

Dynasty Warriors 2

Platform:
PlayStation 2

Publisher: Koei

Price: $49.99

ESRB: Teen

Dynasty Warriors 2 is a single-player, action/strategy hybrid that forces you to get out of the war room and join the front line as you fight for control of ancient China. The action part of this game is a lot of fun as you join your army in hand-to-hand combat against (literally) hundreds of enemies. The gorgeous graphics will astound you by the sheer number of moving characters on-screen at one time — you'll really feel like you're in the midst of a battlefield with dozens of attackers trying to do you in! The strategy part of this game prevents it from becoming a mindless button-masher, for you must coordinate your attacks and movements with those of the rest of your army (and keep its morale up!) to defeat the opposing forces. *Dynasty Warriors 2* is an excellent adventure game that requires both brains and brawn.

Did You Know? — *Dynasty Warriors* picks up where Koei's *Romance of the Three Kingdoms* strategy series leaves off. The original *Dynasty Warriors* came out for the original PlayStation.

Fear Effect 2: Retro Helix

Platform:
PlayStation/PS one
Publisher: Eidos
Price: $39.99
ESRB: Mature

Fear Effect: Retro Helix features a visually stunning combination of computer-rendered and hand-drawn animated elements — it's almost like playing *Resident Evil* with cartoon characters. In *Retro Helix*, you guide four heroes through an engrossing story that involves tough puzzle-solving and intense action. Excellent aesthetic elements aside, the dialogue also shines with some of the sharpest quips that you've ever heard in a video game. The game's only stumbling block is the controls — especially the clumsy weapon selection menu that makes you cycle through several weapons until you find the one that you want. *Retro Helix* isn't for all gamers, though. There's some pretty mature subject matter and a few disturbing scenes, which more than earn this title's Mature rating.

Legacy of Kain: Soul Reaver

Platform:
PlayStation/PS one
Publisher: Eidos
Price: $19.99
ESRB: Teen

In *Soul Reaver,* you get to play as the bad guy for a change! In this adventure title, you're Raziel, a vampire who seeks revenge on his former evil master who tried to destroy him. But instead of feeding on blood, Raziel thirsts for souls, which he can devour after defeating an opponent. *Reaver's* full 3-D environments are ripe for exploration — something for which the adjustable camera is key — and loaded with cool visual effects. Yet the real star here is the gameplay. You can dispatch of your enemies in various nasty ways with a variety of weapons, and Raziel's climbing and gliding abilities add diversity. If you're looking for a dark change from the usual 3-D-action title, *Soul Reaver* will keep you enthralled for hours with its unholy quest.

Did you know? — *Soul Reaver* is the name of a powerful weapon that was prominently featured in the game *Blood Omen: Legacy of Kain* — the prequel to this title. *Soul Reaver 2,* however, appears on the PlayStation 2.

All Abilities — Pause the game, press and hold L1 or R1, and then press

Up, Up, Down, Down, Right, Right, Left, ●, Right, Left, Down

When you resume playing, you're able to phase through gates, climb walls, fire force projectiles, swim, and wield the Soul Reaver.

Legacy of Kain: Soul Reaver 2

Platform:
PlayStation 2

Publisher: Eidos

Price: $49.99

ESRB: Rating
pending

Life is tough for undead vampire Raziel. He used to be the commanding officer for Kain, ruler of the dark fantasy world called Nosgoth, but fell out of favor and was turned into a walking corpse with awesome powers (but only half his mouth — yuck). Now Raziel must travel back in time before Kain conquered Nosgoth to seek his revenge on Kain, but his only source of nourishment is to suck out the souls of his victims. As the Soul Reaver, you explore gorgeous, vast 3-D environments, accomplish specific tasks, search out hidden items, and use your wits to unravel story-oriented puzzles that help move along the tale. For instance, instead of just pushing boxes or finding hidden items, one puzzle requires you to reflect light to kindle a fire in a forge — complex stuff. You know what it's like to be a vampire after flying a mile in his leathery wings.

Medievil 11

Platform:
PlayStation/PS one
Publisher: Sony
Price: $19.99
ESRB: Teen

Poor Sir Dan. He was a valiant knight, but now that he's passed on, he still can't rest in peace. In *Medievil II,* our reluctant hero has been brought back to life — in skeleton form, no less — for one last showdown with evil forces. The humorous 3-D adventure title pieces together a balanced combination of hack-n-slash, exploration, puzzle-solving, and platform gameplay. You can move the camera in either a third-person or first-person view, and tight controls enable you to use 17 weapons to hack, slash, and shoot with pinpoint precision. But don't expect brawn to win out over brains; you must put some thought into which weapons to use against particular adversaries. The visuals put on an impressive and entertaining show, while the sounds hold up their end nicely, especially the voices that accurately capture the personalities of the quirky characters.

Cheat Menu — Pause the game, press and hold L2, and then press

▲, ●, ▲, ●, ●, ▲, Left, ●, Up, Down, Right, ●, Left, Left, ▲, Right, ●, Left, Left, ▲, ●, Down, ●, ●, Right

If you enter the code correctly, a Cheats option appears in the pause menu. Inside the Cheats menu are several options, including a level skip, invincibility, and more.

Nightmare Creatures

Platform:
PlayStation/PS one
Publisher:
Activision
Price: $19.99
ESRB: Mature

Nightmare Creatures is one of the fastest — and bloodiest — adventure games for the PlayStation. It's like *Tomb Raider* meets *Night of the Living Dead.* Using a behind-the-character view, you play as one of two monster killers — a wandering holy man and a female fencer. Both characters hack-and-slash through turn-of-the-century London, which happens to be loaded with monstrous mutations and powerful evil creatures, all minions of the infamous necromancer, Dr. Crowley. The explicit gore definitely earns a Mature rating, but a good portion of the game's appeal comes from the level design that features darkly lit haunted city streets that create a very effective fear factor. Seasoned vets will find the game a formidable challenge, but novice players may find the ramped-up difficulty frustrating.

Stage Select — At the Options screen, press

L1, L1, L2, R1, R1, R2

If you enter the code correctly, you'll hear a confirming sound. Start a new game and a Stage Select option will appear.

Mega Man Legends 2

Platform: PlayStation/PS one

Publisher: Capcom

Price: $19.99

ESRB: Everyone

Mega Man started as a side-scrolling 2-D hero, but the *Legends* series spins him off into another story line, with another style of gameplay, and even another person known as *Mega Man! Legends 2* adds improved 3-D action/adventure gameplay and satisfying exploration-style adventure as *Mega Man* tries to locate some lost explorers. You quickly cross paths with Tronn Bone and her Reaverbots — the bad guys — who try and thwart your every move. Complete with solid 360-degree 3-D gameplay, *Legends 2* moves at a laid-back pace thanks to a good mix of brain-stumping puzzles and character conversations that reveal key clues. *Mega Man Legends 2* nicely fits the requirements for a satisfying 3-D adventure title that doesn't rely on blistering your thumbs.

Metal Gear Solid

Platform:
PlayStation/PS one

Publisher: Konami

Price: $19.99

ESRB: Mature

Metal Gear Solid is the culmination of 10 years of work and dedication — and it shows. *MGS* is one of the top adventure offerings for the PlayStation, due to its intense and addictive action as well as its engrossing story line. You play as Solid Snake, an elite soldier sent to stop terrorists from gaining control of a deadly weapon. Not only can you dispatch your adversaries with a plethora of awesome weapons, but you can also eliminate them with your bare hands, and must often use stealth tactics to survive (including hiding under a cardboard box — really!). In addition to a polished play engine is an intriguing narrative that's brought to life by some of the finest voice-acting ever recorded for a video game. You'll never feel safe around a cardboard box again.

Did You Know? — *Metal Gear Solid* spawned both a quick sequel (*Metal Gear Solid: VR Missions,* an in-depth series of training exercises) and an impressive line of highly detailed action figures from McFarlane Toys.

Metal Gear Solid 2: Sons of Liberty

Platform:
PlayStation 2
Publisher: Konami
Price: $49.99
ESRB: Rating
pending

You're Solid Snake, super secret-agent supreme, and it's your mission to infiltrate an oil rig off the coast of New York. Make no mistake, this game isn't just another shoot-em-up where you can pull a Rambo and blast away at your opponents. Stealth, patience, and strategy are the keys to success as you go solo against an army of opponents. This awesome adventure game revs the PlayStation 2's engine by delivering a very realistic experience with cinematic graphics and sound, detailed controls, and in-depth gameplay in which you truly become the character on-screen. You may actually end up getting shot a couple times when you stop inadvertently to enjoy the incredible graphic eye-candy. *MGS2* is the reason many gamers are buying PS2's in the first place!

Did You Know? — The *Metal Gear* franchise started on the original 8-bit Nintendo Entertainment System in the early '90s. Although the graphics and gameplay were chunky and simplistic, that version was one of the first games to offer more than just shoot-em-up action; it also required strategy and stealth for success. The franchise really took off when Solid Snake returned in full 3-D glory in *Metal Gear Solid* and *Metal Gear Solid: VR Missions* for the PlayStation.

Oddworld: Abe's Exoddus

Platform:
PlayStation/PS one

Publisher:
GT Interactive

Price: $19.99

ESRB: Teen

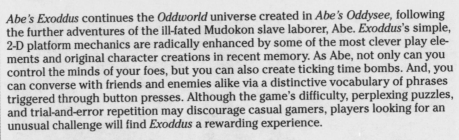

Abe's Exoddus continues the *Oddworld* universe created in *Abe's Oddysee,* following the further adventures of the ill-fated Mudokon slave laborer, Abe. *Exoddus*'s simple, 2-D platform mechanics are radically enhanced by some of the most clever play elements and original character creations in recent memory. As Abe, not only can you control the minds of your foes, but you can also create ticking time bombs. And, you can converse with friends and enemies alike via a distinctive vocabulary of phrases triggered through button presses. Although the game's difficulty, perplexing puzzles, and trial-and-error repetition may discourage casual gamers, players looking for an unusual challenge will find *Exoddus* a rewarding experience.

Unlock All Levels in the Game — At the title screen where Abe says "Hello," press and hold R1 while you press

Down, Up, Left, Right, ▲, ■, ●, ▲, ■, ●, Down, Up, Left, Right

If you enter the code correctly, Abe will say, "Okay" and a level-select option will appear.

Spider-Man

On the whole, video games based on superhero exploits have been pretty lame. Thankfully, *Spider-Man* breaks the losing streak with one of the best comic-character based video games ever created. You play as Marvel's popular everyhero Spider-Man, a super-strong guy who spins webs to swing between Manhattan's skyscrapers and can crawl on walls. In this 3-D adventure, ol' web-head takes on a host of his arch-foes — Rhino, Carnage, Scorpion, Dr. Octopus, and others — in several gigantic locales. A solid combat engine gives you multiple nonlethal options, including web balls, an explosive web shield, and web-based spikes. Your Spider Sense always lets you know when you're about to enter a dangerous situation — courtesy of a tingling sensation from the Dual Shock controller. Play on, true believers!

Platform:
PlayStation/PS one

Publisher:
Activision

Price: $39.99

ESRB: Everyone

Invulnerability — At the main menu, choose Special, and then select Cheats. Input the code **RUSTCRST**. If you enter the code correctly, the screen will shake and the name of the cheat will appear at the top of the screen. Now you can't be defeated by enemy attacks.

Onimusha: Warlords

Platform:
PlayStation 2
Publisher: Capcom
Price: $49.99
ESRB: Mature

Capcom, the video game company that revolutionized the action/adventure gaming genre on the PlayStation with the *Resident Evil* and *Dino Crisis* series, sets a new standard with *Onimusha: Warlords.* This solo adventure game pits you as the samurai warrior, Samanosuke, who must battle relentless hordes of zombie samurais, wall-crawling demons, and other monsters in order to rescue a kidnapped princess. Samanosuke can execute a large variety of combat moves, but the game delves deeper than a simple hack-and-slash game. Your weapon of choice is your samurai sword, but you can also attack with the powers of three magic gems: wind, thunder, and fire. The graphics are simply gorgeous, bringing ancient feudal Japan to full-color glory.

Did you know? — Capcom spared no expense to make *Onimusha* as realistic an experience as possible. Samanosuke's face and voice are modeled after those of Takeshi Kaneshiro, one of Japan's hottest action-movie stars, and Capcom employed a 200-piece orchestra to create the game's cinema-quality soundtrack.

Portal Runner

Platform:
PlayStation 2
Publisher: 3DO
Price: $49.99
ESRB: Rating pending

Springing forth from the insanely popular *Army Men* video game series comes the first standout solo character — and the army man is a lady at that! Vikki's boyfriend Sarge is captured by the villainous Brigitte Bleu, so Vikki has to jump through inter-dimensional portals to three diverse alternate worlds to his rescue. Armed with just her bow and seven powered arrows, it's Vikki to the rescue. You can use the bow to shoot opponents, start fires, blow up obstacles, and even conjure up magic. Lush, fully rendered 3-D graphics bring the fantasy worlds to life, and tight controls make you mistress of her domain. On some levels, you even control Vikki's occasional sidekick, Leo the lion. Even though she may be primarily green, this adventure is red hot.

Did you know? — 3DO wants to establish Vikki as a virtual star, so look for a *Portal Runner* comic book, an action figure line, and an animated cartoon series. The company has even signed former *Playboy* Playmate, Heather Kezar, to represent Vikki at live events.

Resident Evil 2: Dual Shock Version

Platform:
PlayStation/PS one
Publisher: Capcom
Price: $19.99
ESRB: Mature

The *Resident Evil* series is one of the most popular for the PlayStation, and with *Resident Evil 2,* it's easy to see why. Playing as one of two characters, you must escape a monster-infested city while collecting weapons to defend yourself. *RE2*'s strength isn't theme, but rather it's execution that grabs the glory. Not only does *RE2* feature pulse-pounding action, but it also features enough replay value to keep you riveted to the edge of your seat for days. The game is loaded with horrific images and eye-popping special effects — not to mention a story line that's just plain, well, evil. Although the controls and the 3-D, prerendered visual scheme require some getting used to, *RE2* is one scary — and very Mature — game experience you won't forget.

Did you know? — When *Resident Evil 2* was originally developed, the creative team wasn't pleased with the game's progress. So they scrapped everything — the game was about 68 percent complete — and started over. The fabled *Resident Evil 1.5* was never released.

FUN FACTS

Silent Hill

Platform:
PlayStation/PS one
Publisher: Konami
Price: $19.99
ESRB: Mature

In the bloody 3-D adventure *Silent Hill,* fright is the star. Via a third-person view, you control Harry Mason, an ordinary guy who's stranded in a extraordinarily haunted town. Not only must you do battle with various monsters and collect key items, but several mind-numbing puzzles also bar your way to freedom. What the premise lacks in creativity, the game more than compensates for with creepy level designs, gross-out special effects, and creative use of the Dual Shock controller that rhythmically sends out a heartbeat tremor. The game does have its share of flaws, including no on-screen life-bar, excessive fog in the visuals, and awful voice-over acting. Although these factors are distracting, they don't break the game's atmospheric spell.

Did you know? — *Silent Hill 2* is currently in development for the PlayStation 2.

Soul of the Samurai

Platform:
PlayStation/PS one
Publisher: Konami
Price: $19.99
ESRB: Mature

Soul of the Samurai is a violent slash-em-up that takes place within a compelling tale set in ancient Japan. You play as one of two selectable samurai warriors, each with his own distinctive story line. Viewed against a backdrop of prerendered environments and forced camera angles similar to those of the *Resident Evil* games, the combat is fast, furious, and frequent, with successful swordplay depending on technique and fast button-pressing. Although each character can execute several types of attacks and magic spells, and while the emphasis is on action, the game also has several perplexing puzzles to solve. The only hitch in this sharp title is the controls, which take patience and practice to master.

Syphon Filter 2

Platform:
PlayStation/PS one

Publisher:
989 Studios

Price: $39.99

ESRB: Mature

If you're looking for the action and excitement of a 007 flick, *Syphon Filter 2* is one of the best games that the PlayStation has to offer. You're a special agent out to stop a mad scientist from unleashing a deadly virus. No mere carbon copy of its predecessor, *Syphon Filter 2* spans two CDs and 20 missions, sizzling with two-player deathmatches, a captivating plot, sleek animation, cinematic music, an improved save system, and more. If you liked *Metal Gear Solid* and are looking for a worthy next mission, *Syphon Filter 2* is your game.

Level Skip — Pause the game, highlight Map, and simultaneously press and hold

Right, L2, R2, ●, ■, ✖

Choose Options, choose Cheats, and then select End Level. Poof! On to the next mission.

Tenchu 2: Birth of the Stealth Assassins

Platform:
PlayStation/PS one

Publisher:
Activision

Price: $39.99

ESRB: Mature

If you want to know what it's like to be a ninja, *Tenchu 2* gives you a pretty good idea. You can play as a male or female stealth operative, and each character has his or her own narrative and levels. This 3-D adventure title features a behind-the-character view, but the gameplay emphasis is on sneaking around instead of action — moving quietly and invisibly is the key to success. *Tenchu 2*'s intriguing premise should keep most gamers hooked — just beware of some powerful end-level bosses who can quickly send you to the Game Over screen. *Tenchu 2* also features a very cool level creator, so you can construct your own ninja challenges. Action gamers looking for a change of pace will find *Tenchu 2* a cut above other offerings.

All Items — Start any mission other than the Training Course. At the Items screen at the beginning of the mission, press

■, ■, ■, ●, ■, ●, ●, Left, Up, Down, Right, R2, R2

If you enter the code correctly, all items become available.

Tomb Raider: The Last Revelation

Platform:
PlayStation/PS one
Publisher: Eidos
Price: $39.99
ESRB: Teen

Even if you haven't played *Tomb Raider,* you've probably heard of Lara Croft, the famous female Indiana Jones-esque archaeologist and adventure seeker. *The Last Revelation* is a good opportunity to become acquainted with Croft's adventure-filled world, complete with its labyrinthine 3-D catacombs and ancient, mysterious civilizations. As Lara, you run, jump, crawl, and blast our heroine through several booby-trapped levels and frustrating, nail-biting situations where the smallest error means instant death. The game delivers the visual goods, but the controls may prove frustrating to newbies. And in truth, all the *Tomb Raider* games play fairly alike.

All Weapons, Infinite Ammo, and Infinite Medipacks — At the Inventory screen, highlight the Timex-TMX. Simultaneously press and hold

L1, L2, R1, R2, and Up, and then press ▲

If you enter the code correctly, you'll automatically exit the Inventory screen and resume the game. You now have all weapons available in the current mission, plus unlimited ammo and Medipacks.

The World Is Not Enough

Platform:
PlayStation/PS one

Publisher:
Electronic Arts

Price: $39.99

ESRB: Teen

Fans of the James Bond movie series will be pleasantly entertained by this game adaptation of the latest 007 adventure. Playing as MI-6's famed secret agent, you embark on several multiobjective missions that more-or-less follow the movie's narrative (scenes from the movie are included) via a first-person view. Of course, it wouldn't be Bond without gadgets and action, and *The World is Not Enough* delivers a healthy share of both elements. When you aren't saving the world, you can take on three of your friends in the deathmatch mode. Despite the game's choppy, flawed visuals and loose controls, adventure fans and corridor-shooters alike will find *TWINE* a fun way to kill some extra hours with the 007 license.

Win at Cards — When playing Blackjack during Russian Roulette, you generally win the first few hands, so bet it all and early.

Chapter 8
Brain Games

*T*he famed philosopher René Descartes once said, "It is not enough to have a good mind. The main thing is to use it well." Word up, dude. René predated video games by about four hundred years, but I tend to think he'd find a few games of interest on the PlayStation 2. Whether you're looking for perplexing puzzles, a strategic workout, a digital take on a classic board game, or even a creative musical challenge, there's a brain game that's right for you.

In This Chapter . . .

Ballistic

Ballistic is a great puzzle game for kids or newbies. You control a globe-shooting turret at the center of the screen. Meanwhile, colored balls form a chain that spirals toward you, creeping ever inward. The goal is to prevent the stream of spheres from reaching the center by firing balls from your cannon. If you match up three or more balls of the same color in the encroaching spiral, that set disappears and the chain is shortened, buying you a little more breathing room. The game offers three play modes, including a head-to-head mode that allows you to mix it up with a friend. *Ballistic* combines the quick thinking of a puzzle game with the reflexes of a shooting game. If dropping blocks in *Tetris* doesn't sound interesting, *Ballistic* could be more your style.

Platform:
PlayStation/PS one
Publisher:
Infogrames
Price: $29.99
ESRB: Everyone

Bust-A-Groove

Bust-A-Groove is structured as a ladder-style dance tournament. You control your rendered counterpart through a library of smooth moves by matching the button icons and directional arrows that appear on-screen with the ones on your controller — all while keeping the beat. When you manage to string together a series of steps, you create a combo that boosts your rating. The true charm of *Bust-A-Groove* is the characters and their music — each with its own style (house, disco, old-style hip hop, techno). It's amazing how well each of those styles merge as you play. Laid-back Frieda does just as well dancing to Hiro's disco as to Gas-O's hardcore techno. Pure fun and non-violent, *Bust-A-Groove* is especially popular among female gamers.

Did You Know? — Like many PlayStation games, *Bust-A-Groove* was first released in Japan (under the title *Bust-A-Move*). The developer sought out some of the hottest Japanese recording artists to create one of the best game soundtracks. Prior to the game's release in the U.S., most of the tracks were converted to English.

Platform:
PlayStation/PS one
Publisher: Sony
Price: $39.99
ESRB: Everyone

Platform:
PlayStation/PS one

Publisher: Acclaim

Price: $19.99

ESRB: Everyone

Bust-A-Move '99

Bust-A-Move '99 is part of a long line of quality puzzle games that prove surprisingly addictive. Bubbles descend from the ceiling, inching closer and closer to the bottom. When a bubble hits the bottom, it's game over. By matching up three or more bubbles of the same color, you pop them and make them disappear; the more you can gather and dissipate at once, the higher your score. While the premise may not sound like fun, the quick-thinking gameplay is nevertheless strangely addicting — plus, the bounced angle shots may improve your billiards skills. There are numerous games in this series, but *B-A-M '99* is one of the best and most affordable.

Did You Know? — *Bust-A-Move* is known overseas as *Bubble Bobble*. In 1998, a Japanese dancing game entitled (strangely enough) *Bust-A-Move* boogied onto the scene as well. When that game came stateside, its name had to be changed, of course; but the name chosen was *Bust-A-Groove*. Talk about an identity crisis.

Platform:
PlayStation/PS one

Publisher:
Activision

Price: $14.99

ESRB: Everyone

Civilization II

Ever look around at society and say, "You know, I could've done this better?" *Civilization II* enables you to build culture from the ground up. You start off with a small settlement, and play God (or at least supreme ruler) by choosing what they build and how they use their resources. Here's a hint: Pick a site that has easy access to water, or you won't be able to grow enough food to feed your population. Advisors pop up to offer suggestions, but you alone are responsible for your people's destiny. You must balance science, defense, entertainment, and foreign policy or you may wind up at the business end of a spear. *Civilization II* is a real time sink; as your society's years pass in hours of gameplay, you may find real hours passing in what feels like mere minutes.

Did You Know? — *Civilization II* was created by Sid Meier, one of a handful of acknowledged game-design masters. He's also responsible for the PC hits *Pirates* and *Alpha Centauri*.

Command & Conquer: Red Alert — Retaliation

Platform:
PlayStation/PS one
Publisher:
Westwood
Price: $19.99
ESRB: Teen

Calling all armchair warriors! *Command & Conquer: Red Alert — Retaliation* shows off the stellar gameplay of this series' famed real-time strategy. It's like a game of *Risk* on steroids — build your base, command your troops, and send them around the virtual battlefield to vanquish the enemy. *Retaliation* is set in the aftermath of World War II when Allied and Soviet forces are fighting over what's left of Europe. In this revisionist past, you deploy advanced weapons like nuclear bombs through a simple point-and-click interface. The key to *Retaliation* is the excellent options. Plus, this entry in the *C&C* series offers a simple control mode to get you in the action faster, as well as support for the PlayStation mouse, which affords even greater precision.

Get the Nuke — Enter this code during gameplay (not while paused):

Highlight ● and press ●, highlight ✖ and press ●, highlight ● and press ●, highlight ● and press ●, highlight ✖ and press ●, highlight ■ and press ●

Dance Dance Revolution

Platform:
PlayStation/PS one
Publisher: Konami
Price: $39.99
ESRB: Everyone

One of the hottest games in Japanese arcades, *Dance Dance Revolution,* is making its way into American homes. A dance game similar to *Bust-A-Groove, Revolution* takes it one step further (pun intended). You can purchase an add-on controller — a vinyl dance mat that mimics the arcade version's disco floor. Now you can jump around trying to step on the correct directional arrow at the correct time without humiliating yourself in public! You can play *Dance Dance* with a standard controller, but it's not nearly as much fun. The soundtrack features over 30 songs, from laid-back pop to blistering techno. A two-player mode enables you to cooperate or compete with a friend, while a bonus workout mode lets you count the calories you lose as you shake your groove thing.

Did You Know? — *Dance Dance Revolution* — *DDR* to its serious fans — is part of a musical game series in Japan called *Bemani*. Other entries include *Guitar Freaks, Drummania,* and *Hiphopmania,* the last of which gives you a virtual turntable and makes you the DJ!

Devil Dice

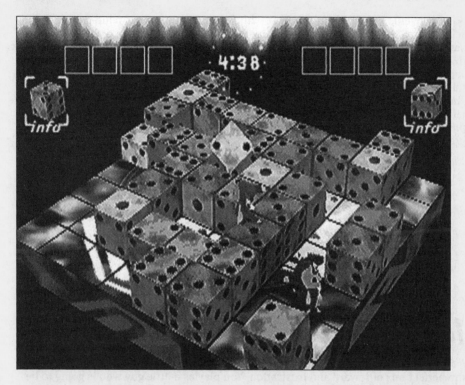

Platform:
PlayStation/PS one
Publisher: THQ
Price: $19.95
ESRB: Everyone

Unlike all the stale *Tetris* clones out there, *Devil Dice* puts a new spin on the 3-D puzzle game. *Devil Dice* features five types of dice, each with unique properties that affect gameplay and strategy. To make the dice disappear, players must flip the dice on the screen by directing their on-screen character to walk on them and match their faces. The action can become pretty hairy at times, especially in multiplayer games (up to five players at once) and War mode contests, where quick turns of the dice are a must. *Devil Dice* requires concentration and strategy to get the dice rolling your way. As with most good puzzlers, you'll quickly find the gameplay addictive. This one is truly Devilish.

Platform:
PlayStation 2
Publisher: Sony
Price: $49.99
ESRB: Everyone

Fantavision

Sony reinvents the puzzle game genre with *Fantavision,* a unique mind-twister that relies on quick wits and reflexes to link similar colored firework-buds in midair and set up multicolored chain reactions in the skies. Wait too long, and the fireworks fizzle out; detonate too early, and you get fewer points. As a game that was born in Japan, *Fantavision* may seem a bit unusual, but it's all innocent fun. The controls take some getting used to, but after that, they're responsible and reliable. *Fantavision* is really a simple 2-D game hiding behind 3-D, fully rendered graphic effects. While it won't go down on record as a classic like *Tetris, Fantavision* does provide some fun for gamers of all ages and abilities, and it shows off the PS2's graphics quite nicely.

Platform:
PlayStation/PS one
Publisher: Sony
Price: $39.99
ESRB: Everyone

Intelligent Qube

Intelligent Qube is a wildly challenging and exciting game that manages to provide the perfect mix of reward and frustration. You play as a little guy who is going to be crushed or knocked off the world unless he can capture the giant blocks that flip toward him. Not all killer cubes are created equal — some cubes can actually harm you if you capture them. And if you let too many cubes escape, your platform becomes shorter. It's easy to immerse yourself in this game, especially with its ticking clock. The pounding soundtrack perfectly complements the game's intensity, and really, this game is all about stress. It's a crushing way to up your IQ!

Jeopardy!

The answer: A console version of a TV game show that lives up to its license. "What is *Jeopardy!*, Alex?" If you spend evenings trying to out-shout friends and family while watching the pre-eminent TV trivia game, this virtual version is for you. Complete with the classic "This is *Jeopardy!*" opening by Johnny Gilbert, this three-person game (with the multitap) gives you the true competitive experience. A bonus is that *Jeopardy!* enables you to develop the one skill that will be useful if you're actually chosen to appear on the show — buzzer smarts. You may know all the answers, but unless you're first on the draw, you get nada. And with 3500 *Jeopardy!*-caliber questions, you can strut your brainy stuff at home. Just make sure to answer in the form of a question.

Platform:
PlayStation/PS one

Publisher:
Hasbro Interactive

Price: $29.99

ESRB: Everyone

Kessen

Military strategists will love *Kessen,* which pits you against hordes of ancient Japanese warlords for total domination of Japan. Although the game features gorgeous cinematics of massive armies charging into battle, *Kessen* is really a fancy electronic board game that requires attention to detail, strategic placement of troops, and forces to master. Upon making your moves, you are treated to mini-movies of the battles and their results based upon your decisions. You can't actually participate in the battles as in *Dynasty Warriors 2* (see Chapter 7), so it may get monotonous watching the repetitive battle scenes from the sidelines. Only true fans of Japanese historical battles will get the most out of this game, but the eye candy is easy for anyone to appreciate.

Did You Know? — The developer of *Kessen,* Koei, is legendary for its intense military strategy series, including *Nobunaga's Ambition* and *Romance of the Three Kingdoms.*

Platform:
PlayStation 2

Publisher:
Electronic Arts

Price: $49.99

ESRB: Teen

Jungle Book: Rhythm 'n Groove

Platform:
PlayStation/PS one

Publisher: Ubi Soft

Price: $59.99

ESRB: Everyone

One of the hottest current game genres is dancing games in which you mimic on-screen dance moves with your control pad or on the enclosed special mat controller. So it was only a matter of time before Disney jumped on this Big Band-wagon. Based on the classic animated movie, *The Jungle Book*, *Rhythm* enables you to play as Mowgli, Baloo, King Louie, and seven other characters from the film in nine magical environments. Play solo against computerized characters or against a friend to see who has the best hand-eye coordination and the ability to keep on the beat. Your ears are treated to classic songs like "The Bare Necessities" and "I Wanna Be Like You" while your eyes feast on Mowgli and crew in full 3-D. Now, who's a monkey's uncle?

Did You Know? — For better or worse, Lou Bega, the artist responsible for that repetitive dance diddy, "Mambo No. 5," does a remake of the classic "I Wanna Be Like You." The game disc even comes with a Lou Bega music video of the song.

Monster Rancher 2

Platform:
PlayStation/PS one
Publisher: Tecmo
Price: $29.99
ESRB: Everyone

A cross between virtual pets and *Pokémon, Monster Rancher 2* challenges you to raise and train virtual creatures to become virtual fighting machines. To create one, you have to insert music CDs in your PlayStation. The kind of original creature that appears on-screen depends on the type of music you choose. You can have fun comparing a Mozart monster to a Limp Bizkit lizard. After you have your little warriors, you need to train them to up their battle skills with a series of 12 exercises. You then send them to the arena where you discover whether you have a winner or a wimp. This game skews young, but it may be perfect for kids who like the idea of a virtual pet but want more action beyond just care and feeding.

MTV Music Generator

Platform:
PlayStation/PS one

Publisher:
Codemasters

Price: $19.99

ESRB: Everyone

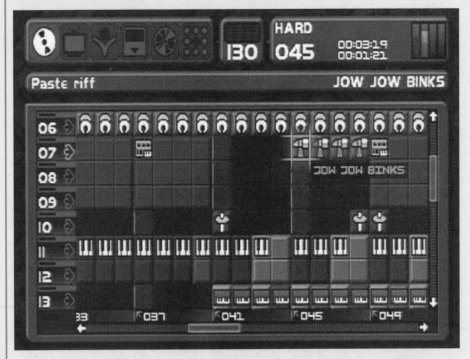

If you want to see your PlayStation do the impossible, check out the unbelievable *MTV Music Generator,* a mind-blowing sonic concoction that enables your inner mix-master to run wild. This is no mere game, it's actually a sophisticated, yet simple, multitrack sound studio. You have 24 tracks that you can fill with over 8000 samples, from full-on funky bass lines to heart-stopping techno drum loops. Mix and match as you please: You can edit existing riffs one note at a time, or even insert your favorite music CD and sample a phrase or key riff. This is a deceptively powerful, unusually creative tool that could bring out your hidden musical genius. With a multitap, you and up to three friends can hook up for a jam session. Rock on!

The Next Tetris

Tetris is perhaps the best puzzle game in existence. As oddly-shaped bricks fall from the sky, you have to fit them together to create full lines, which causes them to disappear. It's hard to improve on the original, though countless people have tried. Often, the new incarnations lose the classic, simple gameplay in overly complicated add-ons. *The Next Tetris* does it right, however, by keeping the basic line-clearing model and offering other modes with different shapes. For those of you who have not already been inducted into the cult of *Tetris* addicts, welcome to a game with a short learning curve that will supply hours of entertainment. A rival for *Solitaire* on desktop computers, *Tetris* is one of the top time-wasters in the country. True fun for all.

Did You Know? — The original *Tetris* was created by Russian programmer Alexey Pajitnov — on company time. So the rights to the game actually belong to the government of the former Soviet Union. Although the game is insanely popular worldwide and one of the most cloned games of all time, Pajitnov made virtually no money on it.

Platform:
PlayStation/PS one

Publisher:
Hasbro Interactive

Price: $19.99

ESRB: Everyone

PaRappa the Rappa

"Kick, punch, it's all in the mind." This genre-breaker made history in 1997 with its collection of bizarre, paper-thin 2-D characters in a 3-D world. PaRappa, a down-with-it cartoon dog, wants to go on a date with Sunny, a cheerful flower. Still with me? In order to make it to the date, PaRappa must master certain skills that he learns through wildly catchy raps. Teachers such as Chop-Chop Master Onion — the martial arts sensei, who is, in fact, an onion — lead the rap while you follow, matching the right button press to the right cue in the right rhythm. The game becomes progressively harder and more bizarre until one of the final stages actually takes place in a line for a bathroom. You must rap your way to the head of the line or have an "accident." The positive moral is all about believing in yourself, and the tunes will stick in your head long after you've stopped playing.

Platform:
PlayStation/PS one

Publisher: Sony

Price: $19.99

ESRB: Everyone

Q-Ball Billiards

Platform:
PlayStation 2

Publisher:
Take 2 Interactive

Price: $49.99

ESRB: Everyone

You can rack 'em up on your PS2 in this virtual reality pool hall. Play solo or with a friend in a variety of pool games, including U.S. Nine Ball, International Nine Ball, Eight Ball, Straight Pool, Rotation, and Frozen. Challenge yourself or one of the many computer opponents to sharpen your game. Super crisp graphics bring each pool table to life with camera views that range from an overhead wide-angle view of the whole table to close-ups of the chalk on your pool cue. Real-world physics apply, so you must consider friction, roll, speed, and collision in your gameplay. Although it could never replace the real thing, *Q-Ball Billiards* makes a good case for cyber-pool hustling.

Real Pool

All the fun and intricacy of playing pool comes to life in this game, with beautiful life-like graphics and smooth controls. You can play solo or start a pick up a game with a friend. Choose from several pool games including Eight Ball, Nine Ball, Rotation, and specialty games like Carom and Bowliards. In-depth features enable you to start and cultivate a career versus eight computer opponents to become a true, shrewd digital-pool shark. To test your skills, a unique Puzzle mode provides over 25 odd-shaped tables, such as triangles, stars, and other forms. Real-world physics, gorgeous graphics, and an intricate control system jam an entire pool hall onto your TV screen. You still need your smarts, a good sense of angles, and a delicate touch to run the table.

Platform:
PlayStation 2

Publisher:
Infogrames

Price: $49.99

ESRB: Everyone

Return Fire

Everyone remembers playing Capture-the-Flag at some time or another, but how would you like to up the ante? That's what *Return Fire* does, enabling you and one friend to pursue flags not by running around among trees and bushes, but by taking control of a tank or a helicopter in cities that are just waiting to be reduced to rubble. The goal is still the same — capture your opponent's piece of cloth — but the means are just slightly altered . . . to decimating bridges, using AAV drop mines, decoys, traps, and so on (unless this is the way you already play in your neighbor-hood). *Return Fire* has more than 100 levels, a superb classical music soundtrack, solid controls, and detailed visuals.

Platform:
PlayStation/PS one

Publisher:
Time Warner
Interactive

Price: $19.99

ESRB: Kids-to-Adults

Did You Know? — The soundtrack to *Return Fire* came through a licensing deal with classical music record label Angel. The game features major symphonic pieces such as Wagner's *Ride of the Valkyries* and Holst's *Mars* to lend the proceedings a truly regal air.

Platform:
PlayStation/PS one

Publisher:
Hasbro Interactive

Price: $39.99

ESRB: Everyone

Scrabble

If you've ever wanted to hone your *Scrabble* skills, this game is for you. With its very useful Hint option, you'll find yourself making words that you don't understand. But never mind that — your score will be higher than ever before! You can also practice against up to four computer opponents, or even play for real against four human beings. A virtual dictionary calms those tense moments ("What do you mean, 'XQMW' is not a word?!"), and the game's artificial intelligence automatically reshuffles your letters until muddled thinkers can actually discern the traces of a word. Multiple difficulty settings and the fact that you'll never, ever lose a letter make *Scrabble* for your PlayStation a really fun buy.

Did You Know? — *Quartzy* is purportedly the highest-scoring word in *Scrabble*, though I've never had the pleasure of actually testing this theory out. (On the other hand, I can guarantee that *an* is not worth the effort.)

South Park: Chef's Luv Shack

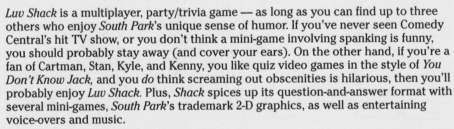

Platform:
PlayStation/PS one

Publisher: Acclaim

Price: $19.99

ESRB: Mature

Luv Shack is a multiplayer, party/trivia game — as long as you can find up to three others who enjoy *South Park*'s unique sense of humor. If you've never seen Comedy Central's hit TV show, or you don't think a mini-game involving spanking is funny, you should probably stay away (and cover your ears). On the other hand, if you're a fan of Cartman, Stan, Kyle, and Kenny, you like quiz video games in the style of *You Don't Know Jack,* and you *do* think screaming out obscenities is hilarious, then you'll probably enjoy *Luv Shack*. Plus, *Shack* spices up its question-and-answer format with several mini-games, *South Park*'s trademark 2-D graphics, as well as entertaining voice-overs and music.

Did You Know? — In case you missed it, *South Park* is a multimedia phenomenon. It has already spawned three video games (including a racing game and a first-person shooter), a feature length film (*South Park: Bigger, Longer, and Uncut*), toys, records, and so on. The creators of *South Park* are Trey Parker and Matt Stone, who have also made three live action films, which are available on DVD (and therefore watchable on your PS2).

Super Bust-A-Move

Puzzle gaming fans that love *Tetris* will instantly latch onto *Super Bust-A-Move,* an arcade classic that has already been successfully translated for various other gaming systems. But it has never looked or sounded better than it does on the PS2. The concept is simple: Line up three or more similar colored falling bubbles to *bust* them off the playing field before they descend to the bottom of the screen. Play against a friend, and you can send your burst bubbles over to his screen. *Super Bust-A-Move* is one of those cool games that you can instantly play but may never master because of the speed that the bubbles fall. The levels are endless and special trick bubbles that have unique abilities just add to the addictive factor of this fun game.

Platform:
PlayStation 2
Publisher: Acclaim
Price: $49.99
ESRB: Everyone

Theme Hospital

If you've ever had to spend an afternoon (or longer) in a hospital waiting room, now's your time for revenge. *Theme Hospital* (the sequel to *Theme Park*) enables you to design the hospital of your dreams — or the virtual public's ultimate torture chamber. You can manage everything: fire, hire, adjust room temperature ("No, no — not 125 degrees!"), and create the hospital floor plan. One of your goals is to make money (when is the national health care game coming out?) while you take care of patients who have bizarre diseases like *King Complex* (Elvis Envy, that is). Be warned, however; *Theme Hospital* is a true sim and will take some concentration before it becomes second nature — and hilarious.

Platform:
PlayStation/PS one
Publisher:
Electronic Arts
Price: $39.95
ESRB: Everyone

Unlock Level Passwords — In order to skip to the following levels, use these button presses:

Skip to Level 2: Press ✖, ●, ■, ▲, ▲, ●, ■, ✖

Skip to Level 3: Press ●, ●, ▲, ■, ✖, ▲, ●, ▲

Skip to Level 4: Press ■, ▲, ●, ■, ✖, ✖, ▲, ●

Skip to Level 5: Press ●, ▲, ■, ●, ✖, ▲, ●, ■

Skip to Level 6: Press ■, ▲, ■, ●, ✖, ■, ✖, ●

Skip to Level 7: Press ■, ▲, ▲, ●, ✖, ■, ▲, ●

Super Puzzle Fighter II Turbo

Platform:
PlayStation/PS one

Publisher: Capcom

Price: $39.99

ESRB: Kids-to-
Adults

Street Fighter — just the name commands a hushed sense of awe from fighting game fans. So naturally, its appearance in the puzzle section looks a little weird. Stranger still, the cartoonish *Super Puzzle Fighter II Turbo* is one of the most addictive puzzle games ever made! This *Street Fighter* spin-off features hours of *Tetris*-style fun for one or two players as they scheme and plot to keep their side of the screen free of colored gems. Specific combinations of similarly colored objects will cause them to disappear, thus keeping your playfield clear, while the 2-D graphics should satisfy younger gamers. The characters are familiar and the controls are spot-on, so start duking it out in puzzle format.

Play as Hidden Character Akuma — Go to the Player Select Screen and enter the following button presses:

> Player One: Put the cursor on Morrigan, and then press and hold Select. While holding Select, press Down, Down, Down, Left, Left, Left, ●.

> Player Two: Put the cursor on Felicia, and then press and hold Select. While holding Select, press Down, Down, Down, Right, Right, Right, ●.

Note: These codes work in all modes except Street Puzzle mode.

Theme Park Roller Coaster

If you can't go to the amusement park, bring the amusement park to you with *Theme Park Roller Coaster.* This one-player game allows you to play a theme-park baron as you create your ideal fantasyland with roller coasters, concession stands, and sideshows. You control everything from placement of attractions to money management in order to achieve maximum profitability. You can also sit back and watch Lilliputian customers move about your park going from attraction to attraction — or jump into their shoes and experience the park yourself. Being able to ride your coaster creations and view every stomach-churning twist and turn through a first-person view is almost worth the price of admission itself.

Platform:
PlayStation 2
Publisher:
Electronic Arts
Price: $49.99
ESRB: Everyone

Um Jammer Lammy

Made by the same music-happy video gamers responsible for *PaRappa the Rappa, Um Jammer Lammy* wants you to have fun playing virtual guitar. But no, the game doesn't supply you with an actual video-guitar; instead, you let your fingers do the playing on the PlayStation's controller, with the ✖ and ▲ buttons becoming the chords of your virtual instrument. As you attempt to strum your way to success, you'll listen to music in a variety of styles, from classic rock-and-roll to super-charged heavy metal — and in the process hear some of the goofiest lyrics this side of a *Simpsons* episode. The game looks psychedelic, in a two-dimensional way, but you'll be so involved with following the on-screen cues that you probably won't even notice the game's graphics. *Um Jammer Lammy* is a good game for lovers of music and the unusual.

Did You Know? — To give you an idea of the craziness that *Um Jammer Lammy* contains, all you have to do is read the following names of the game's guitar "teachers": Cathy Piller, Teriyaki Yoko, Paul Chuck, Chief Puddle, Captain Fussenpepper, and, last but not least, PaRappa's old *sensei* Chop Chop Master Onion.

Platform:
PlayStation/PS one
Publisher: Sony
Price: $19.99
ESRB: Everyone

Platform:
PlayStation/PS one

Publisher: Hasbro
Interactive

Price: $29.99

ESRB: Everyone

Wheel of Fortune

Admit it — you've sat at home watching *Wheel of Fortune* and thought, "Man, I knew that! I could be on this show!" Well, you're probably right — but there's a huge waiting list (somewhere in the vicinity of two years!) to get on, plus you either have to wait for them to come to your town on a tour or you have to get your butt out to California. So, isn't getting the PlayStation version easier? Maybe *Wheel of Fortune* — the game — doesn't need a high-tech treatment to be fun, but Hasbro's packed it with television-style graphics, 2000 puzzles, tons of prizes, and, of course, hostess Vanna White herself, who appears in video clips. Weirdest of all, the Dual Shock controller vibrates with every spin of the wheel!

Platform:
PlayStation/PS one

Publisher: Sony

Price: $39.99

ESRB: Everyone

Who Wants To Be a Millionaire
2nd Edition

By now, the question is *Who* Doesn't *Want To Be a Millionaire*. The TV show is already part of Americana (even though it started in Britain), and the video game does it justice. If you don't have the patience to call 10,000 times to get on the real show, you may want to participate virtually. Of course, the money you win isn't real (um, *duh*), but the video game's reproduction of the show's set and presentation is well done, so at least you feel like the experience is authentic, right down to Regis's voice-overs. You can also play against a friend as you answer all 600 questions. The down side is that you end up answering the same question repeatedly because the game doesn't keep track of which questions it's already asked.

Did You Know? — *Who Wants To Be a Millionaire* began in the United Kingdom back in September 1998 and migrated to the United States roughly a year later. During the 1999/2000 TV season, it averaged about 29 million viewers a night. Believe it or not, at the time of this book's writing, only 14 contestants worldwide had come home with the elusive million: six in the United States, two in France, and one each in Israel, Japan, Portugal, South Africa, England, and Spain.

You Don't Know Jack

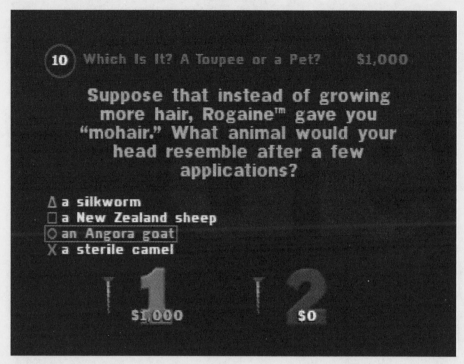

Platform:
PlayStation/PS one
Publisher:
Berkeley Systems
Price: $19.99
ESRB: Teen

First there was trivia. And it was boring. Then came *You Don't Know Jack,* which added sarcasm and pop culture to the mix, and the rules suddenly changed. Set up like a fake game show, *YDKJ* players get to decipher sarcastic queries and rediscover useless information in parts of the brain that have long since ceased to function. In fact, this process can be fun — particularly if you're playing with one or two others, as *Jack* allows. Most of the questions concern pop-culture, but sometimes high-culture "legitimate" knowledge is called for. In other words, you may be lured in by a *Brady Bunch* reference, but wind up answering a question about Shakespeare. One of *Jack*'s more insidious features is the ability to sabotage your competitors by forcing them to respond to questions that you're sure, or practically sure, they won't be able to answer (insert diabolical laugh here). *YDKJ* is a must-play!

Did You Know? — The original *You Don't Know Jack* started on the PC as an attempt to utilize CD-ROM's greatest untapped asset: Crystal clear audio. As a result, every *Jack* game has dozens of hours of human speech — almost all of it sarcastic.

Chapter 9

Racing, Driving, and Flying Games

*L*adies and gentlemen, start your engines! This chapter introduces you to the games in which the big machinery is fired up — sports cars, Indy racers, fighter jets, tough off-roaders, space fighters, and other cool vehicles you may not expect to see in a racing game. Drive fast, fly fast, go fast, game fast!

In This Chapter . . .

4 x 4 Evolution

00:03.942

Explorer Sport Trac - Pro   Press the START button to continue

Platform:
PlayStation 2
Publisher:
Gathering of
Developers
Price: $49.99
ESRB: Everyone

Terminal Reality, the developer behind the *Monster Truck Madness* series of racing games on the PC, brings its special blend of racing and off-road excitement to the world of SUVs in *4 x 4 Evolution*. Players vie on 16 tracks with a variety of licensed trucks and SUVs, including the Nissan Pathfinder, Toyota 4-Runner, and Lexus LX 470. The racing environments are completely wide open — this isn't just pretend off-road like some other games; you really can drive anywhere you like throughout the game's levels. Look for accurate car models as well as vehicle physics — but the realism isn't so heavy that it ruins the fun of zooming around in a souped-up truck.

Did You Know? — When it came out for Sega's Dreamcast, *4 x 4 Evolution* became the first game that allowed PC and Mac players to simultaneously race against console gamers over the Internet.

Ace Combat 3: Electrosphere

Platform:
PlayStation/PS one
Publisher: Namco
Price: $19.99
ESRB: Everyone

Air Combat was the first flight simulator for the PlayStation; *Ace Combat 3: Electrosphere* is its most impressive and entertaining sequel yet. *Ace Combat 3* targets the future of aerial combat by featuring cutting-edge aircraft like the F16XF Grayfalcon, state-of-the-art weaponry, and missions that range from the seas to the skies (and even into the stratosphere). One player suits up for 26 missions against a variety of land-based and aerial opponents. Earn your wings on the initial easier missions; then earn the right to upgrade to more powerful planes and weaponry. Special tasks such as night missions, landings on aircraft carriers, and mid-air refueling add to the challenge and fun. Enhanced graphics, fluid controls, and a vast payload of planes, weapons, and missions set this game apart.

Did You Know? — In Japan, the *Ace Combat* series is known as *Air Combat*. Why the title was changed when it crossed the Pacific is anyone's guess.

ATV Offroad Fury

ATV Offroad Fury puts you in the saddle of a 4 x 4 all-terrain vehicle, and then takes you deep into the dirt for competitions filled with jumps, bumps, tricks, wrecks, and more. This game provides ATVs from Honda, Yamaha, and Polaris for action on more than 20 tracks that range from supercross-style stadiums to tricky outdoor circuits to wide-open heats where you blast across two square miles of terrain. The action focuses less on the mechanics of cornering and more on the timing of jumps. Visually, *ATV* looks pretty sharp with sleek terrain, awesome vehicle models, and some of the coolest lighting yet for the PS2. A kicking soundtrack paces the action with tunes from bands such as Primus, Soundgarden, and Alice in Chains.

Platform:
PlayStation 2
Publisher: Sony
Price: $49.99
ESRB: Everyone

Colony Wars

This intense, fast-action space-combat game features a solid story and some of the best looking PS one graphics this side of the solar system. You play a fighter pilot caught in the middle of a massive war deep in space. Missions require you to destroy capital ships with torpedoes, dogfight with enemy fighters, and protect allies on escort runs. The game strikes a good balance between simulation and arcade-style gameplay, and the branching plot lines make it very replayable. The sequels are fine, but the original makes the best entry point into the series. *Colony Wars* is the kind of high-quality game that action gamers and sci-fi fans shouldn't pass up.

Invincibility — Having a little trouble defeating your enemies? Enter the password **Hestas*Retort** exactly as shown. You'll never be shot down again.

Platform:
PlayStation/PS one
Publisher: Sony
Price: $19.99
ESRB: Teen

Platform:
PlayStation/PS one
Publisher: Sony
Price: $19.99
ESRB: Everyone

Crash Team Racing

Crash Team Racing personifies the kart racing genre: Cute, large-headed mascots speed around in tiny cars and blast each other with comical weapons as they race for the finish line. *CTR* surpasses its competition through its execution. Starring Crash Bandicoot and his cartoonish pals, *CTR* controls better, plays faster and, in many instances, looks better than its peers, whether they be on PlayStation or any other system. Adventure, Arcade, Versus, Battle, and Time Trial modes keep the gameplay fresh, and with tons of secret tricks to discover, *Crash* fans will never run out of stuff to do. If you're new to the genre, *Crash Team Racing* is the game with which to start.

Unlock More Characters — At the main menu, simultaneously hold R1 and L1, and press the following buttons to unlock secret characters:

Dr. N. Tropy: Press Down, Left, Right, Up, Down, Right, Right

Komodo Joe: Press Down, Left, Right, Up, Down, Right

Ripper Roo: Press Right, ●, ●, Down, Up, Down, Right

The unlocked characters are not available in Adventure mode, but you can use them in Arcade, Versus, and Battle modes.

Platform:
PlayStation/PS one
Publisher:
Midway Home
Entertainment
Price: $39.99
ESRB: Everyone

Destruction Derby Raw

Admit it — deep down, you have a burning desire to smash up some cars! *Destruction Derby Raw* finally gives you the opportunity with all the fun of the real thing and none of the whiplash. *DDR* drops willing drivers into races on 31 tracks with 17 cars. Only the strong survive — to prove their strength, other drivers giddily slam into you at high speeds. If you're incapacitated before you can reach the finish line, you're out. A tight physics engine makes the cars easy to control, and slick graphics provide sweet visuals. You may want to turn down the techno-heavy sound-track, but the noise won't ruin an otherwise smashingly good game.

Driver

Driver slams onto the PlayStation with some of the hottest cops-and-robbers action since *Starsky and Hutch.* By combining the realistic racing physics of *Gran Turismo* with the devastating action of *Destruction Derby* (and adding lots of cinematic flair), *Driver* gives gamers an exciting thrill-ride they won't soon forget. You play an under-cover cop, posing as a getaway man for hire, who's on a mission to take down a big criminal organization. Realistic physics and damage combined with plenty of traffic and pedestrians (not to mention a sweet soundtrack) make tearing through the city streets a real kick. A host of extra game modes and a very cool Director mode, in which you can edit your own *Driver* movies, make this is a must-buy game for virtual drivers.

Invincibility — At the main menu screen, quickly press

   L2, L2, R2, R2, L2, R2, L2, L1, R2, R1, L2, L1, L1

You hear a sound effect if you enter the code correctly. Then go to the Cheats menu (from the main menu) to activate the cheat, you cheater!

Platform:
PlayStation/PS one

Publisher:
Infogrames

Price: $19.99

ESRB: Teen

F1 Championship Season 2000

F1 Championship Season 2000 is Electronic Arts' next-generation follow-up to *F1 2000,* its first Formula 1 racing title. EA has consistently brought out some of the most realistic sports games, and *F1 Championship Season* is no exception to the rule — this game strives for authenticity at every hairpin turn. The game features hyper-detailed graphics, ranging from detailed reflections to vehicle paint damage. The game keeps things real with actual Formula 1 drivers, licensed cars, recognizable announcers and tracks, realistic physics and the full schedule for the actual 2000 F1 racing season. *F1 Championship Season* also sports a split-screen two-player mode for head-to-head competition that pits two human players against a whole lineup of computer-controlled cars.

Platform:
PlayStation 2

Publisher:
Electronic Arts

Price: $49.99

ESRB: Everyone

Driving Emotion Type S

Platform:
PlayStation 2

Publisher:
Square EA

Price: $49.99

ESRB: Everyone

The PlayStation 2 racing genre is very crowded, so it takes a lot for a game to stand out. *Driving Emotion Type S* is a serious contender from developer Squaresoft, a company better known for its role-playing adventures than its automotive romps. All the standard features for racing titles are here, and the game's added bonus is the inclusion of various race circuits from Japan as well as cars native to that country. But with *Gran Turismo 3* shining so brightly beside it, the hardcore simulation gameplay of *Type S* may limit its appeal to casual gamers. It's still worth checking out, however, especially for fans of serious sim-style racers.

Gran Turismo 2

Highly anticipated, eagerly awaited sequels to million-selling blockbusters usually disappoint, but *Gran Turismo 2*, the PlayStation's premier racing simulation game, is bigger and better than its predecessor. This highly refined driving simulation features over 500 cars (!) from auto makers such as Volkswagen, Audi, Dodge, Nissan, and Mercedes-Benz. The vehicles handle with challenging but engaging realism, and impeccable controls keep you in the action. Amazing car physics, outstanding graphics, and an excellent soundtrack make this a premiere driving package. But this is a simulation — you have to earn your driver's license by passing several performance tests! Don't let the release of *Gran Turismo 3* discourage you — *GT2* is still very much worth taking for a test drive.

Platform:
PlayStation/PS one
Publisher: Sony
Price: $19.99
ESRB: Everyone

Gran Turismo 3

Gran Turismo 3 is undoubtedly the highest profile racing game for the PlayStation 2, mixing the real-life car physics found in the first two versions with sharper visuals and brand new features. Smooth car models handle without fault, and the tracks, featuring beautiful and realistic lighting, look great. *GT3* has 150 fully licensed cars, 15 tracks (including the Monte Carlo and Tokyo Racing Circuits), weather conditions like fog, heat-waves, and rain, and a fresh soundtrack that comes with a mix of big-name bands and up-and-coming hits. Additionally, up to six people can play at once by using the ilink cable. This is Sony's flagship racing title, and it shows — *Gran Turismo 3* really showcases the power of the PlayStation 2.

Did You Know? — The first two *Gran Turismo* games for the PlayStation inspired three audio CDs: a soundtrack for each game as well as the title of the Cardigans' trip-hop album, *Gran Turismo*. Next time you hear the band's song "My Favorite Game," you'll know exactly what they're talking about.

Platform:
PlayStation 2
Publisher: Sony
Price: $49.99
ESRB: Everyone

Midnight Club: Street Racing

Platform:
PlayStation 2

Publisher:
Rockstar

Price: $49.99

ESRB: Teen

Racing games have come a long way since Atari's old *Night Driver* in 1979. The racing still takes place in the dark, but now there are complete cities to explore and roam freely. *Midnight Club*'s virtual representations of London and New York feature full traffic and realistic geography — you can zoom through landmarks like Times Square and power over the River Thames! Of course, you can't just go toolin' around big cities at top speed, or the cops will be after you the moment they see you hot-rodding. With city traffic, other racers, secret shortcuts, non-linear gameplay, and the long arm of the law crowding the streets, *Midnight Club* offers a racing experience so exciting that it should be illegal . . . and it is!

Drive on the USS Enterprise — Choose the New York map. From the starting point, go forward one block; take a right; take the second left; go one block; take a soft right. Go as fast as you can for one block. Go straight through the stoplight into the building that sits beside the water, up the ramp, and into the opening in the side of the aircraft carrier. A ramp at the far end of the hangar leads to the top of the ship.

Moto GP

Platform:
PlayStation 2
Publisher: Namco
Price: $49.99
ESRB: Everyone

Moto GP is a slick racing-bike simulation game that enables you to hop on authentic motorcycles from big names like Honda and BMW to go against well-known bikers such as Kenny Roberts and Max Biaggi. The breakneck action takes you through five game modes (Season, Versus, Challenge, Arcade, and Time Trial) on real-life tracks such as Suzuka, Donington, and Jarez. With the solid sounds of growling horsepower under your seat and the cheering crowd in the stands, you'll be thrilled by the detailed bikes and tracks (especially noticeable in the replays). *Moto GP* is a simulation of real motor bike racing so the difficulty level is rather high; if you want something with an easier, more arcade-like feel, try the *Moto Racer* series for the PS one.

Did You Know? — Namco produces many games for the arcades and its specialty is large, interactive machines. The arcade game that *Moto GP* is based on features a life-size bike that you lean to the right or left sides to control, much as you would a real bike. If you're lucky, perhaps the local arcade near you has this original version.

Platform:
PlayStation/PS one

Publisher:
Electronic Arts

Price: $19.99

ESRB: Everyone

Moto Racer 2

Moto Racer 2, which features both dirt and road tracks, blends a solid physics model and very fast graphics to deliver a thrilling motorcycle racing game. A third-person view gives you a good picture of what lies on the road ahead, but the first-person view is awesome, putting you in the driver's seat with a frighteningly realistic view of the road. An excellent track editor enables you to build custom tracks, so you'll almost never become bored with the game. Equally suitable for casual fans and serious motorheads alike, the high-revving road rockets in *Moto Racer 2* offer something for every racing fan.

Platform:
PlayStation 2

Publisher:
Electronic Arts

Price: $19.99

ESRB: Everyone

NASCAR 2001

EA's *NASCAR 2001* is a simulation for the hardcore NASCAR racing fan who doesn't mind getting his hands dirty in the virtual garage first. *NASCAR 2001* enables you to tweak just about every car setting imaginable for maximum speed. On the track, the game is a white-knuckle ride. Realistic physics make drafting behind other cars a must, and caution is just as important as bravery — one slip and you'll be kissing the wall (and kissing that lead goodbye). The NASCAR license comes with official tracks (including Daytona, for the first time in EA's game series), drivers, and cars, plus you can create your own driver to compete against NASCAR's greatest racing minds. The two-player split-screen mode makes for great showdowns with friends, too. Ho-hum sounds mean it's not perfect, but it's close enough to surely thrill stock-car fans.

NASCAR Rumble

Imagine an arcade kart racing game crossed with a NASCAR simulation game, and you have a good idea of what *NASCAR Rumble* is all about. You can mix it up with over 30 NASCAR racers, such as Jeff Gordon, Rusty Wallace, and Dale Earnhardt, as you bump and grind through some seriously twisted tracks including Daytona Beach and the Sierra Nevada mountains. Most of the tracks feature hidden time-shaving shortcuts and axle-bending road obstacles. You can also pick up crazy power-ups like battering rams and weather-based attacks to help you cross the finish line first. Where else can you watch Rusty Wallace ram Kyle Petty off the road, and then see both of them swallowed up by a tornado?

Platform:
PlayStation/PS one

Publisher:
Electronic Arts

Price: $19.99

ESRB: Everyone

All Cars, Drivers, and Tracks — At the main menu, choose Game Options. Highlight Load and Save, press Left, and then press ✖ to enter the password screen. Enter **C9P5AU8NAA** as the password. If you enter the password correctly, a message asks if you want to replace the current password. Choose Yes. All cars, drivers, and tracks are now available.

Need for Speed: High Stakes

Need For Speed: High Stakes puts you behind the wheel of some insanely fast sports cars, including Porsches, Ferraris, and Lamborghinis, for wild street races — until the police catch up and arrest you! In addition to *pink slip races*, in which the winner receives both participants' cars, *High Stakes* lets you play as the cops in Hot Pursuit mode, nailing speeders by calling for backup, setting up roadblocks, and laying down spike belts. A two-player split-screen option enables you and a bud to battle on both sides of the law, too. In single-player mode, you can use the cash you win in tournaments for repairs, upgrades, and new cars. Nice graphics and great audio make *High Stakes* a high priority for sports car fanatics.

Platform:
PlayStation/PS one

Publisher:
Electronic Arts

Price: $19.99

ESRB: Everyone

No Fear Downhill Mountain Bike Racing

Platform:
PlayStation/PS one

Publisher:
Codemasters

Price: $19.99

ESRB: Everyone

Of all the extreme sports, downhill mountain biking has to be one of the most terrifying, dangerous, and suicidal. Can't wait to try it, can you? In *No Fear,* it's leg power that prevails as you compete against pro riders in a series of races. You can also go head-to-head against a friend. In Trick Trial, you can show off by grabbing air and ripping tricks for points. But the game features serious simulation elements, too. You must tune your bike to match conditions and courses; tires, gears, and suspension are all adjustable. It's not a perfect game by any means, but solid controls, good graphics, and its unique brand of racing make it worth checking out.

All Upgrades — At the main menu, choose Time Trial. Answer Yes when asked `Use Competition Access Code?` Enter the password **LOTSOFGEAR** to outfit your bike with every upgrade possible.

Nuclear Strike

This fast-action combat game puts you in the pilot seat of a powerful helicopter and other aircraft as you attempt to avert nuclear disaster and save the world from a terrorist threat. Just another day at the office, right? *Nuclear Strike*'s shoot-em-up style of gameplay affords relatively simple controls — your altitude is automatically adjusted, so you don't have to worry about hitting the ground — yet the variety of missions and the evolving plot keep the game challenging. Lots of stuff to blow up, tough enemies to battle, and nicely created cinematic sequences make this one of the best shooters for the PlayStation.

Infinite Lives — Enter the password **LAZARUS** to remove the fear of running out of chances before you can finish your missions.

Platform:
PlayStation/PS one

Publisher:
Electronic Arts

Price: $19.99

ESRB: Teen

Rally Cross 2

Slogging through the mud and grinding on the pavement takes a new twist in this highly enjoyable on- and off-road racing game. *Rally Cross 2* lets you take control of rally style trucks and cars for fast competition with tough game-generated drivers or with a friend. Tracks vary from serene mountains to noisy stadiums; naturally, there are plenty of high-flying jumps, secret pathways, and tricky corners to navigate, as well as obstacles like puddles, rocks, and potholes. After you master the pre-made tracks, an easy-to-use editor enables you to make up your own challenging courses. Easy to pick up and play, *Rally Cross 2* is a muddy good time.

Drive Any Car — From the main menu, choose Race, and then go into Season. Start a New Season and enter **moobmoob** as your player name (that's *boomboom* backwards). At the Season menu, choose Select Car, and you can drive any car in the game.

Platform:
PlayStation/PS one

Publisher: Sony

Price: $19.99

ESRB: Everyone

Ridge Racer V

Platform:
PlayStation 2

Publisher: Namco

Price: $49.99

ESRB: Everyone

The first *Ridge Racer* was a launch title for the PlayStation back in 1995, so it's appropriate that the newest *Ridge Racer* game, *Ridge Racer V,* is also one of the first titles available for the PS2. The game features Grand Prix, Time Attack, and two-player Versus modes for racing. The driving in *Ridge Racer V* is tough, especially for newcomers to the *Ridge Racer* games, so newbies should bump down the difficulty level, or they'll find themselves frustrated fast. Still, *Ridge Racer V* is one of the highest-profile racing games for the PS2 and is definitely one of the best racing games available (especially with a few practice laps under your seatbelt). It sticks a little too close to tradition to be a real breakthrough title for Namco, but fans of the series and newcomers will love it.

Did You Know? — Stranger than Fiction department: The digital female model seen on the game's cover and in the game's opening cinema isn't based on a woman at all — the male artist scanned his own face into the game and turned the image into that of a girl using digital art tools. Weird!

Road Rash Jailbreak

Biker gangs run amok in this wild motorcycle racing game, which has some combat thrown in for good measure. In the world of *Road Rash,* dirty tricks are encouraged, so you can bump, smack, and trip up opponents with weapons ranging from heavy pipes to chains (clearly, this one is not for younger gamers). A great two-player cooperative mode lets one player drive while the other lends a hand while riding in a sidecar. Gamers can also play as the fuzz and try to stop the lawless bikers. *Road Rash Jailbreak* has a twisted sense of humor and offers a wild time for gamers who want to hit the open road on two wheels.

Platform:
PlayStation/PS one
Publisher:
Electronic Arts
Price: $19.99
ESRB: Teen

Rollcage Stage II

Warning to gamers who get carsick: Stay far away from *Rollcage!* Gorgeous, fast graphics and a thumping techno soundtrack highlight this science-fiction combat racer. In *Rollcage Stage II,* you race vehicles with serious four-wheel drive, which enables them to climb walls and basically go anywhere — sort of like those cool remote control cars with the oversized tires that you can't stop. Behind the wheel, you compete against A.I. opponents or a friend, picking up power-ups and weapons to foil your competition as you tear around the fantasy tracks at truly insane speeds. The sound could be better, but *Rollcage Stage II's* impressive frame rate doesn't disappoint when it comes to the blindingly fast visuals. *Rollcage II* isn't just fun — it's *stomach-churning* fun!

Platform:
PlayStation/PS one
Publisher:
Midway Home
Entertainment
Price: $19.99
ESRB: Everyone

Platform:
PlayStation 2
Publisher:
Activision
Price: $49.99
ESRB: Everyone

Sky Odyssey

Take to the skies in aircraft from the past and present for some virtual flying fun. In *Sky Odyssey,* you soar in ten planes, from the elegant and efficient biplane to the nearly invisible (to radar at least) stealth jet, in over 40 challenging missions. The massive 3-D maps make for nice eye-candy and, for all you sunny day pilots that take to the skies only on partially cloudy evenings, you can customize weather conditions and time of day to your liking. The planes are easy to control, which enables you to look around and appreciate the various landscapes. The graphics could be nicer, but the gameplay is solid. *Sky Odyssey* may fly PlayStation 2 pilots to cloud nine.

Platform:
PlayStation/PS one
Publisher:
Electronic Arts
Price: $19.99
ESRB: Everyone

Sled Storm

Brother, it's cold out there! Don your mittens for some winter-weather racing action on snowmobiles. Excellent physics and fine controls make this challenging game a blast to play. Hidden shortcuts, big jumps, and great-looking outdoor scenery keep the gameplay fresh. Not only do you have to arrive at the finish line first, but you also have to rack up points by pulling off tricks, smashing fences, and plowing through snowmen and other obstacles that appear on the track. *Sled Storm* was something of a sleeper when it came out, but it's worth tracking down. Brrrrrrrrrrring on the c-c-c-c-ompetition!

Cheap Upgrades — Go to the Password screen beneath the Load/Save option from the main menu; then press

    ✖, L1, ●, ▲, ■, ■, ▲, L2

If you enter the cheat correctly, the screen will read `Password Accepted` and you'll be able to upgrade your snowmobile for less cash.

Smuggler's Run

Platform:
PlayStation 2
Publisher:
Rockstar
Price: $49.99
ESRB: Teen

Rockstar's *Smuggler's Run* combines off-roading and capture-the-flag fun to create an exciting, entertaining driving game for the rule-breaker that lurks inside you. You take the wheel of awesome dune buggies, jeeps, and other rugged vehicles as you cavort across treacherous terrain in order to grab packs of loot and smuggle it to your delivery zone. Thanks to the PlayStation 2, you can literally drive anywhere — if you spot mountains in the distance and have the patience, you can drive over there and climb 'em. You have to perfect your off-roading skills, though, because lawmen and rival smuggler gangs will try to take you down and steal your contraband. *Smuggler's Run* is the off-roading fan's dream come true, and one of the most enjoyable racing games around.

Invisibility — Pause the game and press

R1, L1, L1, R2, L1, L1, L2

If you enter the code correctly, you hear a noise. The cheat takes effect when you resume the game. The cops can't catch you if they can't see you!

SSX

Platform:
PlayStation 2

Publisher:
Electronic Arts

Price: $49.99

ESRB: Everyone

Hailed by many as the number one PlayStation 2 launch title, *SSX* is one awesome action/extreme sports game. In *SSX* (short for Snowboard Supercross), you race down giant snow-covered mountains on cool-looking snowboards to a wicked sound-track. *SSX* is all about wild stunts, and super-sick courses, complete with loops, ramps, and secret trails to give you plenty of places to shred. Levels include French slopes, snowed-in cities, and even one level that looks and acts like the inside of a pinball machine. Snowboard fans will love being able to catch huge air while bolting down the slopes, and racing fans will enjoy edging out the competition. If you're into arcade-style, trick-happy snowboarding action, then take it to the hills with *SSX*.

Unlock All Boards and Characters — At the Select Mode screen, press ■ to enter the Options screen. At the Options screen, simultaneously press and hold L1, L2, R1, R2; then press

> Down, Left, Up, Right, ✖, ●, ▲, ■

If you enter the code correctly, you hear a sound. All boards and characters are now available.

Test Drive 5

Platform:
PlayStation/PS one

Publisher:
Infogrames

Price: $19.99

ESRB: Kids to
Adults

This arcade style racer offers high-class, real-world cars for you to drive, but the physics and vehicle handling are from another planet. That's okay, as long as you don't expect a serious simulation game when you hop into the driver's seat of *Test Drive 5*. Choose from '60s muscle cars and ultra modern sedans in a number of varied competitions, including a drag race. You also have to dodge police and oncoming traffic as you race for the finish. A rocking soundtrack featuring Fear Factory backs the solid graphics. It may not be like a real-life test drive, but *Test Drive 5* offers another racing option if the *Need for Speed* series leaves you, well, in need of an alternative.

Three Bonus Cars — Select Full Race from the main menu, and then choose Select Race Type. Go to Time Trials and enter the password **NOLIFE**. Next time you start a race, you'll find three additional cars: Chris's Beast, Mighty Maul, and Pitbull Special.

Star Wars Starfighter

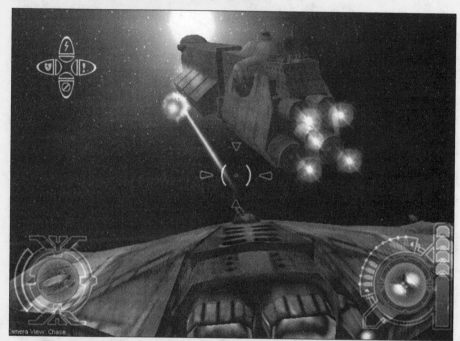

Platform:
PlayStation 2
Publisher:
LucasArts
Price: $49.99
ESRB: Teen

Starfighter puts you in the cockpit of three *Star Wars* ships as you battle the Trade Federation from *Episode I.* You pilot either a Naboo N-1, the most agile dogfighter of the bunch, the Guardian, a fast ship with a cloaking device and advanced sensors, or the Havoc, a powerful bomber with a rotating gun turret. You pilot them all through tight canyons, while blasting enemies, defending against a Trade Federation assault on your base, and engaging in all kinds of dogfighting and bombing action. As an added bonus for *Star Wars* fans, the final battle in *Episode I,* complete with droid-piloted fighters and large capital ships, is recreated in the game's grand finale.

Star Wars Super Bombad Racing

Platform:
PlayStation 2

Publisher:
Lucas Learning

Price: $49.99

ESRB: Everyone

You know what they say: Every good franchise deserves a good, big-headed, kart racing game. Not one to be left in the dust, LucasArts introduces *Star Wars Super Bombad Racing* for the PlayStation 2. Up to four players simultaneously race, hover, and fly around tracks taken from a number of locales in *Episode I* as they collect over 25 power-ups while attempting to squelch their unwary competitors. Stylized versions of Obi-Wan Kenobi, Sebulba, Queen Amidala, and that lovable little scamp Darth Maul are all along for the ride, all with big heads and big eyes, looking cuter than ever. If your little ones love *Star Wars* and racing, this game may be what they've been waiting for.

Twisted Metal 2

One of the most beloved games to come out on the PlayStation, *Twisted Metal 2* blends driving and combat into a seriously addictive mix. There are no races per-se; instead, you battle in vehicular fights to the finish. The last man standing wins in these brutal battles, which take place in global scenarios like downtown Paris and Hong Kong. Each character/vehicle has special attacks and abilities, and weapons like rockets and bombs litter the battle arenas. Excellent graphics, audio, and fierce two-player action make this game a continual fan favorite.

Hyper Machine Gun — During gameplay, press and hold R2 while you press

Up, Down, Left, Right, Right, Left, Down, Up

If you enter the code correctly, your machine guns fire faster and do more damage.

Platform:
PlayStation/PS one
Publisher:
989 Studios
Price: $19.99
ESRB: Teen

Twisted Metal: Black

From the depths of madness comes *Twisted Metal: Black,* a high-octane mix of a shooter and a demolition-derby racer. This is the fifth *Twisted Metal* game in the series and as its name implies, it's darker and even more twisted than the last two *TM* discs. The evil overlord Calypso is back, and this time, he's gathered yet another bunch of lunatics together to compete for the ultimate prize: One wish granted, no questions asked. Of course, this competition comes down to blasting whatever enemies happen to drive by, and the PS2 enables combat carnage to go down at a level of detail and realism unseen on previous consoles. With crazier cars, faster action, and a much more dark and disturbing feel, *Twisted Metal: Black* may be the game more mature racers have been waiting for.

Platform:
PlayStation 2
Publisher: Sony
Price: $49.99
ESRB: Teen

Vigilante 8

Platform:
PlayStation/PS one
Publisher:
Activision
Price: $19.99
ESRB: Teen

Like the *Twisted Metal* games, *Vigilante 8* is about car combat, not racing. Set in an alternative version of the 1970s, this funkified automotive assault lets you duke it out in a series of single-player missions in Quest mode or enables you to jump right in for a quick melee. Levels vary from downtown Las Vegas to a slippery ski slope. Smooth and fast graphics keep the RPMs revving high in this classic game, and the '70s style is dy-no-mite. *Vigilante 8* is one of the most unique and exciting games for the PlayStation, and some say it's even better than the legendary *Twisted Metal* series.

All Drivers and Cars — Go into the Options menu, highlight Game Status, press ✖, and then press ●. Enter the password **WMNNWLHTSCUCLH** to unlock all the drivers and cars you would normally have to earn by playing through the game.

Wild Wild Racing

Platform:
PlayStation 2
Publisher:
Interplay
Price: $49.99
ESRB: Everyone

In *Wild Wild Racing,* you crouch in the cockpit of a mud-slinging dune buggy as you tear around massive, checkpoint-based tracks that test the limits of your racing skills and endurance. You take on all comers on mud tracks in the U.S., Iceland, and India, with adverse conditions like night driving, snow, and thunderstorms. If driving in circles isn't your thing, you can to access three additional modes: Quest mode (in which you must collect letters hidden throughout the tracks), Skill mode (push a ball to the goal within the time allotted), and Stunt mode (complete stunt challenges in the time allotted). It's not as strong a game as *Smuggler's Run,* but it features more gameplay variety.

World Destruction League: Thunder Tanks

Platform: PlayStation 2

Publisher: 3DO

Price: $49.99

ESRB: Teen

World Destruction League: Thunder Tanks is for gamers who like mindlessly blowing stuff up and watching the resulting fireworks. You drive a tank in a silly tournament-style game show, simultaneously blasting other tanks and pesky turrets. You can choose from several massive vehicles, but the many crazy weapons (guided missiles, mines, even nukes) really make it worthwhile. Not surprisingly, the screen is constantly filled with explosions and over-the-top visual effects — each shot emits a bright halo of light. Similarly, your ears ring with a cacophony of crashing missiles and cannon fire, though the commentary is among the most insipid you'll ever hear. If you want a low-brainer shoot-em-up with lots of explosions, *World Destruction League: Thunder Tanks* delivers plenty of electronic bang for your buck.

Did You Know? — *World Destruction League: Thunder Tanks* is actually the third game in the *Battletanx* series, though 3DO has abandoned the *Battletanx* name. *Battletanx* and *Battletanx: Global Assault* were released for the original PlayStation.

FUN FACTS

World Destruction League: WarJetz

Platform:
PlayStation 2

Publisher: 3DO

Price: $49.99

ESRB: Teen

3DO's *World Destruction League* series powers forward, this time ditching the tanks and taking to the skies. *WarJetz* takes place in the future when game shows have evolved from casual contests in which housewives spin wheels for cash or brainiacs match wits for a million bucks — to all-out warfare. Futuristic aerial assault vehicles swoop and dive through skyscrapers, all itching to blow their opponents out of the skies for big bucks. You play as one of the daredevil pilots, flying for glory and greed. Get ready for airborne combat like you've never seen before.

Wipeout 3

The original *Wipeout* was a huge hit when the PlayStation made its debut, and the third game in the series is even better. In *Wipeout 3*, you race high-speed hovercraft on a variety of wild tracks that have huge jumps, narrow chutes, spirals, and hairpin turns. You can pick up weapon power-ups like rockets and mines to use against opponents as well as boosts, autopilots, and shields to help you get to the finish first. Thankfully, *Wipeout 3* features some major improvements to the controls, so it's not nearly as squirrelly or difficult to control as its forebears. The futuristic setting, amazing graphics, and thumping techno soundtrack make the *Wipeout 3* experience one that's not to be missed.

Infinite Shields and Hyperthrust — Choose Options from the main menu screen; then proceed to Game Setup and select Default Names. Enter your default name as **GEORDIE** to give your racer a decidedly unfair advantage in defense and speed.

Platform:
PlayStation/PS one
Publisher:
Psygnosis
Price: $19.99
ESRB: Everyone

Wipeout Fusion

The *Wipeout* series of hover-racing games got its start with the original PlayStation. While the series didn't make its way onto the PS2 until recently, it's still one of the fastest, futuristic racing titles around. In this, the latest sequel in the series, the year is 2150 and the new F9000 racing league has been born, promising new technology, free-form tracks, and blinding speed. *Wipeout Fusion*'s physics model has been completely overhauled for the PS2, and the addition of individual pilot characters with unique personalities and preferences will affect every race's outcome. If you're into racing hovercraft and listening to cutting-edge music, *Wipeout Fusion* is a title well worth looking into.

Platform:
PlayStation 2
Publisher: Sony
Price: $49.99
ESRB: Everyone

Chapter 10
Fighting Games

Put up your dukes, pal — it's time to go *mano a mano* with some of the roughest, toughest brawlers known to man. Because most civilized humans never dirty their hands with base fisticuffs, fighting games offer a safe outlet for aggressions and some good, old-fashioned hero fantasies. Or maybe you just like beating stuff up. Either way, you have plenty of games to choose from for your PlayStation 2.

In This Chapter . . .

Bloody Roar

You've never heard of a death zoo? It's just like a regular zoo, only with more . . . death. This cult favorite's biggest draw is the fact that your fighters, when they become enraged at being hurled against the arena wall for the upteen-millionth time, can turn into vicious, bloodthirsty animals who then turn around to even the score. *Bloody Roar* sports some very polished fighters, smoothly blended polygons, and breakneck speed. The easy-to-use button configuration keeps things simple, while your punches, kicks, and transforms are all a tap away. It looks like a PS2 sequel is hovering on the distant horizon, but for now, this is a solid, unique 3-D fighter. *Bloody Roar* is fast, easy to play, and the title doesn't lie (note the Teen rating).

Platform: PlayStation/PS one
Publisher: Sony
Price: $19.99
ESRB: Teen

Marvel Super Heroes vs. Street Fighter

While it certainly doesn't have the playable punch of Capcom's most solid fighting games, this crossover fighting game hits the PlayStation with more muscle than its predecessor, *X-Men vs. Street Fighter*. *Marvel vs. SF* has all the trademark elements of Capcom 2-D fighting — intense action, easy-to-learn controls, special attacks that fill the screen with big, loud, and shiny effects, and a huge selection of appealing characters, including some of your favorite Marvel Comics characters (Spider-Man, Captain America, and Wolverine). In their supreme folly, however, the reckless folks over at Capcom didn't realize that bringing the Marvel and *Street Fighter* worlds together would open up a cosmic can of worms, leading to black holes, temporal paradoxes, and other such unpleasant time-space anomalies. That stuff always happens in comics.

Platform: PlayStation/PS one
Publisher: Capcom
Price: $39.99
ESRB: Teen

Bushido Blade 2

Platform:
PlayStation/PS one

Publisher:
Square EA

Price: $19.99

ESRB: Teen

You can think of *Bushido Blade 2* as the thinking man's fighting game. Featuring a realistic fighting engine based on true-to-life samurai swordplay, the game emphasizes finesse and control over combos and button-mashing — sort of the anti-*Tekken,* if you will. A single, well-placed blow could end the match, and players are encouraged to follow the "code of bushido" — meaning no back stabbing, head starts, or similarly nefarious chicanery. Plus, it's ridiculously fun to run around with a samurai sword slicing down stalks of bamboo. If this fighting sequel bears a striking resemblance to *Kengo: Master of Bushido* for the PS2, there's a reason: They were developed by the same team.

Did You Know? — *The Bushido Blade* series was the second foray into the realm of the fighting genre by SquareSoft, the folks who turned console role-playing games on their ear with the extraordinarily popular *Final Fantasy* series. SquareSoft's first fighter? A weird little fighting/role-playing hybrid called *Tobal No. 1.*

Darkstalkers 3

Platform:
PlayStation/PS one
Publisher: Capcom
Price: $39.99
ESRB: Teen

If you like your fighting games on the more whimsical side, you can't go wrong with Capcom's *Darkstalkers 3*. In a stylish, cartoony bent, the third game in the *Darkstalkers* series features a cast of vampires, werewolves, mummies, ghosts, and other famous mythical monsters. Gameplay resembles the same old-school, 2-D fighting action that made the *Street Fighter* series a star. The fights are fast, furious, easy to control, and loaded with color and splashy visual effects. Sure, *Darkstalkers 3* can't disguise the fact that it's really just another *Street Fighter* game in a Halloween costume — but there's nothing wrong with wearing a disguise every now and then.

Dead or Alive 2: Hardcore

Platform:
PlayStation 2
Publisher: Tecmo
Price: $49.99
ESRB: Teen

Dead or Alive 2 first turned heads as an arcade title that was later ported to the Dreamcast. But this PS2 incarnation is the definitive and most full-featured version of the game (hence the term, "Hardcore"); in fact, this high-quality title is in a battle with *Tekken Tag Tournament* to see which is the king of the PS2 fighting games. *DOA2* is definitely the most visually captivating of them all (though some of its fame comes from the . . . "healthy" female fighters that populate the game). In terms of gameplay, *DOA2* features a solid fighting engine with a unique attack reversal system: It's great fun to watch as your opponent tries to deliver a kick to your head — only to see your character grab the attacker's foot in midair and throw him down to the ground with a painful thud. *Tekken Tag Tournament* may be slightly better known, but *Dead or Alive 2: Hardcore* is the sleeper hit of PS2 fighters.

Guilty Gear

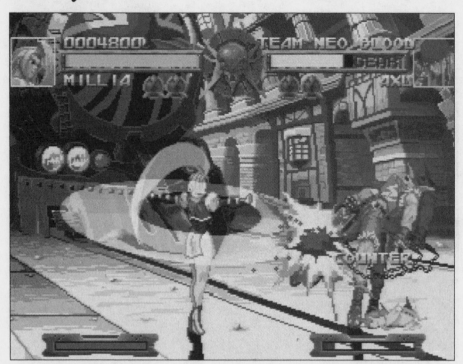

Platform:
PlayStation/PS one
Publisher: Atlus
Price: $49.99
ESRB: Teen

Take everything that old-school 2-D fighters have ever been, hurl them into a giant pot, stir for thirty seconds, and *voila!* Here's your *Guilty Gear,* Monsieur. Borrowing characters and environments from just about everywhere — including the streets of the *Street Fighter* series along with the velvet-laced castles, hair-whipping femme fatales, and sword-wielding knights of *Darkstalkers* — this brawler is like the bizarre, yet strangely appetizing casserole some grandmas make from Thanksgiving left-overs. You'll find nothing new here, but luckily, everything has been expertly ripped off; it's sort of the culmination of the 2-D fighting genre as a whole. *Guilty Gear* is weird, has plenty of variety, and, if nothing else, has one of the silliest titles ever put to a pixel.

Kengo: Master of Bushido

Platform:
PlayStation 2

Publisher: Crave
Entertainment

Price: $54.99

ESRB: Mature

Kengo: Master of Bushido, set in the feudal era in Japan when samurai and shogun
reigned supreme, is unique — it's one of the most realistic swordfighting titles on the
market. Featuring 20 characters to fight in 20 stages along with interactive elements
and environments, *Kengo* offers a wide range of sword attacks, stances, and offensive strategies culled from real-life martial arts. *Kengo* also includes a character-
growth system: After each fight, you gain more strength, speed, and agility, or learn
more sword combinations. Part of *Kengo*'s claim to fame is the infamous one-hit
fatality — run a sword through your opponent's heart, and he won't just lose a few
hit points . . . he'll drop dead (hence the Mature rating). Just like in the movies!

Did You Know? — If this game looks and sounds a little familiar, that's because
Kengo was developed by the same team that created the first two *Bushido Blade*
games for the PlayStation, both of which employ the same realistic style of
swordfighting.

Mortal Kombat 4

The first three installments in this series of brutal 2-D fighting games are, when all is said and done, basically the same game (which is why it wasn't very difficult to assemble them into one title, *Mortal Kombat Trilogy*). After the third installment, fans of *MK* were clamoring for Midway to breathe polygonal, 3-D life into their series before it went the way of the dodo. Midway's answer to the fans' call is *Mortal Kombat 4,* which brings all the blood, guts, and Fatalities of the *Kombat* series into the third dimension — and lo and behold, Midway did it right. By maintaining the look and feel of the series, Midway made *MK4* fast, furious, and fun, while the introduction of weapons into the fray added depth to the already vast oceans of brawler blood. After *MK4,* Midway put the series on ice for a few years, but rumblings say that another one is in the works, deep down in some dungeon.

Did You Know? — *MK4* is the first time that the popular four-armed boss Goro has been available as a playable character. He's still a secret, though.

Platform:
PlayStation/PS one

Publisher:
Midway Home
Entertainment

Price: $19.99

ESRB: Mature

Mortal Kombat Trilogy

Hide your children — because Midway has taken all three original 2-D *Mortal Kombat* games and united them into one! Fighting game fans either love the *MK* series to death or curse its name — but no one denies its impact. The *Mortal Kombat* games introduced concepts such as Fatalities and buckets of blood to fighting games, a realm in which violence and pain had previously been expressed only through colorful, cartoonish lines of surprise hovering over characters' heads. Some fighting game veterans can't stand *Mortal Kombat* due to the cookie-cutter nature of its characters and what they see as shallow, stiff gameplay. Other gamers find great satisfaction in the more strategic *MK* fighting dance. One man's trash is another man's treasure. Be warned: Not only does the game fully earn its Mature rating, but it's one of the few games that Sony says isn't 100 percent compatible with your PS2. It works, but it may lock up now and then, causing you to reset the machine. No permanent damage, mind you, but it can be a bit annoying.

Platform:
PlayStation

Publisher:
Midway Home
Entertainment

Price: $19.99

ESRB: Mature

Play as Chameleon — To play as the hidden fighter Chameleon, at the fighter select screen select Human Smoke. Then press and hold

> Left, L1, R2, ■, and ▲

Keep these buttons held until the fight starts. When the match starts, Human Smoke explodes into Chameleon, who has the powers of Classic Sub-Zero, Rain, Smoke, Ermac, Scorpion, and Noob Saibot.

Pocket Fighter

Platform:
PlayStation/PS one

Publisher: Capcom

Price: $39.99

ESRB: Everyone

In the grand tradition of *Muppet Babies*, *Young Frankenstein*, and *Flintstones Kids* comes *Pocket Fighter,* the fighting game that proves size really does matter! *Pocket Fighter* takes characters from *Darkstalkers* and *Street Fighter* and super-deforms (big heads, small bodies) them into cuddly little tykes — but don't let their looks fool you. These pint-sized pugilists have enough special moves, techniques, and combos to send the most seasoned *Street Fighter* vets back to basic training. In addition to intense hand-to-hand, one-on-one fighting, you can grab gems during a fight (to power up special moves) and throw objects like bombs. Plus, the characters are loaded with humorous and witty animations, which makes *Pocket* as entertaining to watch as it is to play. Good things do come in small packages.

Did You Know? — This isn't the only time these *Street Fighter* Jr.'s duked it out on a video game screen; you can also catch them lining up colored jewels in the awesome multiplayer puzzle game *Super Puzzle Fighter II Turbo* (see Chapter 8).

Rival Schools: United By Fate

Platform:
PlayStation/PS one

Publisher: Capcom

Price: $39.99

ESRB: Teen

Rival Schools is more than an excellent home translation of an arcade brawler — its bonuses and secrets place it on the fighting-game honor roll. In the grand Capcom tradition, this 2-D *Street Fighter*–style game features 3-D polygonal characters, animated backgrounds, and plenty of fireball-spewing. The twist? The game focuses on the conflict between two competing high schools, which means all the characters run off to do their homework after the final round comes to a close. The school aspect is a unique, funny variation on the whole fighting scene — to see the school's star baseball player square off against the stern-looking school principal is a riot. Getting beaten up after school may actually be fun for a change.

Hidden Characters — This cheat works for the Evolution Disc only: Each time you finish a one-player game, one hidden fighter becomes unlocked. At the Character Select screen, put the cursor on the box under Kyoko, press ●, and then press Left or Right to select any of the unlocked hidden characters.

Soul Blade

Platform:
PlayStation/PS one
Publisher: Namco
Price: $19.99
ESRB: Teen

"Welcome to the stage of history!" (Or at least, that's how the game says hello when you start it up.) The focus of this now-classic 3-D fighting game from Namco (the makers of *Tekken*) isn't special moves, finesse, or strategy — it's weapons! Sure, *Soul Blade* (or *Soul Edge* as it was known in the arcades) has all that other good stuff, but its trademark is the unique array weapons and fighting style that went hand-in-hand with each character: Mitsurugi has his katana; Li Long has his nunchakus; and Siegfried the knight has his giant, armor-cleaving claymore. *Soul Blade* has also spawned an awesome sequel, *Soul Calibur* (not on a Sony system yet), which takes the weapons concept to dizzying new heights. Watch for a *Soul Calibur* game on PS2.

Play as SoulEdge — To play as SoulEdge, finish the game in Arcade mode on any skill setting with all 10 characters. At the Fighter Select screen, SoulEdge should appear between Mitsurugi and Siegfried.

Street Fighter Alpha 3

Platform:
PlayStation/PS one

Publisher: Capcom

Price: $19.99

ESRB: Teen

Street Fighter Alpha 3 is a truly great 2-D arcade fighting game, and the PlayStation version is a great translation of it. *Alpha*'s main appeal has always been its multitude of fighting choices, updated animation, and no-nonsense fighting attitude. A whopping 31 characters from the *Street Fighter* series appear here to duke it out, and each can choose from one of three fighting styles — that's a lot of variety. If you've already got another *Street Fighter* game in your collection, *Alpha 3* may not be what you're looking for, but it does offer deeper strategy and greater rewards to players who choose technique over random button-mashing. Not that there's anything wrong with that.

Play as Evil Ryu, Guile, and Powerful Akuma — Start a World Tour game and build your fighter to Level 32. At the Select Player screen, Evil Ryu and Guile are now selectable characters; you can select Powerful Akuma by highlighting Akuma and pressing L2.

Street Fighter EX3

Platform:
PlayStation 2
Publisher: Capcom
Price: $49.99
ESRB: Teen

Here, folks, is the game that started it all. Well, okay, here's the eight-zillionth sequel to the game that started it all. *Street Fighter EX3* is a strange combination of 3-D graphics and the traditional, "old school" 2-D-fighting, fireball-hurling, dragon-punching mechanics that made the series so huge in the first place. Thanks to the horsepower of the PS2, instead of the usual one-on-one or tag-team fights, *SF EX3* has many kinds of multiplayer brawls — one-on-three, two-on-one, and even four-player free-for-alls — if you have a PS2 multitap. The game also features 16 characters, nine unlockable secret personages, and a character editor that enables you to create a custom fighter. If this incarnation of the game doesn't float your fighting boat, just remember that there's always another *Street Fighter* game on the horizon.

Did You know? — Counting all the Alphas, Golds, EX's, Pluses, sequels, Impacts, and Strikes, *SF EX3* marks the 24th fighting game to feature the *Street Fighter* lineup. Add in puzzle games *(Super Puzzle Fighter II Turbo)* and spin-offs *(Pocket Fighter, Rival Schools)*, and variations for different console systems, and that number just gets ridiculous.

Tekken 3

Platform:
PlayStation/PS one
Publisher: Namco
Price: $19.99
ESRB: Teen

Namco's flagship 3-D fighting game series reaches its PlayStation summit with the arrival of *Tekken 3*, the fastest, deepest, and most intricate fighting game the system has ever seen. *Tekken 3* comes with over 100 moves per character, a ton of hidden (and really weird) characters, multihit combos (all *T3* fighters can pull off 10-hitters), outstanding graphics, and seamless gameplay that includes juggles, counters, and linking moves. You don't get much better than *Tekken 3*. To augment *T3*'s replayability, Namco has thrown in some exciting extras not found in the arcade version, like Tekken Force mode (a side-scrolling mini-adventure), an extensive and helpful Practice mode, and the bizarre, undeniably fun, volleyball fighting-frenzy of Beach Ball mode.

Play as Tiger — Finish the Arcade mode with 16 different characters. At the Fighter Select screen, highlight Eddy Gordo and press Start.

Tekken Tag Tournament

Platform:
PlayStation 2
Publisher: Tecmo
Price: $49.99
ESRB: Teen

The *Tekken* series is one of the longest-running series of 3-D brawlers out there. *Tekken* games are characterized by their awesome computer-generated movie openings, huge cast of characters, and lightning-fast gameplay that emphasizes a more realistic blend of combos, reflexes, and efficiency over fireballs and flashy special-effect moves. *Tekken Tag Tournament* is the most complete version of the game yet, enabling up to four players to take part in a single tag-team style match. You'll also discover a ton of secrets, ranging from art galleries to *Tekken* bowling . . . yes, bowling! Easily frightened players take note: The extremely bizarre non-sequitur endings you see when you beat the game have been known to produce uncomfortable, baffled confusion in those souls who have borne witness to them.

Ultimate Fighting Championship

Platform:
PlayStation 2 and
PlayStation/PS one

Publisher: Crave
Entertainment

Price: $39.99

ESRB: Teen

The fighters are ready, the judges are ready, and developer Crave is ready to bring you some of the best fighting action since Grognog invented the portable beatin' stick back in the Stone Age. Just like the brawling league on which it's based — where the fighting is never faked and all disciplines, from matrial arts to wrestling to street fighting, are represented — *Ultimate Fighting Championship* is raw, brutal, realistic, and very cool. Both the PlayStation and PlayStation 2 versions have all the fighters and action you'd expect from *UFC*, including a Tournament mode, Create-A-Fighter, and more. When you put aside the pomp and circumstance of wrestling and the beat-mania button-mashing of games like *Tekken,* you end up with *Ultimate Fighting Championship.* This is, hands-down, one of the best fighting/wrestling games.

Did You Know? — The Ultimate Fighting Championship tournaments have thrived as pay-per-view events, but are too extreme to be on regular television. The league was dominated in the early days by a fighter named Royce Gracie, but he's not represented in the game!

Wu-Tang: Shaolin Style

Platform:
PlayStation/PS one

Publisher:
Activision

Price: $39.99

ESRB: Mature

Get ready for the Wu World Order! Take control of one of the members of the Wu-Tang Clan and battle it out in a four-player brawler that's best described as a button-stompin', weapon-swingin' blast. This persona-based, hip-hop/martial arts fighting game features a fun story (the Clan's master has been kidnapped) and great fighting action with all nine members of the Wu-Tang Clan. One to four players can get in on the action to defeat the villains and recover the master by fighting a variety of very evil looking characters. Graphically, the game is top-notch (it was built on the engine for *Thrill Kill,* a very good but very violent game that was never released) and Wu-Tang fans will recognize their favorite rappers. *Wu-Tang: Shaolin Style* is a great game for kung-fu flick fiends, fighting game enthusiasts, and Wu-Tang Clan fans.

Unlock All Characters — At the main menu, press

Right, Right, Right, Right, Left, Left, Left, Left, ■, ●, ■, ●

If you enter the code correctly, you hear a sound. All characters are now available in Versus mode.

WWF SmackDown 2

Platform: PlayStation
Publisher: THQ
Price: $39.99
ESRB: Teen

The folks at THQ and Yukes (the game's developer) have teamed up to bring PlayStation owners a WWF game that they'll actually want to play again and again. And, like the WWF's Kurt Angle, it has three *I*'s of its own: innovation, ingenuity, and incredible fun. *SmackDown* struts into the ring wielding its revolutionary Season mode, in which you create a superstar and bring him up through the ranks of the WWF, complete with all the soap-opera storylines you see on TV. Through trials and tribulations as well as injury and intrigue, your custom superstar must rise to fame and fortune by grappling with the best superstars of the WWF. Make friends or enemies, and be challenged to defend your title. The player creation feature is incredibly deep — you can change everything from the shape of your face to the style of your boots. If you're looking for a touch of intrigue with your sports entertainment, you can't go wrong with *WWF SmackDown 2.*

X-Men: Mutant Academy

Platform:
PlayStation/PS one

Publisher:
Activision

Price: $39.99

ESRB: Teen

While most hot movie licenses inevitably become horrific to mediocre video games, *X-Men: Mutant Academy* is a rare exception to the rule. After years of awful solo titles and endless crossovers with Capcom fighters, the X-Men finally strike out on their own in a fighting game that dishes out some mad mutant mayhem, combining 3-D graphics with *Street Fighter*–like moves. So what if Storm is battling her beloved mentor Professor X? Big deal if Cyclops is giving laser-death eyes to his best gal Jean Grey. In a fighting game, you don't need a big (or even plausible) story. You just need to get in there and mash some buttons, and that's where this game shines. *Mutant Academy* offers a variety of wild moves, crazy characters, and tons of unlockable hidden goodies, from the *X-Men* movie trailer to extra costumes and production art. You may want to do yourself a favor and enroll in *Mutant Academy*.

The Ultimate Cheat — At the main menu, press

Select, Up, L2, R1, L1, R2

If you enter the code correctly, you hear a strange sound. All ten characters are now playable, and all pictures and movies in Cerebro mode are viewable.

Chapter 11
Role-Playing Games

*R*alph Waldo Emerson once said, "Every hero becomes a bore at last." Clearly, Waldo didn't have a PlayStation 2. Had he been able to go on epic journeys through fantasy lands, casting himself as the central heroic character — had he been able to slay dragons, conjure magic spells, and save princesses aplenty — he may have felt differently. In fact, some of these epic role-playing games (also known as RPGs) are so good that even after you beat them, you may request a re-quest. Ha!

In This Chapter . . .

Alundra 2

The Kingdom of Varuna isn't doing too well. People are turning into monsters, shady people are running the land, and a wooden puppet has replaced the ruler. (You can keep those "So where's the fantasy?" jokes to yourself.) Playing as Flint, a pirate hunter and wanted man, you must help Princess Alexia save her kingdom by destroying the evil Baron Diaz. The game is replete with challenging puzzles and tests scattered throughout underground caverns, sunken ships, volcanoes, and so on. *Alundra 2* is relatively simple to delve into without any confusing elements to hinder your quest. Be prepared to cast cool magical spells by using elemental forces such as water and wind to ward off enemies. *Alundra 2* is an RPG that mixes great action with a great story, and it's a fine start for folks who are new to the genre.

Platform:
PlayStation/PS one
Publisher:
Activision
Price: $19.99
ESRB: Teen

Breath of Fire III

The first two *Breath of Fire* games appeared on the Super Nintendo Entertainment System to much acclaim. The third installment of this popular series (and the first to be released on the PlayStation) upholds that tradition with exceptional gameplay. The game's story is epic, complete with subplots, twists, and turns that keep you guessing to the very end. As a member of the Brood, a clan whose members have the ability to turn into dragons, you're befriended by a pair of thieves, who later disappear. As you try to find them, you become sidetracked with other objectives and are joined by even more characters. The game enables you to travel to mysterious places and battle a variety of creatures in this complex quest.

Platform:
PlayStation/PS one
Publisher: Capcom
Price: $16.99
ESRB: Teen

Did you know? — Every *Breath of Fire* game includes a character named Nina, but each Nina has nothing to do with the others.

FAMILY FRIENDLY

Brave Fencer Musashi

HP· 92/150
BP· 78/150
S 1720
Gunshot
Day: 1 Mon

Platform:
PlayStation/PS one

Publisher:
Square EA

Price: $19.99

ESRB: Everyone

The name may sound odd, but this light-hearted, refreshing role-playing game capti-
vates adventurers of all ages with its "less talk, more action" approach. As the legendary warrior, Musashi, you're magically summoned from your world by Princess
Fillet to help restore peace to her kingdom. The setup sounds basic, but the gameplay is unusual — you guide Musashi through a number of detailed levels, splashing
down white-water rapids and racing a monster up the side of a mountain. The game
does feature some traditional RPG elements, such as building Musashi's attributes
and talking to other characters. But the focus is on action, and that's what makes
Musashi unusual and unique.

Breath of Fire IV

In keeping with tradition, the latest in the *Breath of Fire* line contains an intricate story mixed with gameplay that more advanced role-playing gamers will enjoy. You must use strategy during battles to determine who is best to use in your party, to select the best types of magic, and to master your combo attacks (which enable you to attack more than once in a single turn). Like the battle system, the story line can be difficult to follow. The plot starts with a search for a missing princess, but quickly focuses on a dragon-transforming figure who seeks to discover his origins. If you're up to playing an engrossing and somewhat trying adventure, *Breath of Fire IV* delivers a memorable RPG experience.

Platform:
PlayStation/PS one

Publisher: Capcom

Price: $39.99

ESRB: Teen

Eternal Ring

As one of the first role-playing games for the PlayStation 2, *Eternal Ring* puts you in control of Cain, a royal emissary sent to the island of Solcia to check up on a research team's hunt for a lost civilization. But when he reaches the island, Cain finds Solcia overrun by mysterious creatures. The research team is unhappy, yet they aren't telling Cain all of their findings. As Cain, you must uncover the research team's secrets and explore every facet of Solcia. Armed with a hefty sword and a wealth of magic rings, you do battle with various monsters along the way. Wondrous visual effects and a rocking soundtrack complete this amazing role-playing game.

Did You Know? — From Software, the developer of *Eternal Ring*, also created the popular *King's Field* series for first-person RPGs on the original PlayStation.

Platform:
PlayStation 2

Publisher: Agetec

Price: $49.99

ESRB: Teen

Chrono Cross

Platform:
PlayStation/PS one

Publisher:
Square EA

Price: $39.99

ESRB: Teen

In *Chrono Cross,* you follow the footsteps of Serge, a young boy who can skip around in time and space. Highlights of the game include nonlinear gameplay and a number of alternate paths. For example, when you find specific items or people, you trigger events or objectives that add more depth to the story. In addition to its beautiful visuals and outstanding soundtrack, *Chrono Cross* has excellent replay value. Experiencing all of the game's diverse scenarios is impossible during a single playthrough. The deep, complex story line and rewarding replayability (there are reportedly nine different endings!) have made *Chrono Cross* an instant classic in the RPG genre.

Did You Know? — *Chrono Cross* is the sequel to the Super Nintendo hit *Chrono Trigger* — you don't need to play the first game to understand or enjoy the second.

Evergrace

If you're known as a fashion plate among your family and friends, then *Evergrace* is perfect for you. The game centers on Sharline and Darius, who awake one day in an odd land and find that a mysterious symbol has been marked on their hands. This symbol endows them with serious power. You have to figure out the importance of the mark by journeying through the land, battling weird creatures, and solving challenging puzzles. Strangest of all, you have to dress correctly to solve the majority of the puzzles, mixing and matching your clothes according to the clues you're given. This aspect of the game may sound a bit whimsical, but *Evergrace* handles the unique premise well.

Platform: PlayStation 2

Publisher: Agetec

Price: $49.99

ESRB: Teen

Final Fantasy VII

Final Fantasy VII is considered one of the best role-playing games of all time, and was the first *FF* title to appear on the Sony PlayStation. The tale (which does not build on the earlier Final Fantasy games — they're all independent tales) centers around a sword-wielding mercenary named Cloud Strife and a motley band of revolutionaries, called Avalanche, who are trying to prevent the evil Shinra Corporation from draining their world's energy. Easy-to-use menu systems enable you to battle with a slew of magic and weapon attacks, while the eye-popping graphics (including gorgeous pre-rendered backgrounds) and sensational music complete this adventure of epic proportions.

Did you know? — *Final Fantasy VII* required a staff of over 100 people and approximately $20 million to create.

Platform: PlayStation/PS one

Publisher: Sony

Price: $19.99

ESRB: Teen

Final Fantasy VIII

Platform:
PlayStation/PS one

Publisher:
Square EA

Price: $19.99

ESRB: Teen

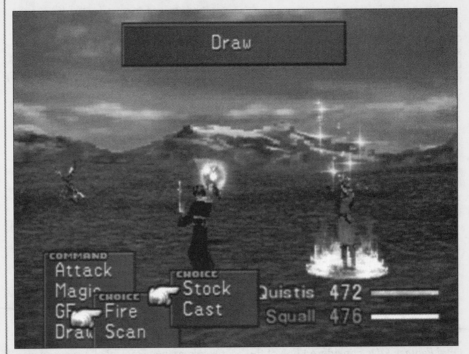

Final Fantasy VIII offers a completely independent story from the hit *Final Fantasy VII* — same universe, different world, so to speak. The eighth chapter takes place at a school that trains cadets to become soldiers. The game focuses on a hero named Squall and his five colleagues, who become involved with a resistance group and are eventually embroiled in a battle to save time itself. You travel to wondrous, beautifully detailed lands, to outer space, and even through time, all while facing adversities in a story full of touching moments, humor, double-crosses, and surprises. The game spans four CDs, which means it takes over 60 hours to finish, and also includes one of the best soundtracks of any RPG to date.

Final Fantasy IX

Platform:
PlayStation/PS one
Publisher:
Square EA
Price: $39.99
ESRB: Teen

Final Fantasy IX, which is the latest *Final Fantasy* game and the last installment for the PlayStation, is a more light-hearted, fantasy-based adventure than its predecessors. Instead of one main protagonist, *FFIX* weaves the lives of eight characters into a single story line. The characters explore moral issues as their homelands are trapped in a war with each other. It's this deep, rich tapestry of emotion that allows *FFIX* to transcend the usual RPG save-the-world story, creating a true narrative accomplishment for a video game. Like the previous two *Final Fantasy* games, players should expect painstaking detail in the graphics and splendid tunes throughout. *Final Fantasy IX* raises the stakes of what makes a great RPG and is a worthy finale to possibly the greatest series for the PlayStation.

Did you know? — Why are the games named *Final Fantasy* when none of them signifies an end to the series? After creating four unsuccessful games for the old Nintendo Entertainment System, the director of the development team, Hironobu Sakaguchi, thought that his next game was going to be his last one — so he dubbed his role-playing adventure *Final Fantasy*. Not only was *FF* an enormous hit, but it spawned one of the best role-playing series in video game history.

Front Mission 3

Platform:
PlayStation/PS one

Publisher:
Square EA

Price: $39.99

ESRB: Teen

Front Mission 3 walks a thin line between strategy and role-playing adventure. The setting is futuristic Japan, where you're a test pilot for Kirishima Industries, creators of war machines (in this case, giant robots). From an overhead view, your sights focus on the battlefield as you determine what units go where and who should go on the offensive or defensive. In this combat-heavy game, it can take anywhere from five to 30 minutes to complete a battle. You also have to deal with many menus, as you place characters, change weapons, and access items. *Front Mission 3* isn't for everyone, but if you enjoy the sci-fi aspects and have a healthy attention span, *FM3* can be quite engaging.

Kagero: Deception II

Platform:
PlayStation/PS one
Publisher: Tecmo
Price: $42.99
ESRB: Mature

In *Kagero,* you're Millenia, a human who's been brainwashed and transformed into an assassin by a strange race of blue-skinned creatures. Your job is to kill ambitious humans who dare approach the castle (make no mistake, this is one game that deserves the Mature rating). The catch is that Millenia can't bear arms. Instead, she must lure humans into a series of traps, which can be set on the ceiling, floor, or wall. Adding to the sinister premise, the more humans decapitated, the more experience points you receive. As the levels progress, you need to contend with tougher opponents who learn to avoid your deadly contraptions. While an original idea, the game consists of simply setting traps for unwanted intruders, and can get old quickly if you don't share the game's dark sense of humor.

The Legend of Dragoon

Platform:
PlayStation/PS one

Publisher: Sony

Price: $39.99

ESRB: Teen

With high-caliber visuals and a powerful story, *The Legend of Dragoon* is truly a modern role-playing classic. To fulfill an end-of-days prophecy, Emperor Diaz wants to unleash total destruction and bring forth a new dominant species of creatures upon the land. It's up to the hero, Dart — that is, you — to stop him and bring peace to everyone. Along the way, you must acquire gems that give you power to transform into a mythical Dragoon — one who can control dragons — which in turn enables you to cast spells and deliver destructive blows with your weapon. The game contains fantastic scenery in a vivid and colorful world, plus a sweeping music score plays to the very end. Beginners will have no problem learning the easy controls and simple battle system.

Legend of Legaia

Platform:
PlayStation/PS one

Publisher: Sony

Price: $19.99

ESRB: Everyone

Legend of Legaia is an unusually eco-friendly adventure that puts you in control of young hunter Vahn, who is determined to rid the world of an evil mist that brings death and madness to whatever it touches. To return Legaia to normal, you must find and revive the seven life-giving Genesis Trees and destroy the three mist generators. Unique to this game is the battle system: You just can't attack an enemy, but must also specify what area of the enemy to hit. This system is innovative and creates entirely new strategies. With the addition of colorful graphics and a mood-inspiring soundtrack, this is one RPG that shouldn't be missed.

Lunar 2: Eternal Blue Complete

Platform:
PlayStation/PS one
Publisher: Working
Designs
Price: $59.99
ESRB: Teen

This popular RPG was originally released on the Sega CD video game system, and its gameplay holds up well in its PlayStation reissue. With a revamp of its sound and graphics, *Lunar 2* looks, sounds, and feels like a can't-miss adventure. You follow the journey of Hiro and his companion, Ruby, as they seek to unlock the mystery behind the Blue Spire, a crystal that strangely encapsulates a young girl. Of course, evil is never too far off, and you're challenged by dark forces who will stop at nothing to revive Zophar, a menacing entity who could plunge the Lunar world into eternal darkness. It may not look as flashy as some other role-playing games on the system, but make no mistake: Lunar is a great, traditional RPG.

FAMILY FRIENDLY

Ogre Battle Limited Edition: The March of the Black Queen

Platform:
PlayStation/PS one

Publisher: Atlus

Price:
$19.99–$29.99

ESRB: Kids to Adults

THUNDER FLARE

In *Ogre Battle,* you fight as the leader of the Rebellion army, trying to reclaim land stolen by the evil Highland Empire. You move your troops along a number of maps and missions as you conquer enemy territory, liberate cities, and discover a host of hidden characters, spells, and weapons. Adding to the replay value are 13 possible endings that vary depending upon what type of leader you are, what path you take, and what characters and items you uncover on your journey. Because *Ogre Battle* came out almost four years ago, don't expect any eye-popping graphics. Still, with a great story line and tons of secrets to uncover, the game is addicting (especially if you like strategy/RPG hybrids).

Orphen: Scion of Sorcery

While not the strongest role-playing game for the PlayStation 2, *Orphen* has enough gameplay spunk to entice even the most cautious newbie to the role-playing world. In this game based on a popular Japanese cartoon series, you take on the role of Orphen, a wannabe-teen-idol sorcerer who inadvertently travels to Chaos Island after being forced off course by a sea monster. During your quest to help people living on the island, you're joined by two sidekicks, who you can also control as you battle villainous monsters and cast strangely named spells. One of the coolest features of *Orphen* is that you can take multiple paths. In other words, when replaying the game, you can discover an entirely new story to play.

Did You Know? — In Japan, the animated series on which the game is based is called *Orphen: Sorcerous Stabber*. Eewww — it's no surprise that title was changed for the game.

Platform:
PlayStation 2

Publisher:
Activision

Price: $49.99

ESRB: Teen

Wild Arms 2

A sequel to the 1997 PlayStation hit, *Wild Arms 2* continues the legacy with a fantastic story that everyone can identify with. The game puts you in control of three heroes who are chosen to unite the people of the planet Filgaia in order to save it from an evil force. As the journey progresses, you find that your role as hero is muddled by your missions, and the people you meet always have ulterior motives. Using your might and magic is relatively easy, which helps move the gameplay at a good pace. *Wild Arms 2* is one of the few role-playing games that people of all ages can sit down and enjoy to the very end.

Platform:
PlayStation/PS one

Publisher: Sony

Price: $39.99

ESRB: Everyone

Parasite Eve

Platform:
PlayStation/PS one

Publisher:
Square EA

Price: $39.99

ESRB: Teen

273/763
AT
HP
PE

Parasite Eve breaks the traditional role-playing mold by emphasizing intense action along with the traditional character development. You're Aya Brea, a New York City cop who discovers that the human body's cell structure is starting a revolution that people can't seem to resist. The result: NYC must be evacuated, and Aya must put a stop to Eve, the parasitic super being that starts it all. *Parasite Eve* has heavy firefights with mutated animals and other freaky creatures at every turn, so it may be too scary for younger gamers — but it also features some of the most beautiful, movie-quality cinemas around. *Parasite Eve* leaves you thrilled, chilled, and wanting a bit more due to its short length, but it's well worth the price of admission.

Did You Know? — Madonna's movie production company, Maverick, optioned the rights to *Parasite Eve* to make it into a movie. That doesn't guarantee that *Parasite Eve* will make it to the silver screen, but it's a good sign that Hollywood understands the appeal of gaming's storytelling.

Revelations: Persona

Set in modern-day Tokyo, *Revelations: Persona* takes you on an incredible journey through different dimensions to fight demons. In your quest, you're armed with swords, guns, and magical abilities called personas. You start the game as a normal teenager, but as you adopt personas during gameplay, you acquire supernatural powers — exactly what every adolescent dreams! The adventure consists of over 300 monsters, multiple plot twists, and several possible endings, giving this game great replay value. The visuals look surprisingly smooth despite its four-year-old age, and gameplay is easy, even with all the personas that are available. The tone of the story may be a little dark for the younger crowd, though.

Platform:
PlayStation/PS one
Publisher: Atlus
Price: $19.99
ESRB: Kids to Adults

Summoner

Platform:
PlayStation 2
Publisher: THQ
Price: $49.99
ESRB: Teen

Summoner is a fine example of how deep and engaging a role-playing game can be. As Joseph, a simple farmer born with the power to summon demons, you must lead a band of adventurers and scour the land in search of several magical rings. During your search throughout the humongous world, you encounter a myriad of mini-games and challenges that don't necessarily connect to your final objective, but which serve to make the story and gameplay deep and engrossing. You can also expect to converse with a large number of people populating the world as you slowly learn the land's tumultuous history and burgeoning future. Intense, somewhat tedious battles come often, but along with engaging story lines, battles are what serious role-playing is all about.

Vagrant Story

Platform:
PlayStation/PS one

Publisher:
Square EA

Price: $39.99

ESRB: Teen

From the opening cinema to the dramatic, twisty conclusion, *Vagrant Story* hits all the right RPG notes. You play as Ashley Riot, whose memories have been altered and who must now find out his real identity. To get the answers, Ashley has to pursue his nemesis, Sydney, through the creepy bowels of the abandoned city of Lea Monde and its surrounding areas in search of the Gran Grimoire — the ultimate dark weapon. *Vagrant Story,* which features intense battles, creepy visuals, and haunting sounds, was one of the best RPGs of 2000.

Chapter 12
Sports Games

Hut one . . . hut two . . . hike! I mean, um, two men on, two men out, bottom of the ninth, and the home team is down by . . . er . . . a field goal. Oh! And the right fielder has been given two minutes in the penalty box for tripping! That means, um, the point guard will shoot two free throws, after which he'll attempt to set a world record for the long jump. Or something. Go team!

In This Chapter . . .

All-Star Baseball 2002

Acclaim's take on the national pastime thrilled Nintendo 64 owners with its delicate balance of gritty simulation-style realism and home-run heroics. PlayStation 2 fans can look forward to a style of baseball that lets you adjust how detailed you want the game to be, six modes of play (including a home-run derby and all-star play), a General Manager setting, customizing options, environmental effects, real-world stadiums, and jaw-dropping visuals. *ASB 2002* features stunning graphics — in fact, more polygons are used in the player model's head alone than were used to create entire stadiums in previous *ASB* games. And now that *All-Star* is no longer limited by the space of N64 cartridges, there's a lot more room for color commentary. Bob Brenly (now manager of the Arizona Diamondbacks) joins his former play-by-play partner Thom Brennaman, while the voice of the Texas Rangers, Chuck Morgan, lends his talents as the announcer. Break out the peanuts and Cracker Jacks and play ball!

Did You Know? — The year 2002 marks the *All-Star Baseball* series' fifth year. The first game appeared in 1997 with Frank "The Big Hurt" Thomas as its spokesman.

Platform: PlayStation 2

Publisher: Acclaim

Price: $49.99

ESRB: Everyone

FIFA 2001: Major League Soccer

Long known as the best-playing soccer series out there, *FIFA 2001* carries on that tradition with its PS2 debut. While it's not as ground-breaking as *NHL 2001* or *Madden 2001,* the latest *FIFA* incarnation is a stellar soccer game that will delight fans of the sport. As always, *FIFA* packs in an obscene amount of teams, tournaments, and leagues — everything from the MLS to the English Premier League to all the national squads. The gameplay feels realistic, and deep, intuitive controls back up the action all the way. All told, *FIFA 2001* delivers a fine performance. It's not the instant classic that some of EA's other titles are, but if you're a fan of the world's most popular sport, you'll be glued to the controller.

Did you know? — Wondering what in the world a *FIFA* is? That'd be Fédération Internationale de Football Association, the world's international governing body of soccer. Or *football,* as the rest of the world calls it!

Platform: PlayStation 2

Publisher: Electronic Arts

Price: $49.99

ESRB: Everyone

FAMILY FRIENDLY

ESPN International Track & Field

Platform:
PlayStation 2
Publisher: Konami
Price: $49.99
ESRB: Everyone

Konami's thumb-battering *Track & Field* series began in the arcades in the '80s, and this version retains that familiar gameplay while delivering the glorious graphics that are synonymous with the PS2. The basic premise of the gameplay involves alternately hammering a pair of buttons to make your athlete surge to victory. *ESPN International Track & Field* provides 10 events that range from 100m hurdles to weightlifting to the horizontal bar. The game really gets fun with a group of players who can bruise their thumbs together in pursuit of the gold medal. While the PS2 version definitely isn't a must-have for every gamer, it's great for track and field fans or anyone looking for a good multiplayer party game.

FUN FACTS

Did you know? — The first *Track & Field* was released in the arcades in 1983 — right before the Summer Games in L.A. and right after *Chariots of Fire* (you know, the movie that made running seem like fun?) raked in multiple Oscars. No wonder it was such a smashing success!

ESPN Winter X Games Snowboarding

Platform:
PlayStation 2
Publisher: Konami
Price: $49.99
ESRB: Everyone

If you're interested in PS2 snowboarding, your first stop should be EA SPORTS' awesome *SSX* title. For those of you who aren't satisfied with that, Konami is hitting the slopes with *ESPN Winter X Games Snowboarding*. This game appeals to those who are really serious about snowboarding and would enjoy a more technically oriented simulation. If that's you, *EWXGS* straps on the board for tournaments, frenzied boardercross races, trick-busting frenzies in the half-pipe, and more. You can even build your boarder from scratch, choosing everything from goggles to lift tickets. While the graphics and sounds are fairly solid, the main stumbling block is the controls, which are tough to master. But experienced gamers who live to board will probably find a lot of enjoy in *EWXGS*.

Did you know? — ESPN's X Games may seem like a new, trendy sensation, but the first event was held in June 1995 in Rhode Island and Vermont. The first Winter X Games, however, wasn't held until January 1997 in Big Bear Lake, California.

Hot Shots Golf 2

Platform:
PlayStation/PS one

Publisher: Sony

Price: $39.99

ESRB: Everyone

Even without any pro golfers or courses, *Hot Shots Golf 2* is the best golf game on the PlayStation. Its accessible action will reel in golfers of all calibers with gameplay that's both fun and easy to learn. At its most basic level, you can play *Hot Shots 2* by tapping just one button. But if you're looking for depth, you can also control advanced elements like draw, fade, backspin, power shots, and so on. Additionally, the game's smooth, beautiful graphics will draw crowds. The Tiger Woods PS one games are good, but if you're looking for a fast, fun, and challenging tee time, *Hot Shots Golf 2* is the original PlayStation's best.

Unlock Everything — At the main menu, choose New Game, and enter **2GSH** as your name. If you enter the code correctly, all courses, characters, clubs, and balls become available the next time you play.

Knockout Kings 2001

Platform:
PlayStation 2

Publisher:
Electronic Arts

Price: $49.99

ESRB: Teen

Knockout Kings has ruled the ring since it debuted two years ago, and this PS2 version will only tighten the champ's grip on the top spot. *KO Kings* delivers a huge lineup of boxers ranging from Rocky Marciano to Lennox Lewis. Other stars such as Oscar De La Hoya, Shane Mosley, and Fernando Vargas can trade punches with historical greats like Muhammad Ali, Joe Louis, and more. *KO Kings* provides both novice-friendly Slugfest bouts and a more challenging Career mode, where you create and train a boxer, and then battle up through the ranks. The gameplay sizzles with ferocious fights, and the controls, though a little complicated for rookies, offer a great lineup of moves ranging from clinches to low blows to haymakers.

Did You Know? — While boxing fans will find almost every imaginable star in *Knockout Kings 2001,* two notable names are missing: Roy Jones, Jr., and the world's most renowned ear-chomper, Mike Tyson. Both athletes have exclusive deals for other boxing games.

Madden NFL 2001

Madden NFL 2001 has more glitz and glamour than the Dallas Cowboy cheerleaders. Yes, you get all 31 teams, 50 NFL hall-of-famers, and every All-Madden team. You can also build your own fantasy franchise with trades and free-agent signings, and you can even create your own players. But face it, the first thing you notice about this game is the eye-popping graphics. When you see defensive linemen in a four-point stance crab-crawl when the line shifts, you're basically sold. But Madden made its rep with gameplay, and 2001 raises the bar on that tradition. EA SPORTS played it smart by making *Madden NFL 2001* a football powerhouse, as well as the first PS2 football game.

Madden Cards — Cheats in *Madden NFL 2001* are activated via a new feature called Madden Cards. To earn the cards, activate the Madden Challenge on the Team Select screen. When you earn enough points in the Madden Challenge, you're able to buy and collect packs of cards that activate cheats that boost player stats, unlock hidden teams, and more.

Platform:
PlayStation 2

Publisher:
Electronic Arts

Price: $49.99

ESRB: Everyone

NBA Hoopz

NBA Hoopz hits the courts for the lighter side of b-ball as gamers dive into three-on-three action loaded with over-the-top dunks, wild alley-oops, and bone-shattering shoves. If the name *NBA Hoopz* doesn't ring a bell, perhaps *NBA Jam* does — *Hoopz* is the latest in the famous arcade dynasty that began with *Jam*. *Hoopz* improves over *Jam* by including a fourth button (that enables you to pass to a CPU teammate and make them hold it until you're in position for an alley-oop or other big play), team creation, and mini-games like a three-point shootout, around the world, and more. Midway is also souping up the graphics with new facial animations and motion capture by Shaquille O'Neal. If you like your hoops on the informal side, get ready to hit the court.

Did you know? — *NBA Hoopz* is the latest in the hallowed video basketball series that began in 1993 with *NBA Jam*. In arcades, the original *NBA Jam* grossed $1 billion in quarters before it was even released for a home console system!

Platform:
PlayStation 2

Publisher:
Midway Home Entertainment

Price: $49.99

ESRB: Everyone

NBA Live 2001

Platform:
PlayStation 2

Publisher:
Electronic Arts

Price: $49.99

ESRB: Everyone

NBA Live 2001 — the latest in the most respected, longest-running hoops franchise — packs style to spare. *Live 2001* sizzles with incredibly detailed player models, unbelievably realistic stadiums, and player interactions you usually see and hear only when you're in Jack Nicholson's courtside seats at Staples Center. But no one is going to judge *Live 2001* on looks alone — Allen Iverson's cornrows wouldn't mean a thing if he didn't have all that game. *NBA Live* on the PS2 sticks to the playbook mapped out by the PlayStation version of the game. They're similar in control scheme, gameplay, and options, but (of course) PS2 owners get a big boost in the graphics and audio departments. With TV-style presentation, motion capture of Minnesota Timberwolves forward Kevin Garnett, and a plethora of post moves, the game is well suited for one-on-one match-ups. Extra game modes include a playground game versus Michael Jordan, and the NBA Challenge, which has you complete specific tasks like logging a triple-double.

NBA ShootOut 2001

Platform:
PlayStation 2

Publisher:
989 Sports

Price: $49.99

ESRB: Everyone

NBA ShootOut 2001 is another video game sports franchise from Sony. The game includes rosters featuring veteran and rookie players from all 29 NBA teams, real NBA arenas, and various playbooks with strategies in the style of those actually used by some pro teams (upwards of 450 individual plays). You can also play the NBA All-Star game, the NBA Playoffs, and the NBA Finals. You don't get any player versus coach tirades or superstars whining because they aren't getting their touches with the ball as in the real NBA, but that's one of the best aspects of a video game.

Did You Know? — Okay, sports fans, see if your pals can recognize the moves of Jason Kidd from the Phoenix Suns, Brevin Knight from the Atlanta Hawks, or Chris Webber from the Sacramento Kings, who all contributed motion-captured moves to the 400 player animations in this game.

NBA Showtime: NBA on NBC

With fast gameplay and tons of secret codes and characters, *NBA Showtime* has the fantasy stuff that action/sports gamers crave. The PlayStation version retains the original arcade game's two-on-two full court game with a lot of fast breaks and crazy dunks. Not only are the 3-D graphics impressive, but four-player games and a create-a-player option will keep your interest for a long time. *Showtime* bends the NBA rules a little bit — you can get away with shoving opponents to make them give up the ball. But the game tracks fouls, and free throws are pretty easy to make, so you'll only pay in the end on the scoreboard!

Secret Midway Court — For the hidden Midway black-and-red court, hold Shoot and Pass while pushing Up on the directional pad as you select your teammate.

Platform:
PlayStation/PS one

Publisher:
Midway Home
Entertainment

Price: $39.99

ESRB: Everyone

NCAA Final Four 2001

NCAA Final Four 2001 includes more than 300 Division I-A schools representing 31 different conferences, and team-specific playbooks mean you'll be able to use the exact same strategies your favorite schools use when they're on the court. The game also sports a smooth graphics frame rate (the action zips by at 60 frames per second — more than twice the rate of motion pictures) and sharp resolution, with over 1,000 motion-captured moves including fresh elements like the one-handed bounce pass and a behind-the-back dish. Unfortunately, those moves could be better animated, and a number of the other key elements look rushed as well (chalk it up to PS2 growing pains). Hardcore college hoops addicts should check out *Final Four* on PS2 for themselves to decide whether the shortcomings are that important.

Did You Know? — The official Web site for the NCAA Basketball Championship is `www.finalfour.net`.

Platform:
PlayStation 2

Publisher:
989 Sports

Price: $49.99

ESRB: Everyone

Platform:
PlayStation/PS one

Publisher:
Electronic Arts

Price: $39.99

ESRB: Everyone

NCAA Football 2001

Fire up the fight songs! EA keeps college football alive on the PlayStation with the 2001 edition of *NCAA Football.* This year's model features deeper gameplay than ever before, the most complete statistics tracking of any sports game, and a locker room full of options. If for some reason the 140 Division I-A and I-AA teams and 25 all-time great squads aren't enough for you, you can create your own gridiron squad and take to the turf with a custom team. The game has a few flaws — the animation seems a little stiff, which is where 989 Sports' *NCAA GameBreaker* shines — but if you're a stickler for details and statistics, this is the choice for you. Rent both and decide for yourself.

Did You Know? — The 25 all-time great teams in *NCAA Football 2001* were chosen by fans who visited the EA Web site. Power to the people!

Platform:
PlayStation 2

Publisher:
989 Sports

Price: $49.99

ESRB: Everyone

NCAA GameBreaker 2001

If the college bowl system didn't do it for your alma mater this year, you can reshuffle the whole darn thing with *NCAA GameBreaker 2001.* Whether you're a Seminole, a Volunteer, a Cornhusker, or even a Duck, this game packs in 115 Division I-A teams and 21 bowl games. It even wheels announcer Keith Jackson out for some barn-burnin' commentary. As for the video game action, with 1800 plays, this is a real arm-chair coach's game. Like Ivy League college football in real life, you'll find that *GameBreaker*'s offense is dominated by passing instead of running, and you can't always count on your defensive line to perform in a clutch (after all, they've probably got homework on their minds). With pinpoint passing and an impressive Career Mode, this game puts some rah-rah into your PlayStation 2.

Did You Know? — Plays and strategies were supplied by Washington Huskies coach Rick Neuheisel and 1999 Heisman Trophy winner, Ron Dayne, formerly of the Wisconsin Badgers and now with the NFL's New York Giants.

NCAA March Madness 2001

The college basketball franchise from EA SPORTS is the Duke Blue Devils of college hoops video games — it dominates. You can choose from over 150 Men's Division I teams or the sweet 16 of Women's Division I college basketball to play in Exhibition, Tournament, Season, or Dynasty mode. The game features Vern Lundquist and Bill Raftery doing the commentary, and motion-captured moves by former college star and last year's NBA Co-Rookie of the Year, Steve Francis. Even Duke head coach Mike Krzyzewski lent his expertise to make this game as realistic as possible. With fast gameplay, solid controls, and an amazingly realistic soundtrack, *NCAA March Madness 2001* is the reigning national champion of college hoops video games.

Did You Know? — This game's name comes from the nickname for the annual NCAA Division I Men's Basketball Championship tournament, which begins in March.

Platform:
PlayStation/PS one

Publisher:
Electronic Arts

Price: $39.99

ESRB: Everyone

NFL Blitz 2001

Midway offers more radical pigskin action with its popular *NFL Blitz* series, which brings new meaning to the words *fantasy football*. This isn't a game for football diehards who are into in-depth strategies — it's smash-mouth football with exaggerated plays and players, souped up abilities, and bone-crunching, no-refs, no-rules gameplay. Pass interference? No problem! Late hits after the play? No penalties! The 2001 edition features customizable options, the ability to create your own plays and teams, plus a variety of mini-games for when you're not in the mood for a full gridiron battle. Simple three-button controls make this an easy game to just jump in and start heaving long bombs down the field. Hut, hut, hike!

Super Blitz Mode — At the Vs. screen, press the Turbo button four times, the Jump button four times, and the Pass button four times. Then press Up on the directional pad. If you enter the code correctly, you see the name of the mode and hear a chime. When the game begins, you're in super blitz mode!

Platform:
PlayStation/PS One

Publisher:
Midway Home Entertainment

Price: $39.99

ESRB: Everyone

Platform:
PlayStation 2
Publisher:
989 Sports
Price: $49.99
ESRB: Everyone

NFL GameDay 2001

Sony's in-house development studio, 989 Studios, has created a prominent franchise with its *NFL GameDay* series. So, it was understandable that expectations were very high for its premiere on the PlayStation 2 game system. You can play solo or team up with seven other players (with the PlayStation multitap peripheral) for full-on-gridiron on-screen action. The game comes packed full of excellent features, such as all 31 NFL teams, classic teams, customizable rosters, full season and draft modes, authentic playbooks, motion-captured animation, and proportionately-sized players onfield. The framerate is quite high (a brisk 60 frames per second) but a good number of the animations aren't linked together well, and there's a noticeable pause between hits and tackle animations. Still, *GameDay* scores points for solid game options and a larger than life style that injects more action into the gridiron game.

Platform:
PlayStation 2
Publisher:
Electronic Arts
Price: $49.99
ESRB: Everyone

NHL 2001

"The best game ever" is one of those phrases you don't like to see used often, otherwise it loses its potency and meaning. But it's hard to argue that *NHL 2001* by EA SPORTS isn't the best hockey game ever created. EA's years of experience with this series shows: Intuitive controls, strong sounds (including on-ice player chatter and post-game analysis by the commentators), and some incredible cut-scenes (angry players throw water bottles as they stew in the penalty box!) go a long way to recreating a true pro hockey atmosphere. Remarkable graphics, familiar and solid gameplay, tweakable artifical intelligence — NHL 2001 is the pinnacle of video ice hockey.

NHL FaceOff 2001

989 Sports has done fine games in the past, but it's hard to best the offerings from rival EA SPORTS. The PlayStation 2 gives the company its best chance to make its case. The PlayStation version of *NHL FaceOff 2001* showed improvement, offering both arcade and simulation-style gameplay; the PS2 version should follow suit. Watch for all 30 official NHL teams with complete rosters, sharp two-man commentary, plenty of gameplay options (including a new shootout mode that pits one scorer against one goalie in a cold game of one-on-one), and, of course, high-resolution PS2 graphics.

Platform:
PlayStation 2
Publisher:
989 Sports
Price: $49.99
ESRB: Everyone

Ready 2 Rumble Boxing: Round 2

This fast-paced arcade boxing game puts on a clinic for bruisers everywhere with its whimsical and hard-hitting gameplay. For the uninitiated, *Ready 2 Rumble* isn't your typical boxer. You duke it out with 23 off-the-wall brutes, including high-profile celebs Michael Jackson and Shaquille O'Neal, mixing the usual jabs, body blows, and uppercuts. As in the original, stunning visuals feature pugilists who perform hysterical celebratory dances and punch with fluid animation. Adding to the visual excellence is the trademark voice of Michael Buffer, who announces each fight; other vocals lend a well-quipped tongue for funny taunts as well as hilarious intros and endings. If you're craving a nonheavy, nonstrategic PS2 brawler, *Ready 2 Rumble* should be your first contender: It contains all the right elements for just having fun.

Did you know? — Michael Jackson actually approached Midway about being in *Ready 2 Rumble: Round 2.* He's wearing his "History" outfit in the game, and he fights wearing — of course — one sparkling white boxing glove!

Platform:
PlayStation 2
Publisher:
Midway Home
Entertainment
Price: $49.99
ESRB: Teen

Swing Away Golf

Platform:
PlayStation 2

Publisher:
Electronic Arts

Price: $49.99

ESRB: Everyone

Swing Away Golf continues in the tradition of the extremely friendly and playable *Hot Shots Golf* series, but suitably powered up for the PS2. Aside from the obvious boost in visuals, the game's greatest asset is the sheer amount of available play options. Upgraded shoes, special balls, and clubs are a must, and you can unlock new courses and characters along the way as well. Graphically, the game looks great — maybe not revolutionary, but certainly crisp and clean. Although you have great control over the type of swing, the swing meter takes some getting used to, and its speed often seems arbitrary. The unassuming audio won't distract you during crucial shots. The various caddies are all fairly well done, and finding a favorite who will give you good shot advice definitely enhances your experience. If most of your gaming involves four players and sports games, *Swing Away Golf* is almost a sure-fire keeper.

All Characters — At the main menu, press

> L2, R2, L2, R2, Up, Right, Down, Left, L1, R1

If you enter the code correctly, you hear a chime. Select Normal Mode; then choose Stroke. All characters become available.

Tiger Woods PGA Tour 2001

Platform:
PlayStation 2

Publisher:
Electronic Arts

Price: $49.99

ESRB: Everyone

If you want to play golf on your PS2 with real PGA golfers instead of cartoon characters (as in *Swing Away Golf*), *Tiger Woods PGA Tour 2001* is your ticket. *Tiger 2001* has three courses — Pebble Beach, Spyglass Hill, and Poppy Hills — plus six PGA pros, including Justin Leonard, Brad Faxon, and of course, Tiger himself. A new 3-D ball-lie indicator and wind meter will help you keep it on the fairway, and you can choose to use analog-stick swings or the more traditional power meter for your strokes. You're also able to tweak your shots with fade, draw, and spin. With graphics this crisp, why strain your back or risk a sunburn playing real golf? Besides, no one can see you take a mulligan in your living room.

Did You Know? — Tiger Woods's real first name is Eldrick.

Triple Play Baseball

The EA SPORTS *Triple Play* series has owned the PlayStation diamond for a couple years now, but with the move to the PS2, the competition is tougher now that ex–Nintendo 64 superstar *All-Star Baseball* joins the fray. Visually, the *Triple Play* player animations realistically reflect the urgency of the play; the players themselves are composed of a mind-blowing 4,000+ polygons each. On the sound side, Buck Martinez returns to handle the color commentary, but a new play-by-play announcer, Sean McDonough, reports to the broadcast booth. A new pitcher/batter interface has also been added to the game. As for modes and teams, all the MLB teams and players are represented in season or exhibition action. It's not a simulation for hard-core baseball fans, but *Triple Play Baseball* is a fun-to-play, arcade-style look at America's pastime.

Did You Know? — The unassisted triple play, one of the rarest feats in baseball, has been accomplished only 12 times in Major League history. The last player to do it was Oakland Athletics second basemen Randy Velarde against the New York Yankees on May 29, 2000.

Platform:
PlayStation 2
Publisher:
Electronic Arts
Price: $49.99
ESRB: Everyone

Part IV
The Part of Tens

The 5th Wave   By Rich Tennant

"Wait a minute... This is a movie, not a game?! I thought I was the one making Keanu Reeves jump kick in slow motion."

In this part . . .

No Dummies book is complete without the Part of Tens! Here I get to cut loose a bit and talk about a bunch of stuff that just doesn't fit anywhere else. I'll make some recommendations about nifty add-ons that you can buy to enhance your PlayStation 2 experience, show you a little bit of the weird software in Japan, blow away some misconceptions about the PS2, and even offer some gamer-friendly movie recommendations.

Chapter 13

Ten Cool Doodads You Can Buy for Your PS2

Although most people no longer label video games as toys, that doesn't mean that you can't buy toys for your video games! Lots of little gadgets are available that can make your PlayStation 2 experience even better than it is now. It all boils down to two questions: How many doodads do you want, and where will you put all this stuff when you get it?

A DVD Remote

Why Sony chose not to make a remote control for the DVD elements of its PS2 is anybody's guess, but a DVD remote is usually the first extra purchase by movie buffs. After all, you can control the DVD player with the Dual Shock controller, but that has a wire running from it to the machine (whine, moan), and something wireless would be more convenient (moan, whine). Luckily, just about every third-party controller company has jumped on the DVD remote bandwagon, so you have plenty of options.

All DVD remotes provide you with quick, logical access to the DVD's higher film functions, such as subtitles and alternate audio tracks, as well as navigation of the basic menus and rewind/fast forward functions. All models come with two pieces — the remote itself and its own infrared receiver, which must be plugged into one of the PS2 controller ports. Some brands embed that receiver in a *pass-through port*, which means that you can plug your regular controller in through the infrared receiver but still use the remote freely. This port is a convenience if you have two Dual Shocks set up; if not, the port doesn't change anything, because the remote works equally well through port 1 or 2. You can also use the remotes as game controllers if you find a game you like playing with just one hand (such as puzzle games or simple role-playing games).

Remotes generally start at about $10 and go up from there, especially if you're looking for a master remote for your entire entertainment center. One of the nicer ones I've found is the Mad Catz Wireless DVD Remote (see Figure 13-1), which sells for around $20. It doesn't feature a pass-through port and is almost a little too top-heavy, but it's large, so it won't get lost easily. The buttons are big and clearly marked with both the DVD functions and the PlayStation button icons, and it can be programmed to work as a TV and VCR remote. The rubberized grip feels solid and the black and blue color motif matches the PS2 well.

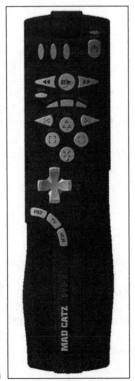

Figure 13-1:
Mad Catz
Wireless
DVD
Remote.

Extra Controllers

The more, the merrier, right? You can't have more players without controllers to match. Sony sells extra Dual Shock 2 controllers for about $35; they're the same as the one that comes in the box (see Figure 13-2). Third-party companies like InterAct, Nyko, and Pelican also sell compatible controllers, usually for a little less money. But many of these are not officially licensed by Sony and not guaranteed to work 100 percent of the time. In reality, the chance that an independent brand gamepad won't work is slim, but every year that *GamePro* magazine has done a big controller roundup (complete with an off-the-wall torture test), the official Sony versions always come out on top in terms of comfort, construction, and reliability.

Some games support two players, while others support up to four — you'll know which games are which by a small box that lists the number of players on the back of the game package. But with only two controller ports, how can four people play at once? Funny you should ask . . . check out the next section for more information.

Figure 13-2:
Sony Dual
Shock 2
Controller
— you need
more of
these if you
want to play
multiplayer
games.

Photo courtesy of Michele Thomas

Multitap

Games such as *TimeSplitters, Street Fighter EX3,* and *Unreal Tournament* offer multiplayer modes for up to four gamers at once. But to take advantage of those modes, you need a *multitap* (see Figure 13-3). The multitap plugs into player one's controller port, which then enables you to plug four gamepads or joysticks into a single slot. The doohickey is $35 from Sony, though, like controllers, you can get third-party versions. On the original PlayStation, however, a number of games wouldn't work with anything but an official Sony tap. You may be able to skimp on the spare controllers, but don't take a chance with the multitap. Go with Sony.

Figure 13-3:
Sony
PlayStation
2 Multitap.

Photo courtesy of Michele Thomas

Deluxe Joystick

Big fighting games like *Tekken Tag Tournament* and *Street Fighter EX3* call for a big arcade-style, heavy-duty joystick to match. After all, what better way to re-create the joy of pounding the pixels out of someone in the arcade than with a sturdy stick at home? InterAct's ShadowBlade Arcade Stick practically redefines "sturdy" thanks to its killer construction and high-quality parts (see Figure 13-4). With its glossy black finish and massive metal base, you can think of the ShadowBlade as the offspring of a Ferrari and an Abrams tank. Like the Dual Shock 2, the buttons are pressure-sensitive, and this joystick is backward compatible with the original PlayStation (as a digital controller, of course). If you're seriously into fighting games, the ShadowBlade is $60 well spent.

Figure 13-4:
InterAct's
Shadow-
Blade
Arcade
Stick makes
your home
feel like an
arcade.

Memory Card

Absolutely, positively, every gamer must have one of these. Most games aren't much fun without a memory card, which is the hardware that enables you to save all your game settings, high scores, and progress (see Figure 13-5). If you actually want to open new courses in *SSX* or work your way through all the missions in *Smuggler's Run,* you'll need one of these (two or more if you're an avid gamer who doesn't want to delete old saved games to make room for new ones). Original PlayStation memory cards won't save PS2 data, so you have to shell out another $35 for Sony's real deal. Again, other companies make memory cards for a few bucks less, but some third-party PlayStation cards are unstable and can lose data. Buying a real Sony card is usually worth the cash for the peace of mind (and really, you should need only one for the first year or so). See Chapter 3 to find out more about memory-card management.

Figure 13-5:
The 8MB
memory
card for
your
PlayStation 2
— don't
play games
without it.

Photo courtesy of Michele Thomas

Horizontal and Vertical Stands

If you've seen any of Sony's photos of the PlayStation 2, you probably noticed a cool little gradient blue border around the bottom. Those blue trim sections are actually $10 to $15 plastic stands that you buy separately and install yourself. The sections come in two flavors — horizontal and vertical — depending on which orientation you want your PS2 to be in. You can't have both sections installed at once, unfortunately, but chances are you've already decided which way you think the PS2 looks better. Without a stand, of course, you can still run the machine in either position; the stand adds a little stability in the vertical position, but it's mostly cosmetic and just adds a little flair of color. Some third parties sell slightly different versions with small compartments for memory cards if you're looking for some extra storage space.

Optical-Ready Speakers

The PlayStation 2 supports fiber optic audio cables for the best possible sound reproduction. Your stereo, however, may not support these cables unless it's really new or was really expensive. A number of speaker companies have jumped in with offerings specifically aimed at PS2 owners. Cambridge Soundworks's PlayWorks PS2000 looks cute and is one of the cheapest options at $200. For full, actual Dolby 5.1 Surround Sound, you may want to invest $500 in MidiLand's S4 8200 speakers (see Figure 13-6). You can find out more detailed information at www.midiland.com.

Figure 13-6:
The
MidiLand
S4 8300
speaker set
offers
outstanding
digital
quality.

USB Keyboard and Mouse

At the launch of the PlayStation 2, only one game took advantage of those intriguing USB ports on the front of the machine: *Unreal Tournament*. Curious gamers who plugged a keyboard and mouse into those ports found — surprise! — that the ports worked just fine, offering more precise aiming and PC-like controls. More games will use this feature in the future (*Half-Life*, among them), and you do get the feeling that Sony put those ports on its PS2 for a reason. Applications for the USB jacks beyond gaming are likely to come soon — specifically when the hard drive and Internet connector are released. A keyboard and mouse will make Web surfing and e-mail access much easier than just using a game controller. USB keyboards run as little as $15, and cheap USB mice cost around $8. As usual, you can spend much more, but you should also consider how much — or in this case, how little — you'll use these accessories with your PS2 until the software supports the peripherals en masse.

The Hard Drive and Internet Connector

You can't buy this set yet, but when you can, you'll want it. Set to debut sometime in 2001, the hard drive and broadband Internet connector will slide into the back of the PS2, behind the little door marked Expansion Bay. The drive will be the same size as a PC hard drive, and the Internet connector will be the same jack found on cable modems and Ethernet network cards. Shortly thereafter, Sony should have its spiffy new high-speed network in place, so PlayStation 2 users will be able to jump onto the Internet and do . . . well, nobody knows just what yet. Sony's plans apparently range from simple head-to-head online gaming and Web surfing all the way up to online movie rentals. Sony has been working so hard to meet launch demand that it hasn't spoken much about its online plans. Cost for the hard drive/Net connector and the cost of the broadband service are, as you might expect, unannounced. Watch the Sony Web site (www.playstation.com) and the *GamePro* home page (www.gamepro.com) for more information on this crucial add-on as it becomes available.

A Subscription to GamePro Magazine

The shameless self-promotion had to come sooner or later. But *GamePro* is my day job, so it's a compulsory plug (see Figure 13-7). No, really! It was very clear that I mention how *GamePro* has been the leading multiplatform video game magazine in America for almost a decade, or there would be serious trouble. (According to what was scribbled on the back of my latest pay stub, I believe the exact words were "dire consequences.") Every month, *GamePro* brings you the newest previews, reviews, features, and news about what's going on in the gaming world — and about what's happening with the PlayStation 2 specifically. So please take a peek at the subscription ad in the back of this book. See how nice and cheap it is to subscribe, and maybe I can keep my job.

Figure 13-7:
GamePro.
Subscribe.
It's cheap.

Chapter 14

Ten Things You Thought the PlayStation 2 Could Do (But It Can't)

*N*o matter how many cool tricks the PlayStation 2 can perform, you can always think up one or two that it can't. This shortcoming is understandable — because the PS2 can play DVDs *and* original PlayStation games *and* audio compact discs, you may assume that it can do your dishes, too. In order to maintain your grip on reality, this chapter lists ten of the more common false assumptions about the PlayStation 2.

Play Foreign DVD Videos

When DVD established itself, movie buffs were thrilled — finally, a high-quality, large-capacity, long-life format for the whole world! Well, sorta. Although the format is used around the globe, every country has its own regional encoding.

Discs sold in the United States and Canada are designated Region 1, Europe and Japan are designated Region 2, and so on around the world — up to Region 8, which is used for in-flight entertainment on airplanes.

Making a DVD adhere to these location-based lockouts is optional, but most major movie studios want to be able to control who sees their movies and when. For instance, movies usually come out in U.S. theaters before they open overseas. Consequently, after a movie's stateside run, its home DVD version may make it to England before the theatrical version actually shows up on the big screen there — a situation the movie studios definitely don't want to occur. So most, if not all, DVDs you buy in the U.S. feature a little icon on the back that says it's a Region 1 disc.

Some of the smaller DVD companies, however, don't bother with regional encoding because they want to be able to sell the same product in multiple countries and save a little money on manufacturing. For instance, Digital Leisure's DVD videos of *Dragon's Lair* and *Space Ace* and MPI Home Video's versions of the Beatles films, *A Hard Day's Night* and *Help!* don't have regional lockouts. Your PS2 will play those "regionless" discs just fine. One amusing footnote: When the PlayStation 2 first went on sale in Japan, people did find a way to play non-Region 2 DVDs with just a few button presses on the controller — but Sony sent out an updated DVD driver to fix that obviously popular bug.

Besides the regional stuff, an older, simpler reason exists for why foreign DVDs won't play on an American PlayStation 2. Japan and the U.S. both use the same standard for television playback (NTSC), but Europe is on the PAL standard (except for France, which uses SECAM), which paints a different number of lines on the screen. So PAL video discs won't play on NTSC players because the encoded information is incorrect for the hardware. But again, you won't even get that far with your PS2. Make sure that any DVDs you buy say Region 1 on the back — particularly if you're buying them while you're abroad — or you'll have spent your money for nothing.

Play Japanese Games

Japanese games may be programmed the same, they may look the same, and they may play the same, but games made for the Japanese market don't run on an American PlayStation 2. Sometimes, this is for the same reason as movies — it's a matter of controlling the content. Other times, it's licensing-based. One group owns the rights to, say, *Speed Racer* in Japan, while another owns them in the U.S. So to protect its investment, one country's games can't play on another's machines. Why do you care? Because American PlayStation 2 units play American games only, and Japanese consoles play Japanese software only.

The downside to this is that many good Japanese games, for whatever reason, don't get translated for release in the U.S. Some gamers want those games so much that they're willing to open up their consoles, solder in some chips and wires, and alter the PS2 circuitry so that their machine can do it all. This process, alternately called *chipping* or *modding*, was fairly common with the original PlayStation, and people have already started using these procedures with their PS2s. But these alterations are terribly risky and void your warranty the moment you open the sleek black casing. If you're really serious about playing Japanese games, save up and buy a Japanese PS2. It will work fine with your U.S. TV set, and you won't risk ruining your American investment.

Play Copied or Bootleg Games

An offshoot of chipping a machine to play international software is that it can often play pirated games: homemade copies of software made by people with a CD-ROM or DVD-ROM burner — and no scruples. Playing games that have been copied in this manner is not only illegal, but it's unethical as well. Plus, pirating games takes money away from the very people who create the games in the first place. No paycheck for them means no cool software for you, and the whole system breaks down. So even though you can, with the right tools, copy the digital data from one PlayStation or PlayStation 2 disc over to a blank CD or DVD, you can't and shouldn't play that bootleg copy on your PlayStation 2.

Play Dreamcast Games

Okay, this assumption has a little history to it. The PlayStation 2 plays original PlayStation/PS one games out of the box — that you already know. Sega's Dreamcast system can also play original PlayStation games through a nifty third-party program called Bleem! (which you can find out about at www.bleem.com). "Wow," thought gamers — "Cool trick!" It's therefore not too much of a leap of logic to think that someone could make a program for the PlayStation 2 that would enable it, in turn, to play Dreamcast games. Is it possible? Yep — the practice of *emulation*, making one computer think and act like another, has been going on for years. The PS2's hardware could certainly handle the task of running Dreamcast games. Is it probable? Nah. Not yet, anyway. Bleem! has had its share of legal disagreements with Sony, so it probably doesn't want to cause more trouble. And other interested parties will probably be scared off by Bleem!'s woes. But hey, never say never. A lot of clever programmers are out there. For now, though, the answer is no.

Play the Multimedia Parts of Enhanced Audio CDs

Wait! Can't the PlayStation 2 play audio CDs? Yes, but discs that feature enhanced CD elements, such as videos, games, or interviews, won't give you those goodies on your PS2. If you pop in Britney Spears's *Baby One More Time*, Offspring's *Americana*, or Sarah McLachlan's *Surfacing* (all of which are ECDs), you hear the music, no problem. But everything else on the enhanced CD works only with a home computer (usually both Windows or Mac). Yes, even if the disc is by a Sony artist.

Play Sony MiniDiscs

Sony has produced much cool technology over the years: The Walkman, Trinitron television sets, and even the failed home video format, Betamax. (Hey, it was fine technology — VHS just caught on faster.) Among the company's many products is MiniDisc, a digital music format that came out in the early '90s, but has yet to catch on in the mainstream. MiniDiscs shrink songs from CDs by compressing the music and removing the frequencies you supposedly wouldn't hear anyway, thereby saving some digital space. Human hearing, however, isn't that easy to quantify — you can *feel* frequencies that you shouldn't necessarily be able to hear. So, to the trained ear, MiniDisc music doesn't sound quite as good as it does on CDs, but it sounds a heck of a lot better than on normal cassette tapes (and I'm not even going to bring up 8-tracks). And because Sony owns both MiniDisc and PlayStation 2 technology, it could light a fire under the format by making the two compatible. But the company has chosen not to do so. If you're looking for that Sony synergy, I'm afraid you won't find it here.

Play PC CD-ROMs

If the PS2 could play CD-ROMS, they'd be called PS2 CD-ROMs. Despite talk of the PlayStation 2 having as much power as a desktop computer, the convergence of game consoles and traditional PCs has not taken this final step — yet. If you pop a copy of, say, the Windows version of *Rollercoaster Tycoon* into your PS2, you'll get a smoky red screen asking you for a proper PlayStation disc instead.

Turn into a Home Computer

When Sony announced the PlayStation 2, it teased the public with plans for the future — plans for a hard drive, plans for Internet capabilities, plans for online banking through the PS2, and plans to be announced. Yet, the company didn't set a time frame for what few details it revealed; and to date, Sony still hasn't. With Sega's Dreamcast offering online connectivity, plus the appearance of the USB and i.Link ports (both of which are standard in the Windows and Mac communities for things like keyboards, mice, scanners, and digital cameras), many consumers thought that they could purchase a PS2 and use it as an affordable, expandable home computer — as well as a killer game machine and home theater appliance. In response to these hopes, I have but two words: Not yet. All those things are possible in the future, and Sony certainly offers tantalizing ideas, but no firm plans have been announced regarding what the PlayStation 2 wants to be when it grows up.

Your Laundry

Nope.

Launch Missiles — Well, Okay It Can

You can file this under *S* for Stranger than Fiction, because this rumor is true. Gamers like the PlayStation 2 because of its awesome graphics power — it can process high-quality images very quickly. Unfortunately, other machines are around that share that capability — namely missile guidance systems. The Emotion Engine, which is the chip that powers the PS2, is so powerful in this respect that Japan's Trade Ministry feared the PS2 could be rewired by an enterprising third-world dictator to wreak worldwide havoc. As a result, the Trade Ministry said that special export restrictions would have to be put in place. Anybody who wanted to send a PS2 out of Japan would have to obtain permission from the Japanese government. Failure to comply would cost almost $20,000. Thankfully, the Japanese export laws were amended so that the PlayStation 2 could be reclassified. Good thing, too. Otherwise, American gamers would have had pretty much no chance of getting the machine. If you know of any third-world dictators, please don't let them spend too much time playing *Kessen*.

Chapter 15

Ten Japanese PS2 Games You'll Probably Never Play in America

There are really only two kinds of PlayStation games in the world: Japanese and not Japanese. Generally, genres like racing and fighting have a global appeal. Whether they're developed in the East or the West, all gamers can get behind the fun of driving a sports car dangerously fast or testing their virtual fighting skills in a digital beat-em-up. Japanese culture, however, spawns its own unique entertainment that often leaves a lot of Americans scratching their heads. So, although Japanese action-oriented games like *Tekken Tag Tournament* and *Ridge Racer V* are no-brainers for a stateside release, some of the other games on the Japanese market will never reach United States soil. Here are ten of the more interesting, unusual, and just plain weird games that have hit Japanese store shelves but will most likely never make it to America.

A-Train 6 (A-Resha De Go 6)

Published by Artdink

If you put *A-Train 6* into perspective, it doesn't sound quite so silly. First, think about big hit games like the town-planning *SimCity;* then consider the popularity of track-design games like *Railroad Tycoon* and *Rollercoaster Tycoon.* Slap them all together, and you've got the train-management simulation, *A-Train 6.* Players plan the routes of city commuter trains, laying track throughout the metropolis and building stations where convenient. The location of trains can affect the citizenship around it. For example, folks may move to be closer to mass transit, which can cause its own problems. Whereas a game like this could possibly succeed in the U.S. (and it was attempted in the late '90s with an American PlayStation game merely called *A-Train,* now out of print), *A-Train 6* didn't go over well with the Japanese press, so there's almost no chance of this particular title having a worldwide release.

All Star Pro-Wrestling

By SquareSoft

Wrestling! Big business in America, right? SquareSoft! One of the most respected game publishers on either side of the ocean. Quality! Not quite. SquareSoft has slowly tried to expand its scope beyond the role-playing games that made it famous (most notably the *Final Fantasy* series) with entries into fighting, driving, and now wrestling. Other grappling games have done great business in Japan, but this one, well, didn't. Poor controls and slow gameplay made fans cry foul and wonder if the company had overstepped its bounds. (Still, you have to give SquareSoft credit for trying something new.) In time, plenty of professional wrestling titles will be available for the American PlayStation 2, but it's almost certain that this game won't be one of them.

Buchigire Kongou

Published by Artdink

When you think of fighting games, you probably think of the big franchises: *Street Fighter, Tekken, Mortal Kombat,* and *Dead or Alive.* You probably *don't* think about bulldozers and cranes. You might, though, if you were in Japan browsing through the software section. *Buchigire Kongou* is a fighting game with construction vehicles. It's not a *Twisted Metal* thing with special weapons and rockets and fast action; no, it's two guys facing off in heavy machinery, trying to smack into each other. Swing your crane to the right; if you miss, try swinging to the left or maybe even moving forward a bit. Except for a few special attacks, uh, that's about it. This title is just too strange to survive on these shores.

Dream Audition

Published by Jaleco

It takes guts to sing karaoke. It usually takes some form of alcohol, too. In Japan, though, karaoke sing-alongs are a huge business and a great deal of fun for those brave enough to pick up a microphone in a crowded restaurant and strut their stuff. *Dream Audition* — originally an arcade game — brings that atonal experience home to the PlayStation 2, complete with a special microphone that plugs into the PS2's USB ports. Over 100 songs are offered on the disc. Even though you're supposed to read the lyrics that scroll by at the bottom of the screen, the words don't really matter — you can read the phone book if you want to — you just have to hit the right tones. If you're off-key, the game cuts you off, and you've essentially failed your *Dream Audition*. For experts, the game has a mode that transposes the key of the song on the fly, so you must constantly change with it. Even if karaoke were a bigger deal in America, this game probably wouldn't be successful. *Dream Audition* is very pricey due to the microphone, and none of the existing songs are in English.

Drummania

Published by Konami

If you've been to a big arcade over the last year, you may have seen one of Konami's music-based Bemani games — unusual, coin-operated machines such as the neon-floor-sporting *Dance Dance Revolution,* the turntable frenzy of *Hiphopmania,* or the six-string fury of *Guitar Freaks.* All three games have come to the PlayStation in Japan, and the fourth in the series — *Drummania —* was the first to launch for PlayStation 2. The goal of the Bemani games is simple: Whatever it is you're doing, whether it's strumming a plastic guitar, stomping on a disco floor, or triggering electronic samples with a fake turntable, you should do it in time with the music and the on-screen graphical cues. *Drummania,* as its name suggests, offers players a compact electronic drumkit, two sticks, and original songs to try to keep up with. If you've never picked up drumsticks before, *Drummania* is fairly uncomfortable at first. On the other hand, if you're an experienced percussionist, it feels even more uncomfortable because you're just hitting electronic pads and not actually playing drums. The game is still great fun, but a patent issue over the electronic drum technology is keeping this one firmly on the other side of the Pacific.

I'm the Supervisor: Pennant Race of the Fierce Fight

Published by Enix

Baseball may be America's pastime, but it's just as popular in Japan. In addition to the action-oriented baseball games you can find in the U.S. — you know, good ol' pitching, catching, batting, and throwing stuff — Japanese gamers also enjoy management-simulation games. Yep, never mind the glory of hitting the game-winning homer — let me be the guy in the dugout with the master plan for winning the pennant. The aptly titled *I'm the Supervisor* uses 12 real Gekikuukan Pro Baseball teams (Japan's professional league) and lets you give the athletes lessons to improve their on-field skills. But first, you have to talk with them to find out what they do well. A cerebral, touchy-feely baseball sim might fly in Japan, but in America, it would probably be out at the plate. That's a shame, too — what a great title!

Mahjong Declaration: Shout and Ron

Published by Taito

Scrabble, Monopoly, Clue, Yahtzee — all Western board game classics. In Japan, only two games really matter: *Go* and *Mahjong*. Strategy game *Go* uses stones as its playing pieces, yet the game is so complex that computer versions rarely do it any justice. *Mahjong* (no matter how you spell it — there are many variants) is a little easier for computers to grasp. The game is played with 144 tiles and features rules similar to those of the card game *Rummy*. Good-looking 2-D tiles are fairly simple to make on a 3-D game system. And, as the name implies, *Mahjong Declaration: Shout and Ron* also features microphone support so that players can call out their commands to the PS2 as they would in a regular table-based game with friends. Great idea, but unless American families decide to turn away from *Pictionary* and pick up some *Mahjong* tiles, this one won't be appearing at your local Wal-Mart.

Sky Surfing

Published by Idea Factory

Extreme sports games such as *Tony Hawk's Pro Skater* and *SSX* have done well as video games . . . so why not one of the most dangerous and exhilarating sports — sky surfing? Maybe you'd call it "air boarding," or maybe you'd just call it crazy, given that participants throw themselves out of airplanes and then execute intricate spins and flips while falling really, really fast. Because most people would never do this in real life, a game simulation sounds safe and interesting. But this one turned out really lousy. Critics slammed the game for weak animation, a flawed combo system, and, worst of all, boring gameplay. Therefore, a stateside release is unlikely. In fact, this game was 100 percent done and ready for the U.S. PlayStation 2 launch, and despite how hungry everybody was to get in on the PS2 action, no American company swooped in for the right to publish it. Enough said.

Stepping Selection

Published by Jaleco

What two words strike fear into the hearts of hardcore gamers? That's right: "Britney" and "Spears." Although dancing games have only recently started to catch on here in the U.S., they've been the rage in Japan for some time. It's no surprise, then, that one of the first games available for the PS2 when it launched in Japan was *Stepping Selection,* a rhythm-based contest offering pop hits past and present, including *Ghostbusters, My Sharona,* the Backstreet Boys's *Larger than Life,* and *Baby, One More Time* by you-know-who (complete with clips from the video). *Stepping Selection* is a fairly simplistic game if you use a Dual Shock controller — just press the buttons in time with the icons on the screen — but it gets a lot harder if you spring for the optional dance mat controller, which requires you to hit colored targets with just two feet instead of ten fingers. Even if dance games were more popular here, this one probably wouldn't make the jump to America due to the tricky music licensing involved. If you do have a hankerin' to shake your groove thing with your PlayStation or PlayStation 2, check out *Dance Dance Revolution* from Konami instead.

Tokimeki Memorial 3

Published by Konami

In addition to the Japanese games featuring dancing, singing, and fake musical instruments, another unusual and alarmingly popular genre that hasn't crossed the Pacific just yet is dating simulation. *Tokimeki Memorial 3* is one of the most popular dating sims on the market in Japan, with two previous incarnations for the PlayStation already out and hugely successful. The setup for the TokiMemo games is fairly simple: The male player enrolls in a high school, only to find that the girl who used to live next door now goes to his new school; she's beautiful and, better still, she likes him! Now his goal is to fall madly in love and make that childhood-sweethearts romance work. To do that, he has to say the right things, buy her the right birthday gifts, and take her to the right places on dates — or she'll dump him like yesterday's garbage. The third game in the series, *Tokimeki Memorial 3* is for the PlayStation 2, so it adds 3-D graphics to the mix. Although the earlier games enjoyed a small but rabid following among Japanese-speaking gamers in the U.S., Konami has repeatedly denied all rumors that the TokiMemo "love RPGs (role-playing games)" are coming to America.

Chapter 16

Ten DVD Rentals for Video Game Fans

*V*ideo games and movies make strange bedfellows. Whether it's a game based on a popular movie, a movie using a video game as source material, or a game that aspires to be an interactive movie, the end result is a mixed bag, at best. Because the PlayStation 2 can play DVD movies, this weird union of two entertainment realms is only going to become weirder. Suddenly, the handful of successful experiments looks awfully important. If you're looking for some movies to watch on your PS2 — whether to start building a collection of favorite flicks or merely to show off the cool tricks your DVD player can perform — you can consider the discs in this chapter as gamer-friendly options.

Dragon's Lair

Not Rated

Cinematronics/Digital Leisure, 1983

Special Features: Playable game, creator interviews

Okay, so the first item on the list isn't really a movie, but it's not just a game, either. When *Dragon's Lair* hit arcades in 1983, most gamers couldn't believe their eyes. While *Pac-Man* and *Asteroids* offered graphics comprised of lines or simple pixels, *Dragon's Lair* let players control the lead character in a feature-film-quality cartoon. Animator Don Bluth (*The Secret of NIMH, An American Tail, Anastasia*) and programmer Rick Dyer created the original arcade game to run from a laserdisc player. So, what better way to experience that game today than on a DVD? The home version, which contains all the scenes and gameplay of the original, runs on any DVD player (including the PlayStation 2). And the simple controls (four directions and an action button) mean that you can play *Dragon's Lair* with nothing more than your remote control; it's even more comfortable with a Dual Shock. You'll notice a slight delay when you enter a move, and the repetitive gameplay can become frustrating, but this is a truly innovative classic. It's worth tracking down if only to watch the footage of its 20-minute, non-interactive, animated movie. Digital Leisure also makes DVD video versions of *Dragon's Lair II: Time Warp* and *Space Ace,* as well as Dyer's later laserdisc projects *Shadoan* and *Hologram Time Traveler* — the latter in 3-D!

The Last Starfighter

Rated PG

Universal, 1984

Special Features: Widescreen version, audio commentary, making-of featurette, trailer

Here's a dirty little secret: Every gamer wants to be Alex Rogan. He's a bright teenager who's an expert at the arcade game *Starfighter,* but he's stuck in a dead-end trailer park with no hope of escape. But when the video game world record he breaks turns out to be the record from another world, Alex is taken into outer space to play the game for real — smack in the middle of an intergalactic war. Lance Guest does a great job as the incredulous Alex, and the esteemed Dan O'Herlihy shines through all his heavy alien makeup as copilot Grig. But the movie belongs to Robert Preston, doing an extraterrestrial twist on the Harold Hill–style fast-talking salesman that made him famous. Cool (if prototypical) computer effects and a family-friendly tone make *Starfighter* a guilty pleasure for joystick jockeys of all ages.

Mortal Kombat

Rated PG-13

New Line, 1995

Special Features: Full-screen and widescreen versions, trailers

When one of the most violent, gory, and controversial video games finally made the jump to the big screen, nobody expected it would be this much *fun.* By loosely translating the game's plot, focusing on only a few main characters, and realizing that what people want to see in a movie based on a fighting game is lots and lots of fighting, *Mortal Kombat* succeeds where a lot of other game movies fail. The world's best fighters convene in a dimension called Outworld for a huge tournament — and that means ample opportunity for high-energy butt-kickin'. The martial arts choreography is excellent throughout (the Johnny Cage/Scorpion fight is a silly but enthralling highlight) and Christopher Lambert (*Highlander*) lends a gentle sense of humor to the good-guy god Rayden. Grab some popcorn and check your brain at the door — this one is pure mind-numbing action. (Warning: Skip the sequel, *Mortal Kombat: Annihilation.* It's stinky.)

The Matrix

Rated R

Warner Bros., 1999

Special Features: Widescreen version, audio commentary, music-only audio track, making-of featurette

What's the biggest-selling DVD to date? So many copies of *The Matrix* have flown off the shelves that Keanu Reeves may never have to say "Whoa!" again as long as he lives. This dense sci-fi thriller suggests that the world we live in is an elaborate computer simulation and that our electronic overlords breed us as nothing more than fleshy batteries. Explaining more would not only ruin the movie but take a heck of a lot more space than I have in this chapter. With incredible visual effects and a digital-friendly plot, *The Matrix* looks, sounds, and just feels right on DVD. Perks like hidden documentaries and behind-the-scenes footage on demand really take advantage of the format's strengths, too. There's a reason *The Matrix* on DVD (and in theatres) is a big hit. Folks who really love the movie can choose from two different deluxe editions. The Platinum Limited Edition DVD Collector's Set comes with lobby cards, a poster, and more. The Limited Edition Collector's Set includes most of the other set's stuff, plus a CD soundtrack and a nice slipcase. The movie is the same in each edition.

Street Fighter

Rated PG-13

Universal, 1994

Special Features: Widescreen version, audio commentary, deleted scenes, making-of featurette, storyboards, trailer

I won't lie to you — this film is terrible. But some films are so bad, they're good. And on that dreadful level, the big-budget, action movie version of Capcom's long-standing fighting game series succeeds. Jean-Claude Van Damme stars as gung-ho commando, Guile, who's trying to rescue hostages from evil dictator M. Bison, played by an extremely gaunt Raul Julia in, depressingly, his last feature film role. No less than 15 of the game's characters are trotted out over the course of this extremely silly film, but it's hard to recognize some of them and, amazingly, almost none of them actually *fight*. *Street Fighter* is so flawed, it comes out howlingly funny. The DVD version, however, is full of interesting extras, such as the film's storyboards and a "making-of" segment, as well as scenes that were so bad they didn't even make the final cut. Because the occasional bad movie is cathartic and many of the other game-based films on this list are high points, it's only fair to show the genre's lowest point. After all, how else can you know good from bad unless you see both? In the strangest twist, this movie based on a game inspired its own game based on the movie based on the game — it, too, tanked.

Street Fighter II: The Animated Movie

Unrated

Sony Music Video, 1995

Special Features: None

If any *Street Fighter* fans were still willing to see a movie based on their favorite video game after the Hollywood disaster, they were rewarded the next year with a much stronger animated feature straight from Japan. Bison is still a maniacal terrorist leader, but the rest of the story focuses on the game's true lead characters, ex-dojomates Ryu and Ken, with a subplot about Chun-Li and Guile. *The Animated Movie* is more grown-up than American cartoons — as the film's fight scenes, strong language, and shower scene attest to — but such are the cultural differences between the U.S. and Japan. Although the DVD is unrated, it falls somewhere between a PG-13 and an R for content, so don't expect a Saturday morning–style slugfest! Shame on Sony for not including any extras in the DVD version and for completely replacing the original Japanese music and dialogue. DVD *can* do multiple audio tracks, so preserving the original soundtrack as an option for serious anime fans would have been a no-brainer. Nevertheless, this disc is more entertaining and coherent than the Van Damme disaster.

Toy Story: The Ultimate Toy Box

Rated G

Disney, 1995 & 1999

Special Features: Widescreen version, audio commentary, making-of featurette, trailers, and too many more to list

When it comes to true modern classics, the *Toy Story* films make the short list. The secret lives of toys is already an entertaining concept, but when those tales are told as the first feature-length computer-animated feature, they practically scream for a deluxe DVD treatment. Because Pixar, the animation studio behind the adventures of Woody and Buzz, likes DVDs almost as much as you do, it has pulled out all the stops for the *Ultimate Toy Box* set. The set includes both *Toy Story* and *Toy Story 2* in all their digital glory, as well as a third disc with lots of extras, hosted by the filmmakers and computer artists themselves. Abandoned concepts, early animation tests, storyboards, character design details, a guide to the hidden jokes in both films . . . when they say, *Ultimate,* they mean it. If you really want to see all that the latest home video technology has to offer, blow the extra bucks on the three-disc set, and you'll see you have a friend in DVD. (Ha!)

Tron

Rated PG

Disney, 1982

Special Features: Widescreen version, trailer

"On the other side of the screen, it all looks so easy. . . ." That line from Jeff Bridges's character, Flynn, pretty much sums up *Tron,* Disney's ground-breaking, and much-maligned foray into the realms of both video games and computer-generated imagery. When a smart-aleck programmer (Bridges) finds himself sucked into the computer realm he helped create, he's forced to play video games from a truly first-person perspective — or die trying. The movie's basic hero-myth is pretty flimsy (all good guys wear blue and all bad guys wear red, for cryin' out loud), but *Tron* still treats the gaming with a certain respect. Unfortunately, the DVD version can't hold a candle to the incredible three-platter laserdisc box set, which revealed the making of the film in incredible detail. Then again, the DVD doesn't cost $125 either. Why not put all that good stuff on the new format, too? Oh, well. *Tron* on DVD is still worth seeing.

Video Essentials

Unrated

Banned from the Ranch/Joe Kane Productions, 1996

Special Features: Not applicable

Setting up your PlayStation 2 was probably hard enough. Now, how do you make it look really good? Setting up your TV and sound system for optimal DVD viewing is no easy task. You have to take into account ambient light, speaker placement, the anomalies of your personal TV set, and tons more. *Video Essentials* walks you through the whole process in an easy-to-follow guided tour that will probably change all the settings on your system that you once thought were right. Although the topics covered are complex, they're broken down into extremely digestible chunks, so you'll never feel lost. The narration comes in three languages, and the disc includes both video and surround-sound tests. If you rent or borrow *Video Essentials,* make sure that you get the little strip of blue film along with the main disc — you'll need it to successfully calibrate your picture tube's color.

WarGames

Rated PG

MGM, 1983

Special Features: Widescreen version, audio commentary, trailer, trivia

David Lightman (Matthew Broderick) is a good-hearted computer hacker with a knack for getting into trouble. When he attempts to break into a game company's system to play its newest titles a little early, he winds up hacking into an entirely different system — the Defense Department's war computer. Thinking he's playing a game, he accidentally triggers a real-life missile crisis — and the only way to stop it is to find the reclusive genius who built the machine (John Wood). Although the ending of the movie is a little preachy, *WarGames* is an enjoyable adventure, and it treats technology with respect. The DVD features an enlightening, alternate audio track by the film's director and screenwriters as well as the original theatrical trailer and a crisp digital transfer of the film. Watch for Michael Madsen's very first movie role as a missile commander in the film's tense opening sequence.

Part V
Appendix

The 5th Wave   By Rich Tennant

"Oh... you mean the controller is supposed to shake like this? I kept stopping the game to see who was paging me!"

In this part . . .

Sooner or later, every game enthusiast asks, "Which game console is better?" With new hardware coming every few years, it's hard not to get the itch to upgrade to the latest model. So now that you've got a PlayStation 2, how long will it be your prized possession? Is there another machine lurking around the corner waiting to make the PS2 no more exciting than a toaster? Here are some helpful tables that show just how the PlayStation 2 stacks up to the competition.

Appendix

PlayStation 2 versus the World

. . . .

. . . .

*P*layStation 2 is the hottest thing going . . . for now. But every game console eventually ages and inevitably is eclipsed by the newest kid on the block. This appendix throws the PlayStation 2 into head-to-head combat with the other consoles — some already on store shelves, some due in late 2001 — to see which has the best chance of winning the war.

Numbers don't lie, but when it comes to computer data, they can be misleading. A machine's clock speed is a representation of how fast the console's main processor can execute an instruction — move this pixel, create this explosion, make this noise, whatever. The faster the clock speed (measured in megahertz — MHz), the more instructions the machine can handle. But other chips inside the game machine share the workload and make their own calculations, which ensures that the main processor doesn't have to work so hard. You can't assume that a faster or slower clock speed immediately means better or worse. After all, it's not about the chips so much as what the programmers do with them.

You may find the information here to be a bit on the technical side. But after throwing all the scary numbers at you, I include some of my own thoughts to soften the edge. You can find really detailed specifications of the PS2 in Chapter 1.

A Tale of Two PlayStations

The PlayStation 2 wouldn't exist without the humble, original PlayStation. That little gray box (and its redesigned, smaller, and cuter successor, the PS one, which has since replaced the old model on store shelves) is currently in about 30 million homes across the country. For some, PlayStation has become synonymous with *video games* the way *Kleenex* has come to mean *tissue*. So just how much better is the PlayStation 2 than its groundbreaking predecessor? Lots. Take a look at Table A-1.

Table A-1	PlayStation/PS one versus PlayStation 2	
Specification	**PlayStation/PS one**	**PlayStation 2**
Year of debut	1995	2000
Main processor	32-bit R3000A RISC processor	128-bit Emotion Engine
CPU clock speed	Approx. 33 MHz	Approx. 300 MHz
Polygons per second	1.5 million	66 million
Number of controller ports	2	2
Price at launch	$299	$299
Price now	$99	$299
Approximate number of games available by Dec. 2000	700	50
Media format	CD-ROM	CD-ROM and DVD-ROM
Audio channels	24 channels	48 channels
DVD video	No	Yes
Backward compatible	No (well, it was Sony's first system)	Yes
Online capable	No	Adapter available soon

The PlayStation/PS one is still capable of some very impressive tricks. Sony didn't sell 30 million machines without having a really good product. If you're on a budget, you can't beat the PlayStation/PS one. The machine is under a hundred bucks, and most of the best games are just $20 each. Nevertheless, it's clear that the video game industry is ready for an upgrade, and the upgrade just happens to be backward compatible.

The Dreamcast Gambit

Sony isn't the only game maker on the block. Sega set the 16-bit standard with its Genesis system, faltered a bit in the 32-bit era with the Saturn, but returned dramatically with the 128-bit Dreamcast in 1999. The Dreamcast has a year's jump on the PS2, and comes with a lower price, more games, and Internet connectivity out of the box. Oh, and it hasn't been particularly impossible to find either. To see how the PS2 stacks up with the Dreamcast, take a look at Table A-2.

Table A-2	Dreamcast versus PlayStation 2	
Specification	*Dreamcast*	*PlayStation 2*
Year of debut	1999	2000
Main processor	Hitachi SH-4 RISC processor	128-bit Emotion Engine
CPU clock speed	Approx. 200 MHz	Approx. 300 MHz
Polygons per second	3 million	66 million
Number of controller ports	4	2
Price at launch	$299	$299
Price now	$149	$299
Approximate number of games available by Dec. 2000	200	50
Media format	Proprietary "GD-ROM"	CD-ROM and DVD-ROM
Audio channels	64 channels	48 channels
DVD video	Not in U.S.	Yes
Backward compatible	No	Yes
Online capable	Built-in 56K modem, with broadband connector optional	Adapter available soon

The Dreamcast is a great gaming machine, pure and simple. Sega is also paving important roads for online console gaming that others will surely follow. But Sega's decision not to bring out a DVD add-on in the U.S. seems short sighted, especially since the company said that the "market was not viable." Tell that to all the people who waited in line for a PlayStation 2 because it could play both games and movies! However, if you really don't care about the DVD connection, the Dreamcast is a very tempting option — even if you already have another game machine in the house.

When I'm Nintendo 64

Nintendo's 64-bit console has been fighting a heated battle with the PlayStation for four years now. But the PS2 is, in almost all respects, a powerful weapon that renders the Nintendo 64 obsolete (see Table A-3).

Table A-3	Nintendo 64 versus PlayStation 2	
Specification	*Nintendo 64*	*PlayStation 2*
Year of debut	1996	2000
Main processor	64-bit custom R4000 RISC processor	128-bit Emotion Engine
CPU clock speed	Approx. 93 MHz	Approx. 300 MHz
Polygons per second	150,000 shaded	66 million
Number of controller ports	4	2
Price at launch	$199	$299
Price now	$99	$299
Approximate number of games available by Dec. 2000	235	50
Media format	Cartridge	CD-ROM and DVD-ROM
Audio channels	24 channels	48 channels
DVD video	No	Yes
Backward compatible	No	Yes
Online capable	Not really	Adapter available soon

The sad truth about the video game biz is that game systems usually have a life cycle of no longer than five years, and the N64 is cashing out at just four. The N64 was simply eclipsed by the competition, and its expensive cartridges didn't help its longevity. The company isn't out yet, however, as you'll see in the next section.

GameCube: Nintendo's Square Deal

With sluggish sales of the Nintendo 64, Nintendo announced the heir to the 64-throne: the six-inch GameCube, easily the funkiest, kitschiest console to come around in a long time. With a color slate including purple, raspberry, and metallic beige, and with a carrying handle sticking out its back, the GameCube resembles a trendy handbag — but don't be fooled. Within the candy-colored exterior beats the heart of a gecko — a 450 MHz IBM processor nicknamed Gekko, anyway. The GameCube is ready to take on the PS2 mano-a-mano (machino-a-machino?), even if that won't be until October 2001 at the earliest. To see how the two compare, take a look at Table A-4.

Table A-4	GameCube versus PlayStation 2	
Specification	*GameCube*	*PlayStation 2*
Year of debut	2001	2000
Main processor	64-bit IBM copper-wire Gekko	128-bit Emotion Engine
CPU clock speed	Approx. 400 MHz	Approx. 300 MHz
Polygons per second	6–12 million (with game effects on)	66 million (raw)
Number of controller ports	4	2
Price at launch	To be determined	$299
Media format	8 cm optical discs	CD-ROM and DVD-ROM
Audio channels	64 channels	48 channels
DVD video	No	Yes
Backward compatible	No	Yes
Online capable	Maybe by winter 2001	Adapter available soon

Nintendo is positioning the GameCube as a serious, dedicated, games-only machine, which means no DVD-video playback. Instead of five-inch compact discs and DVDs, the GameCube will use a proprietary optical disc-based format that should help thwart software pirates. Nintendo will own this format, meaning that not just any yahoo with a CD burner can create a game for his machine. Still, it's a drag that a console aimed so directly at gamers won't offer backward compatibility as one of its features.

X Marks the Microsoft Box

Last, but certainly not least, is Microsoft. When the software monolith announced its intention to get a piece of the console pie back in March 2000, many gamers scoffed. "What does Bill Gates know about video games anyway?

Doesn't he know that three companies are already slugging it out?" Nevertheless, as with anything Microsoft undertakes, the company is ready to fight till the end. Check out the numbers on Microsoft's Xbox (see Table A-5); then snicker if you dare.

Table A-5	Xbox versus PlayStation 2	
Specification	*Xbox*	*PlayStation 2*
Year of debut	2001	2000
Main processor	Modified Intel Pentium III	128-bit Emotion Engine
CPU clock speed	Approx. 733 MHz	Approx. 300 MHz
Polygons per second	150 million	66 million
Number of controller ports	4	2
Price at launch	To be determined	$299
Media format	CD-ROM, DVD-ROM, built-in hard drive	CD-ROM and DVD-ROM
Audio channels	64 channels	48 channels
DVD video	Yes	Yes
Backward compatible	No	Yes
Online capable	Broadband out of the box	Adapter available soon

More than any other PS2 competitor, the Xbox truly seems like a response to the Sony product— meeting or exceeding the PlayStation 2 in most regards (on paper, anyway). For example, the Xbox will be able to generate more polygons. Microsoft is estimating that, even with game effects turned on, the Xbox will still sustain around 100 million triangles a second. The Xbox will also come with a built-in hard drive and broadband connector, which is especially important to game developers who constantly crave more power. The PS2 should have its own hard drive and Ethernet port by next year, but these will be add-ons sold separately. Whereas Sega and Nintendo seem happy to fight it out for the serious gamer, both Sony and Microsoft are making a play for the entertainment consumer with DVD video playback, online access, and high-end gaming all in one box. If any company has the power, money, and sheer chutzpah to make Sony nervous, it's mighty Microsoft. This showdown will be well worth watching when the Xbox debuts in the fall of 2001.

Index

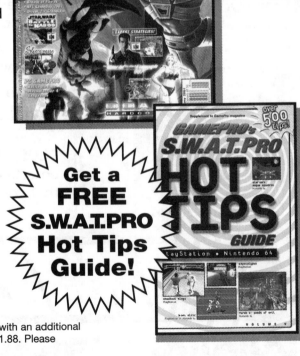

Discover Dummies Online!

The Dummies Web Site is your fun and friendly online resource for the latest information about *For Dummies* books and your favorite topics. The Web site is the place to communicate with us, exchange ideas with other *For Dummies* readers, chat with authors, and have fun!

Ten Fun and Useful Things You Can Do at www.dummies.com

1. Win free *For Dummies* books and more!
2. Register your book and be entered in a prize drawing.
3. Meet your favorite authors through the Hungry Minds Author Chat Series.
4. Exchange helpful information with other *For Dummies* readers.
5. Discover other great *For Dummies* books you must have!
6. Purchase Dummieswear exclusively from our Web site.
7. Buy *For Dummies* books online.
8. Talk to us. Make comments, ask questions, get answers!
9. Download free software.
10. Find additional useful resources from authors.

Link directly to these ten fun and useful things at
www.dummies.com/10useful

For other technology titles from Hungry Minds, go to
www.hungryminds.com

Not on the Web yet? It's easy to get started with *Dummies 101: The Internet For Windows 98* or *The Internet For Dummies* at local retailers everywhere.

Find other *For Dummies* books on these topics:
Business • Career • Databases • Food & Beverage • Games • Gardening
Graphics • Hardware • Health & Fitness • Internet and the World Wide Web
Networking • Office Suites • Operating Systems • Personal Finance • Pets
Programming • Recreation • Sports • Spreadsheets • Teacher Resources
Test Prep • Word Processing

Hungry Minds™

FOR DUMMIES
BOOK REGISTRATION

Register This Book and Win!

We want to hear from you!

Visit **dummies.com** to register this book and tell us how you liked it!

- ✔ Get entered in our monthly prize giveaway.
- ✔ Give us feedback about this book — tell us what you like best, what you like least, or maybe what you'd like to ask the author and us to change!
- ✔ Let us know any other *For Dummies* topics that interest you.

Your feedback helps us determine what books to publish, tells us what coverage to add as we revise our books, and lets us know whether we're meeting your needs as a *For Dummies* reader. You're our most valuable resource, and what you have to say is important to us!

Not on the Web yet? It's easy to get started with *Dummies 101: The Internet For Windows 98* or *The Internet For Dummies* at local retailers everywhere.

Or let us know what you think by sending us a letter at the following address:

For Dummies Book Registration
Dummies Press
10475 Crosspoint Blvd.
Indianapolis, IN 46256

™

FOR DUMMIES

BESTSELLING BOOK SERIES